FRUIT &
VEGETABLE BIBLE

FRUIT & VEGETABLE BIBLE

AUDRA AVIZIENIS, KAREN LAWRENCE, SOPHIE CORNISH-KEEFE

Published by Moseley Road Inc.

© Moseley Road Inc 2019

Created by Moseley Road Inc.
President: Sean Moore
Production Director: Adam Moore
Designer: Philippa Bailel
Layout Designer: Tina Vaughan
Editor: Finn Moore
Picture Researcher: Jo Walton

Printed in China

GENERAL DISCLAIMER

The contents of this book are intended to provide useful information to the general public. All materials, including texts, graphics, and
images, are for informational purposes only and are not a substitute for medical diagnosis, advice, or treatment for specific medical
conditions. All readers should seek expert medical care and consult their own physicians for any general or specific health issues. The
author and publishers do not recommend or endorse specific treatments, procedures, advice, or other information found in this book
and specifically disclaim all responsibility for any and all liability, loss, or risk, personal or otherwise, which is incurred as a consequence,
directly or indirectly, of the use or application of any of the material in this publication.

CONTENTS

CONTENTS

FRUIT & VEGETABLES
WHAT'S THE DIFFERENCE ANYWAY?

When it comes to healthy eating, "Make sure to eat your fruits and vegetables!" is a common mantra. New guidelines suggest that these two food groups should make up half of our daily intake, or between 5 and 7 servings per day. However, though we often hear blanket- statement prescriptions about these two classes of plant-based food, there is a fundamental difference between a fruit and a vegetable. Both have unique botanical properties and nutritional benefits that cannot be found elsewhere. Understanding the differences between a fruit and a vegetable is essential if you want to understand how to get the most out of your diet.

WHAT'S A FRUIT?

On its face, the defining characteristic of a fruit seems straightforward: it is the part of the plant which contains a seed (or seeds). Peaches, strawberries, and apples are all obvious examples of fruits. Less obvious are avocados, cucumbers, olives and tomatoes, which are seed-bearing and therefore technically fruits. Because we think of most fruits as being decidedly sweet, the savory quality of these other fruit-foods often throws people for a loop—and from a culinary standpoint, savory fruits are often treated more like vegetables in their preparation and consumption. However, sweet and savory don't enter the picture when technically classifying a fruit. The simplest benchmark is: if it contains a seed, it's probably a fruit.

WHAT'S A VEGETABLE?

While the defining characteristic of a fruit is relatively simple, what makes a vegetable a vegetable is a little less specific. Essentially, any edible part of the plant that doesn't qualify as its seed-bearing fruit is considered a vegetable. A vegetable can be the leaf of the plant, such as spinach or lettuce; the bud of the plant, such as cauliflower or broccoli; the root of the plant, such as potatoes and turnips; or the stalk of the plant, such as celery. Because the edible part of a given plant varies so widely, it can be difficult to recognize what is a vegetable. The easiest way to know is: if it's an edible part of a plant and there's no seed in sight, it's probably a vegetable.

TYPES OF FRUITS

Now that you know how to recognize a fruit as a fruit, you can begin to break things down a little further. There are a few major categories of fruits, based on exactly how the seeds are organized or contained by the flesh of the fruit, or pericarp. They also are defined by whether the pericarp of the fruit is dry or soft and fleshy. While the classification of certain fruits will seem surprising at first, understanding the basis of these fruit types will help you understand why which fruits pair together so well.

DRUPES

Drupes, known more commonly as stone fruits, are simple, fleshy fruits that contain a single 'stone' or 'pit'. The seed of the fruit is then contained within this hard outer stone.

Examples of these include peaches, avocados, mangos and apricots.

BERRIES

Berries also are defined by their fleshy outer tissue, which is typically sweet and juicy when ripe. Unlike drupes, berries contain multiple seeds. Example of berries include blueberries, grapes, tomatoes, and eggplants.

POMES

A pome contains many seeds within a fleshy pericarp, which is sweet and juicy. Examples include apples and pears.

HESPERIDIA AND PEPOS

Both the hesperidium and pepo fleshy fruits have a leathery rind. Hesperidia include citrus fruits like lemons and oranges, while pepos include cucumbers, cantaloupes, and squash.

LEGUMES

Legumes are 'dry pericarps' which are recognized by their pod-like appearance. They open along two sides releasing several seeds and include peas, beans, and peanuts.

NUTS

Botanically, a nut is a fruit with a hard-shelled outer wall that contains one single seed (or rarely two). True nuts include pecans, chestnuts, acorns and hazelnuts. Peanuts are technically legumes, while cashews, walnuts, and coconuts are all drupes.

TYPES OF VEGETABLES

While the definition of a vegetable is less straightforward than the fruit, breaking down the different categories of vegetables is relatively intuitive. Vegetables are classified by which part of the plant is eaten. In some cases, a plant will fall into multiple categories when multiple parts of the plant are consumed, such as the beetroot plant, the leaves and root of which can both be eaten.

ALLIUM

Allium, or bulbs, usually grow just below the surface of the ground and produce a fleshy, leafy shoot above ground. Bulbs usually consist of layers, or clustered segments, which are the edible part of the plant. They include fennel, garlic, leeks, onions, and shallots.

CRUCIFEROUS

In some instances, the flower or bud of the plant is eaten. These vegetables are known as the cruciferous family. These include the artichoke, cauliflower, broccoli, choi sum, courgetti, and squash flowers.

FUNGI

For culinary purposes, fungi are typically considered to be within the vegetable family. Technically, fungi, like mushrooms and truffles, are incredibly primitive organisms, as they live symbiotically on earthen decay rather than through photosynthesis, like plants. The part of the fungus eaten is the entire fruiting body.

ROOT

In root vegetables, the underground In root vegetables, the underground portion of the plant is harvested and eaten. These commonly include taproots, like beets, carrots, daikon, and turnips; tubers, like potatoes and yams; and rhizomes, like ginger and turmeric.

STEMS

Stem vegetables are perhaps the least commonly occurring category of vegetable, in which the edible above-ground stem of the plant is eaten. Stem vegetables include celery, rhubarb, bamboo, and asparagus.

NUTRITIONAL VALUE

Now that you know the essential difference between fruits and vegetables—and their different subcategories—next you should understand just what's so important about them. New nutritional guidelines recommend that half your plate should consist of fruit and vegetables in each given meal. This is recommended because of the innumerable health-promoting benefits that a single portion of fruit and vegetables can provide. Fruits and vegetables vary widely in the specific nutrients they provide, which is why it's important to eat a diverse variety of plant- based foods as part of your regular diet.

POTASSIUM

Many fruits and vegetables provide a rich source of potassium, which can help the body to maintain healthy blood pressure and improve bone strength. Potassium deficiency can lead to fatigue, weakness, and constipation. Sources of potassium include bananas, spinach, potatoes, soybeans, and some melons.

DIETARY FIBER

Dietary fiber from fruits and vegetables is an important part of a healthy diet. Dietary fiber helps reduce blood cholesterol levels and may lower risk of heart disease. Fiber is also important for proper bowel function. It helps reduce constipation and diverticulosis. Fiber- containing foods also help the body feel full with fewer calories than other foods. Dietary fiber can be found in apples, nuts, beans, citrus fruits and berries.

FOLATE

Folate, or folic acid, is found within a variety of fruits and vegetables. It helps the body form red blood cells. Women who are pregnant or may become pregnant should consume adequate folate from foods, in addition to synthetic folic acid from fortified foods or supplements. This may reduce the risk of neural tube defects, spina bifida, and anencephaly during fetal development. Folate is found in leafy greens, citrus fruits, beans, and lentils.

VITAMINS

Fruits and vegetables are widely regarded as the best source of various vitamins the body needs in frequent, small doses. Eating them in abundance will help prevent vitamin C deficiency, as vitamin C is found only fruits and vegetables. Maintaining a healthy, plant-rich diet is a much better way to getting the vitamins you need than relying on supplements. Vitamin-rich foods include carrots, sweet potatoes, kale, spinach, nuts, and seeds.

PHYSICAL HEALTH BENEFITS OF FRUITS & VEGETABLES

A healthy consumption of vitamins, minerals, fiber, and even other non-essential micronutrients found in plants have been found to have wide-ranging health benefits and preventative outcomes. In addition to providing the necessary nutrients that are vital for our

HEALTHY ORGANS

Eating a diet rich in vegetables and fruits as part of an overall healthy diet may reduce risk of heart disease, including heart attack and stroke. Diets rich in foods containing fiber may reduce the risk of heart disease, obesity, and type 2 diabetes. Eating vegetables and fruits rich in potassium as part of an overall healthy diet may lower blood pressure and may also reduce the risk of developing kidney stones and help to reduce bone loss. Beta-carotene, found in carrots, is converted to vitamin A in the body and helps to maintain healthy eyes and skin.

CANCER PREVENTION

Dietary studies have found innumerable evidence that the consumption of regular amounts of fruits and vegetables may boost your immune system, reducing your risk of

developing some cancers. Red beets offer betacyanin, a plant pigment which may protect against colon cancer. Broccoli is rich in sulforaphane, a similar health-promoting compound. Spinach contains phytochemicals that may boost your immune system and flavonoids, which have antioxidant properties that may be preventative against certain cancers. The deep red pigment found in tomatoes contains the antioxidant lycopene, which is linked with prostate health.

WEIGHT MANAGEMENT

In addition to regular exercise, maintaining a healthy diet is integral to weight management. For a 2,000-calorie diet, it advised that we eat two cups of fruit and 2.5 cups of veggies each day. In addition to their vast health provisions, a diet that relies on fruits and vegetables to provide a large proportion of your daily calorie intake enables you to eat in larger portions than other, less healthy foods. Fruits and vegetables tend to be very low in calories, per cup. Often, eating a large, dinner-sized salad will provide as many calories as a small candy bar.

HOW TO EAT MORE FRUITS AND VEGETABLES

The health benefits derived from fruits and vegetables are many and undeniable. However, meeting the recommended portion guidelines can be a struggle for some, especially when feeding young kids. If you are used to a carb-heavy diet, or one high in artificial sugars, it can be hard to get excited about eating your fruits and vegetables. However, finding fun ways to enjoy them in your diet will make healthy eating easy!

START EARLY

Getting your recommended 5-7 portions of fruits and vegetables daily means incorporating these foods throughout the day, as well as with every meal. Get started early by adding a serving of fruit to your breakfast, like including berries with your yogurt or bananas in your favorite cereal. You can also chop up lots of veggies and add them to eggs with your breakfast.

IN SIGHT IN MIND

Make a practice of keeping lots of already-prepared fruits and vegetables out and visible. Having a bowl of washed fruit out on the counter or keeping carrot sticks in the fridge will make you and your kids more likely to opt for these healthy snacks throughout the day.

Take a little time to prepare the fruits and vegetables in advance, so they are ready to go.

MAKE IT SIMPLE!

Washing, peeling, and chopping vegetables is a major hang-up for those of us looking for a quick and easy meal or snack. However, supermarkets often provide many pre-washed, pre-cut fruit and vegetable options. Canned, frozen and dried fruits and vegetables also provide many of the same nutrients as they do fresh. Keeping fruits and veggies in these forms also means that you have access to them year-round, as they will keep much longer. Making smoothies with frozen fruits is a great way to consume lots of great nutrients with a snack kids will love!

WHAT TO AVOID

While processed and prepared forms of fruits and vegetables might be easier to consume, it is important to be wary of added ingredients. Eating your veggies with calorie-heavy dips or dipping your fruits in chocolate can negate their health benefits, especially if you're looking to lose weight.

ADDED INGREDIENTS

When buying processed fruit and vegetable products, it is extremely important to check your labels for added sugars, sodium, and other ingredients. Fruit juices and ice pops are often loaded with sugars, and products like plantain chips with sodium. If you're looking for convenience, always opt for frozen vegetables before canned ones— the latter of which often strip the vegetable of its nutrients while adding huge amounts of salt. Always look for labels with as few ingredients as possible. Look for packaging that reads "Low Sodium," "No Sodium," or "No Added Sugar."

EAT VARIETY

No single fruit or vegetable can provide all of our necessary daily nutrients. Make sure that you are eating a wide variety of different fruits and vegetables

every day in order to ensure maximum health benefits. When shopping for fruits and vegetables, include a variety of types and colors. Make sure to include plenty of dark, leafy greens, as well as other vegetables such as carrots, peas, and cauliflower.

MAKE IT YOURSELF

Many prepared foods containing fruits or vegetables are easier to make than you think! A can of baked beans is often loaded with sugar and added sodium and chock full of other unrecognizable ingredients. However, with some fresh or canned beans and a handful of other ingredients already in the pantry, you can confidently prepare this dish on your own. Look for healthy recipes online or leave the sugars and salt out when preparing your own dishes.

REPLACE YOUR CARBS

Learning to maintain a diet that relies more heavily on fruits and vegetables means that you should be replacing a component of your diet with these food groups, rather than trying to just add fruits and vegetables to your usual routine. When thinking about a given meal, attempt to replace any processed white carbs with fruits and vegetables. Skip the dinner bread and add a side salad. Replace your white rice with a sweet potato, or legume dish. Try to focus on creating meals where fruits and vegetables take center stage, with a smaller portion of protein and even fewer processed carbs.

SEASONS AND GROWING PATTERNS

Supermarkets have made most fruits and vegetables available year-round, with the help of worldwide shipping, genetic modification, artificial growing, and frozen or canned options. However, the fullest nutritional value will always be derived from fruits and vegetables that are in-season, grown locally, and picked when ripe. Buying fruits and vegetables from farmers markets and local farm stands ensures that the produce you are buying has not been sprayed with pesticides and preservatives. Understanding a little about the growing patterns of different fruits and vegetables will help you to be able to know what you should be buying when.

KNOW YOUR ZONE

Which fruits and vegetables are in season depends on what is known as your "growing zone." Seasonal produce in your area will depend on the growing conditions and specific climate. Fruits that are not available in your growing zone but are found in supermarkets will probably have been treated with preservatives, picked before being ripe, and travelled many miles to get to you. Not only does this rob them of some of their nutritional value, it also creates a large carbon footprint. Learning about what produce is native to your area is a great way to ethically enjoy your fruits and vegetables. Not only this, but the fruits and vegetables grown in season will always taste their best.

GROWING SEASONS

Any given plant or tree will have a specific time of year when it produces its fruit or flower. Leafy greens and root vegetables will only tolerate conditions that are specific to a certain time of year. This means that almost every fruit or vegetable has a specific month, or couple months, when it is "in season". Even in equatorial climates, where sunshine is year- round, seasonal produce will vary by the amount of precipitation in a given month. In the Northeast, we tend to think of a four-season growing cycle, though availability of specific produce will vary month-to-month.

WHEN TO CHEAT

While buying in season will always be the best option for tasty, inexpensive produce, there are some guilt-free ways you can get around this. One tip is to buy seasonal produce in bulk, and then freeze for later. Many fruits and vegetables will retain their nutritional value when frozen, and then you can continue to enjoy them year-round. Some supermarket produce like bananas, celery, and potatoes taste the same throughout the year and remain inexpensive regardless of their growing season.

SPRING FRUITS & VEGETABLES

Depending on your region, growing seasons and crop availability will vary. In the warmest areas, seasons start earlier and last longer. In the most temperate areas, items like greens, carrots, beets, and radishes may be harvested year-round. In colder zones, harvest times start later and end sooner. The following seasonal produce guide is based on a typical growing cycle in North America.

Artichokes
Asparagus
Fava Beans
Fiddleheads
Garlic Scapes (Green Garlic)
Morels
Nettles
Pea Greens
Radicchio
Rhubarb
Spring Onions
Snap Peas, Snow Peas, and Pea Pods
Stinging Nettles
Strawberries
Sweet Onions

SUMMER FRUITS & VEGETABLES

Summer is the most prolific growing season
of the year, regardless of where you live. You
will find the biggest variety and the best fruits
and vegetables during these warm months.
Look for these foods in produce sections
at your local grocer, farmers markets, and
roadside stands. If you like to garden, any of
these would make excellent additions to your
homegrown crops as well.

Basil
Blackberries
Blueberries
Boysenberries, early summer
Cantaloupes, late summer
Chickpeas (Garbanzo Beans), fresh in
summer and dried year-round
Chile Peppers
Corn
Cucumbers
Gooseberries
Mangos
Marionberries
Peaches
Plums and Pluots
Raspberries
Summer Squash
Tomatoes
Watermelons
Zucchini and Zucchini Blossoms

FALL FRUITS & VEGETABLES

Autumn is a peak season for certain fruits and veggies, and you'll find many of these featured at fall harvest festivals. Keep in mind that some of those summer crops extend into or are harvested in early fall, so this short selection is by no means all that you will find at your local markets.

Apples
Artichokes, early fall
Chard
Cranberries
Edamame
Eggplant
Garlic
Green Beans
Grapes
Limes
Melons
Okra
Pears
Pumpkins
Quinces
Sweet Peppers
Potatoes
Shallots
Tomatillos

WINTER FRUITS & VEGETABLES

Winter may be cold in some regions, but it is the peak time for citrus fruits. This is great news if you live in the north because it's like a touch of warm sunshine to get you through those chilly days. A variety of other plants thrive in cooler temperatures too. They begin to peak in fall and are available throughout the winter, up to spring. It's no coincidence that many of these are featured in comforting soups and stews, which are enjoyed throughout the colder months.

Clementines

Mandarins

Pomelos

Tangerines

Brussels Sprouts, late fall into winter

Butternut Squash

Celeriac/Celery Root

Chicories

Delicata Squash

Escarole

Fennel

Horseradish

Kale, available year-round

Leeks

Parsnips

Persimmons

Pomegranates

Radishes

Rutabagas

Salsify

Sweet Potatoes

Sunchokes (Jerusalem Artichokes)

Turnips

Winter Squash

GROWING YOUR OWN FRUIT & VEGETABLES

When you grow your own fruits and vegetables, you get all the fun of gardening plus the garden-to-table goodness and nutrition that only comes from a diet rich in seasonal, local fruit and vegetables. Starting your own vegetable garden can seem daunting, if you aren't someone who considers themselves as having a particularly green thumb. However, if you start simple, you'd be surprised just what you can find yourself capable of harvesting in the coming year.

DON'T START TOO SIMPLE

If this is your first time growing your own fruit or veggies, don't feel like you have to start from square one. Growing plants from seeds is gratifying, but often much less successful than buying pre-started seedlings. Find a local plant store with a good variety of seedlings to choose from and ask for advice on what conditions will be best for your new plants.

USE YOUR SPACE

The specific conditions of your outdoor space will greatly affect what options are best for you when starting your first fruit and vegetable garden. Some plants will require lots of sunlight, while others will do just fine in a shady yard. If you have the ability to put in a whole garden bed, that will be great for some plants,

but plenty will do just fine in pots or hanging planters too. Even city-dwellers have found ways to grow all kinds of produce on rooftop gardens. It just takes a little research into what plants will do best in your space.

CHOOSING WHAT TO GROW

First of all, choose plants that you know you love to eat! There is nothing more gratifying than getting to enjoy your favorite fruits and vegetables grown in your own backyard. Make a list of some of your favorites. Next, you'll need to go through this list and do a little culling. Check which of these plants grow successfully in your region, and what season they will need to be planted. Check how much sunlight and space each plant needs. Cater your garden to what conditions are going to be possible. Carrots, for example, require deep, rich soil to grow well. If you have limited space and sandy soil, you're better off growing surface crops like beetroot.

BEST BETS FOR CONTAINER GROWING

If preparing soil and building raised beds seems like too tall an order for your first time gardening, you can do just fine sticking to container planting. This is great for people who live in apartments and are limited to a balcony or patio. Weeds and pests tend to be less of a problem when growing your plants in pots, too. Look for large open pots for leafy veg like salads, and deep pots for underground veg like carrots and potatoes. You can grow tomatoes and tender veg directly in growbags too. Some of the easiest vegetables to grow successfully in containers include salad greens, radishes, chilies, beetroot, and tomatoes. Fruit bushes are also ideal for containers. Try: strawberries, blueberries, raspberries, cherries, and citrus trees. Growing your herbs in pots is a great way to have fresh, inexpensive and nutritious ingredients to add to your meals, year-round.

PREPARING FRUITS & VEGETABLES

Whether buying or growing your fruits and vegetables, the key to getting the most out of these nutritional wonders is knowing a variety of ways to prepare them. All fruits and vegetables require some proper handling, preparation, or storage in order to maximize their many health benefits. The best way to enjoy these foods, while absorbing their maximum nutrients, will always be eating them raw. However not every fruit or vegetable can be ingested raw, so some case-by-case knowledge is necessary. Since the majority of fruits and vegetables have short growing seasons, processing and preserving techniques can be used to make produce last longer.

KEEPING IT CLEAN

Rinsing all produce in water is a good first step immediately prior to preparing or eating. Even fruits and vegetables with skins should be given a quick rinse to remove any pesticides, bacteria, or insects they may be carrying. Soaking fruits and vegetables in water, however, is never a good idea, as this will dissolve a number of key nutrients.

KEEPING IT FRESH

Baking, boiling, and even chopping your fruits and vegetables will all have some impact on their nutritional output. Whole, fresh, raw produce will always have the highest nutritional value. However, freezing fresh produce is often the next best thing. Freezing produce immediately after it is harvested allows the retention of 95% of most minerals and vitamins and allows you to enjoy many more fruits and vegetables even in the depths of winter.

LEAVE IT WHOLE

Chopping foods into smaller pieces increases the surface area exposed to light, heat and water — three factors that degrade nutrients. In general, try to leave your foods in larger pieces. Keeping peels on foods like potatoes, yams and carrots preserves more nutrients

that tend to concentrate just near the surface. In place of peeling, opt for a good vegetable brush and scrub vegetables thoroughly. Many vegetables are entirely edible and rich in nutrients, so using the entire plant, from root to stem, is a sure way to add nutrients to your day.

COOK SMART

For winter months, when raw veggies just don't appeal, or for vegetables that do require some cooking, the best way to retain nutrients is to use as little cooking time and water as possible. In order to retain water-soluble nutrients, use cooking methods like steaming or stir-frying that use less water, reduce water used in steaming and boiling, and reuse cooking water in soups or sauces to capture escaped nutrients. As a rule of thumb, the longer foods are exposed to heat, the more nutrients are lost. To reduce cooking times, cover the pot to retain heat and avoid evaporation; place vegetables in already boiling water, and learn to enjoy vegetables with a crunchier texture. Since it cuts cooking time and water use, the microwave is a nutrient- friendly kitchen appliance.

FRUIT

From açaí berries and apples to ugli fruit and watermelon, there are countless varieties of fruit that can be found all over the world. As both a vital part of any healthy diet, a colorful addition to a kitchen countertop, and a refreshing side to any meal or dessert, there are few food groups as versatile as fruit.

AÇAÍ BERRY

Euterpe oleraceav

The fruit of the Açaí Palm, açaí (pronounced Ah-sigh-EE) berries have become a very popular health-food of late, as these tiny fruits contain more antioxidants than almost all other berries. These extremely tall palms grow mostly in the floodplains of Brazil, Peru.Suriname, and Trinidad and Tobago. The small, round, and almost-black berries grow in dense clusters.

VARIETIES

AÇAÍ CULTIVARS There are very few varieties—"Branco" ("white") açaí is a very rare variety that only grows in the Amazon estuary—the berries of the Branco stay green when they ripen, and have less antioxidants.

NUTRITIONAL VALUE

serving size 100g
246 Calories
Dietary Fiber 4.8g (19% D.V.)
Potassium 597mg (17% D.V.)
Iron 2.7mg (15% D.V.)
Calcium 70mg (7% D.V.)
Vitamin C 3.6mg (5% D.V.)

HEALTH BENEFITS

Prevents from Some Disease
Heart Health
Immune Health
Energy Source
Skin Health
Promote Weight Loss

IN THE KITCHEN

Açaí smoothie bowls are hugely popular, but also don't usually come cheap. Buy some açaí for your kitchen, and you can enjoy this healthy wonder-food in all kinds of new ways!

 SELECTING
When deciding which processed form of açaí to purchase, it is best to have a specific use in mind. For smoothies, all three forms of acai will work, the powder being most nutrient-dense, while the paste retaining the most flavor

 PREPARING
To make them edible, açaí berries are soaked to soften the tough outer skin and then mashed to form a dark purple paste. This is then frozen, dried or turned into a juice - all of which can be used as is.

 STORING
Frozen acai paste will stay good in the freezer for up to a year. The powdered acai will not go off, though presumably will lose nutritional value at some point.

 PRESERVING
Açaí berries can be purchased as a frozen paste, powder, or juice all of which have already been turned into a preserved form of the fruit.

 USES
Açaí berries are very rarely eaten fresh outside of where they are native, because they spoil very quickly. No more than 10% of the fruit is made up of its skin and flesh, the rest being the large inner seed. This makes these fruits hard to bite into or slice. If you scrape some of the fresh fruit from the seed, the taste is described as being deliciously rich, a cross between dark chocolate and blueberry with hints of hazelnut.

Most often the fruits are soaked, the stones removed, and the flesh is turned into a rich paste, which is sold frozen and can be used as-is, or after being thawed. Most often açaí pulp is used in smoothie-making, blended in with other health-promoting fruits and vegetables. It is also used in a popular exotic-tasting hot chocolate, in which the paste is cooked in with cocoa, milk, vanilla, cinnamon, chilli pepper, and agave nectar. Açaí paste can be cooked with, and is sometimes combined with other fruits to a make a jam.

IN THE GARDEN

Acai berries grow on incredibly tall trees, in rainforests and floodplains, making them quite a challenge for both home and commercial growing.

 CLIMATE
Açaí trees generally grow wild in sub-equatorial rainforests and floodplains. They require low light and wet, swamp-like conditions. They prefer temperatures of at least 70 F and will not tolerate much cooler.

SOIL
Açaí trees will grow in an acidic, moist soil rich in the same type of organic matter which would be plentiful in their natural habitat. Though they like plenty of moisture, they do not like to have wet roots.

PLANTING
Sow seeds indoors 6 to 8 wPlant a young acai tree into the ground once it is one foot tall. The hole should be at least 15" deep.

 GROWING
Water plants twice a week. Fertilize only very poor soil. More text to this point maybe? It seems rather short as it was.

 HARVESTING
Açaí berries grow in large clusters at the tops of the trees. Harvesting this fruit is laborious since the tree has no branches and each cluster of berries needs to be cut and brought down manually in order to preserve the fruit and pulp. They damage very easily.

APPLE

Malus Domestica

Apples are one of the most widely produced and consumed fruits in the world, and are regarded as a miracle food by nutritional experts. Apple trees are cultivated worldwide and are the most widely grown species in the genus Malus. The tree originated in Central Asia, where its wild ancestor, Malus sieversii, is still found today.

VARIETIES

Most apples are bred for eating fresh (known as dessert apples), though some are cultivated specifically for cooking (cooking apples) or for producing cider. Cider apples are typically too tart and astringent to eat fresh, but they give the beverage a rich flavor that dessert apples cannot. Most North Americans and Europeans favor sweet, subacid apples, but tart or sour apples have a strong minority following.

RED DELICIOUS The Red Delicious is one of the most popular apple varieties worldwide. It is heart-shaped, and its skin is bright red with tiny gold strips. It is enjoyed for its crisp texture and sweet taste.

GALA Originating in New Zealand, Gala apples are now grown commercially worldwide. They have a golden skin with orange-pink stripes. Gala apples are crispy and sweet. Good for sauces, salads and pies.

MCINTOSH This well-known cultivar dates back several hundred years. The fruit is deep red, with a green blush at the stem. The flesh is white and tender. McIntosh apples cook well in a sauce or filling.

FUJI Originating in Japan, Fuji have become a household name worldwide. They are bi-colored, alternating stripes of mottled red and green. Flesh firm and sweet in flavor.

GOLDEN DELICIOUS Golden Delicious apples have been growing in popularity since the beginning of the 20th century. They have yellow-green skin and a delicious, sweet taste.

BRAEBURN Braeburn apples are an older variety, popular for their easy growth and shipping. They are versatile apples, whose crisp, sour properties lend themselves well to both cooking and eating.

HONEYCRISP
Honeycrisp are relative newcomers, and have risen quickly as crowd-favorites. They are particularly sweet, juicy and crisp. They stay fresh longer than many other varieties.

CRISPIN
The Crispin is a Japanese variety, also known as a Mutsu. These bright green apples are sweet, refreshing, and crisp. They are great for cooking, with a more tart flavor than most dessert apples.

JAZZ
Jazz are a relatively mild-flavored variety, with a balance of sweetness, bite, and juice. It is medium-sized and typically ruby red with very occasional patches of yellow-green, patches of yellow-green.

MACOUN
The Macoun apple is a fall favorite of commercial orchards in the United States. It has tougher than usual skin, giving way to a crunchy, juicy, very white flesh. They are commonly used for cider.

GRANNY SMITH
Granny Smith apples were first discovered in 1868 by an Australian farmer named Maria Ann Smith. Their popularity grew enormously due to their long shelf life. These apples can be transported over long distances without sustaining much damage or over-ripening. They are light green and have a tart and crunchy taste. They are mainly eaten raw but are also ideal for baking apple pies, cakes, and apple crumble.

IN THE KITCHEN

The widespread availability of apples in supermarket year-round, as well as their long shelf-life, means that a kitchen should almost never go without having a few tasty apples on hand. While perfect as a snacking fruit, they are also a versatile item for a variety of other kitchen uses.

 SELECTING
Look for a plump, fairly firm fruit of a bright, golden orange color throughout the whole surface.

 PREPARING
Apples are often eaten raw, with or without the skin. Some people choose to cut their apples into wedge-shaped slices, discarding the seeds and core, while others prefer to bite into the apple whole, eating around the core.

 STORING
Cold, humid storage ensures that apples maintain their crispness, juicy texture and full flavor. They can be stored in perforated bags in the refrigerator and will keep for six months or longer. If left at room temperature they will soften 10 times faster.

 PRESERVING
Preserving a fresh avocados is virtually impossible. Once cut open, the flesh of the fruit will quickly yellow and lose flavor. Lemon juice can be added to slow down this process, but in general avocados are best enjoyed immediately. 39 Cold, humid storage ensures that apples maintain their crispness, juicy texture and full flavor. They can be stored in perforated bags in the refrigerator and will keep for six months or longer.

 USES
Apples, of course, are delicious enjoyed as a fresh snack, sliced into bite-size segments and eaten as-is. They can also be used fresh, and chopped up to add to oatmeal, yogurt, smoothies, and on top of salads. Apples can be peeled, sliced, and incorporated with a little sugar, as a popular pie filling, with very little preparation of the fruit itself.

When cooked, some apple cultivars cook down very well to form a puree known as apple sauce. Make sure to remove the skins and seeds before turning your apples to apple sauce. Once cooked, apple sauce can be eaten as-is, or refrigerated for later use.

This also makes a great ingredient for homemade baby food. Apple sauce can be frozen in sealed containers for later use. Simply thaw out the frozen puree when you are ready to use it.

Apple sauce can also be turned into apple butter and apple jelly. In order to make a jelly with your apple sauce, transfer the stewed apples into a cheesecloth, suspended over a large bowl. Cover the stewed apples above, to prevent them from attracting bugs, and leave the mixture to strain its liquid for several hours, or overnight. The liquid you obtain below can then be cooked, with some pectin added, and will form a delicious jelly.

IN THE GARDEN

The apple is a hardy, deciduous woody perennial tree that grows in all temperate zones. Apple orchards are hugely popular to visit and pick-your-own, but it's easy to grow apple trees in your own backyard, either from a saved pip (seed), or planting a store-bought sapling.

 CLIMATE
Apples grow best in well-drained loamy soil, although they will still grow in more sandy soil or soil with some clay. They grow best in a neutral soil pH of 6.0-7.0.

SOIL
Apples grow best where there is cold in winter, moderate summer temperatures, and medium to high humidity. They can tolerate winter temperatures as low as -40°F. Apples generally do not grow well close to the ocean where temperatures remain moderate most of the year.

PLANTING
Apple trees can be purchased either bareroot, balled-and-burlapped, or in a container. Bareroot trees are available in the winter and early spring when the trees are dormant and without leaves. Plant bareroot trees in spring as soon as the soil can be worked. Balled-and-burlapped trees are commonly available in spring also; however they may be found later in the year. A container grown tree can be planted any time during the growing season.

 GROWING
Apples are self-incompatible; they must cross-pollinate to develop fruit. Many apples grow readily from seeds. However, more than with most perennial fruits, apples must be propagated asexually by grafting to obtain the sweetness and other desirable characteristics of the parent.

HARVESTING
Crops ripen at different times of the year according to the cultivar. Cultivars that yield their crop in the summer include 'Gala', 'Golden Supreme', and 'McIntosh'; fall producers include 'Fuji', 'Jonagold', and 'Golden Delicious'; winter producers include 'Winesap', 'Granny Smith', 'Greening', and 'Tolman Sweet'.

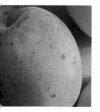

APRICOT

Prunus armeniaca

Believed to have originated in Armenia (where more than fifty varieties grow today) apricots are relatives of peaches. Apricots are small, golden orange fruits, with velvet-like skin, and flesh which is less juicy than peaches, but still smooth and sweet. Apricots grow on trees, and hold a single seed, which is contained within a hard outer shell.

VARIETIES

BLENHEIM A favorite of California apricot growers, these produce medium-large fruits, with a thick yellow-orange which is juicy, sweet, and aromatic. They are wonderful fresh but also can well.

KATY This apricot produces very large fruit withred-blushed skin.. They can be harvested early in the season, for a firmed texture and flavor that is sweet but fairly mild.

AUTUMN ROYAL similar to Blenheim, the Autumn Royal has medium fruit with yellow skin with a slight orange blush; flesh is yellow, slightly acid. Use fresh, canned, or dried. Late harvest into fall.

GOLDCOT Medium to large fruit nearly round with bright gold skin; the thick flesh is orange, firm and sprightly-sweet flavored. Use for processing, canning, or eating fresh. Midseason to late harvest.

PERFECTION The Perfection Apricot,or Goldbeck producesFruits are large and oblong, with a light yellow-orange, mottled skin. Despite its name, the flavor is not nearly as enjoyable as other varieties.

MOORPARK This apricot dates back to the eighteenth century. It is still considered one of the best for its juicy and aromatic properties, and sweet-rich, plum-like taste. It is a mid-season harvest.

IN THE KITCHEN

Apricots are a versatile fruit for eating fresh, cooking with, and preserving. Though they are only fresh during the summer months, they can be enjoyed in other forms year-round.

 SELECTING
Look for a plump, fairly firm fruit of a bright, golden orange color throughout the whole surface.

 PREPARING
Apricots can be eaten raw when picked fresh from the tree. The flesh can be eaten straight off the fruit, or sliced off in half, and the stone discarded.

 STORING
Cover and refrigerate the unwashed, ripe fruit for up to one week. Ripen firm apricots at room temperature until they yield to gentle pressure.

 PRESERVING
Apricots can be canned in a preserving liquid of your choice, whole or sliced. They can also be oven-dried—when dried, the relative concentration of nutrients is increased.

USES
Fresh apricots make a great snacking fruit, eaten whole or sliced in half. Fresh apricots can also be added on top of breakfast cereals, yoghurt, or to smoothies.

Fresh apricots are also very easy to can in a preserving liquid, which can later be used in much the same ways. Fresh apricots also make a great ingredient in many sweet baked treats, such as pies, tarts and crumbles. They require very little preparation or added sugar.

Apricots can be cooked down into a stew, which can be added to sauces or baked with. The stew can also be eaten as-is, and makes a great ingredient to homemade baby food. Stewed apricots can be turned into a delicious jam, as the fruit is rich in natural pectin. It can also be stewed and turned into a jelly.

Apricots are also commonly found dried and canned, though beware or added sugars and sulfites when purchasing apricots in these forms. Dried apricots make a delicious snack straight out the container, but they can also be chopped up and added to breakfast cereals and oatmeals, or as an ingredient in both sweet and savory sauces. When cooked, dried apricots provide a much different texture to the dish than a fresh apricot would.

IN THE GARDEN

Growing an apricot tree from seed is a fun experiment for kids, as you can use the pit of your own just-eaten fruit.

 **CLIMATE**
Hardier than the Peach, Apricots can tolerate temperatures as low as -30C.

SOIL
Apricots prefer deep, moisture-retentive, well-drained, and slightly alkaline soil.

PLANTING
Apricots can be grown from directly seeds. You will need to dry the seeds and allow them to stratify in the refrigerator for 60 days. Plant in small seeding pots under a grow light until they are big enough to transplant into the garden.

 **GROWING**
Apricots prefer deep, moisture-retentive, well-drained, and slightly alkaline soil. When planting the tree, it's important that the soil is nice and firm and settled around the roots.

 HARVESTING
It is best to pick apricots before they are completely ripe, typically in mid summer. They will ripen after being picked, so can be pulled from the tree when slightly underripe.

NUTRITIONAL VALUE

1 serving = 105 g
Vitamin C =18% Recommended Daily Intake
Potassium = 272 mg/serving
Fiber = 2g/serving
Sodium-free = 1 mg/serving
Fat-free = 0.4 g/serving)

HEALTH BENEFITS

Reduced Risk of Diabetes
Reduced Risk of Cancer
Eye Health
Skin Health
Gut Health
Promotes Healthy Blood Pressure

AVOCADO

Persea americana

Avocado's have gained cult status in recent years, both for their versatile taste and texture, but also for their wealth of nutrients and health benefits. Avocados are a stone fruit with a creamy texture that typically grow in warm, equatorial climates. A single avocado is packed with healthy, monounsaturated fats. In 2017, Mexico produced 34% of the world supply of avocados.

VARIETIES

FUERTE Fuertes have an elongated shape and shiny, green skin. They are grown primarily in Mexico and Central America. It is a well-appreciated breed for its easy-to-remove skin.

HASS Hass is the most popular variety of avocado in the world. It produces fruit year-round and accounts for 80% of cultivated avocados in the world. The flavor is more intense than other and the flesh is very creamy, perfect for eating straight from the fruit or mashing.

All 'Hass' trees are descended from a single "mother tree" raised by a Californian mail carrier named Rudolph Hass, who patented his productive tree in 1935. The "mother tree", of uncertain subspecies, died of root rot and was cut down in September, 2002. 'Hass' trees have medium-sized ovate fruit with a black, pebbled skin. The flesh has a nutty, rich flavor with 19% oil.

ETTINGER Cultivated largely in Israel, Ettinger's are very shiny, green avocados with fine skin. They are very soft, and perfect for smoothies. The fleshyellows quickly when ripe, and must be eaten quickly.

IN THE KITCHEN

In recent years avocados have gained cult status in culinary popularity, for their decadent but healthful texture and flavor in a variety of dishes.

SELECTING
When looking for a ripe avocado, look for a shiny, black fruit, that is firm but yields slightly when the skin in pressed. Avoid fruit with dark sunken spots or bruises. The exact color and texture depend on variety. Unripe fruit can be bought and ripened at home by leaving it out at room temperature.

PREPARING
Rinse the avocado and use a knife to cut lengthwise around the pit of the fruit. Gently twist the two sides and the avocado should separate cleanly in two. Remove the pit and scoop the flesh of the avocado from the skin to enjoy. If you are not eating the fruit right away, coat it with lemon juice to prevent browning.

STORING
Avocados ripen (and overripen) more quicklyr when left at room temperature. Ripen firm fruit at room temperature until they yield to slight pressure. Once ripe, your avocado can be kept in the refrigerator for up to five days before turning brown and distasteful.

PRESERVING
Preserving a fresh avocados is virtually impossible. Once cut open, the flesh of the fruit will quickly turn brown and lose flavor. Lemon juice can be added to slow down this process, but in general avocados are best enjoyed immediately.

USES
Avocados are delicious fresh, when they are perfectly ripe. They can be sliced in two and the flesh scooped straight out the skin. This can be eaten as-is with a little salt added, or on top of salads, rice bowls, and other delicious dishes.

The fresh avocado flesh can also be mashed into a deliciously creamy substance, which can be enjoyed as a topping on toast, or quesadillas.

By adding salt, pepper, onions, tomatoes, and lemon, you can make a delicious guacamole, perfect for dipping chips, veggies, and other snacks. Pureed avocado is also a great ingredient for homemade baby food.

IN THE GARDEN

Avocado trees grow best in tropical climates, where temperature remain warm year-round.

CLIMATE
Choose an area with full sun and good drainage, which is protected from wind and frost. Allow plenty of room for the tree to grow.

SOIL
Avocado trees like loose, airy soil which is slightly acidic. Dense, heavy soil will limit root growth.

PLANTING
If you want to turn your an avocado stone into a tree, suspend the seed over a container of water, so half the seed is submerged. Keep your seed in bright light and keep refreshing the water. In 2-6 weeks your seed should produce a sprout, which can then be planted.

GROWING
Give your plant generous water whenever the soil feels dry to the touch. Prune the tree regularly and aggressively to encourage bushy growth.

HARVESTING
Avocado trees can take 5-13 years before producing a successful fruit. Avocados do not ripen on the tree, and should be picked underripe and then left to ripen.

BANANA

Musa acuminata

A staple of the human diet for many centuries, bananas are grown in 150 countries, and are consumed in greater quantities than apples and oranges combined. Bananas contain high quantities of vitamin B_6 (100mg provides 36% of recommended daily value). Contrary to popular belief, they contain only a moderate amount of potassium (360mg or 8% of daily value).

VARIETIES

CAVENDISH Cavendish are the most common variety of banana worldwide. They are a larger, longer shape and bright yellow when ripe. They're often picked underripe, and transport well.

LADIES FINGERS Lady's Finger are smaller and even sweeter than the Cavendish. They are enjoyed in much the same way, but make great smaller sizedsnacks for kids. They are native to Malaysia.

PLANTAINS Plantains, or cooking bananas, are treated more like potatoes in their preparation. They can be roasted, steamed, fried into tasty chips, much like any starchy vegetable. They are sold and used green.

RED BANANA The red banana is shorter and plumper than the Cavendish, sweet tasting andcreamy. They bruise easily and must be handled with greater care.

IN THE KITCHEN

Bananas are one of the most widely consumed fruits worldwide. Many people keep a ripe bunch in the kitchen at all times, for an on-the-go snack.

 SELECTING
Bananas can be enjoyed when under-ripe and slightly green, to perfectly ripe and still firm mellow yellow, to riper deep yellow with a brown spot or two, to super soft and browning. The perfect ripeness depends on personal taste. Super ripe and browning bananas can be thrown in the fridge or freezer to be used later.

 PREPARING
Bananas are often enjoyed fresh when ripe, by pulling down the peel and biting directly down the fruit. They also make great additions to fruit salads and breakfast cereals, when sliced into bite-size rounds. Overripe fruits make great additions to smoothies, cakes, or breads.

 STORING
Ripe bananas can be kept at room temperature for 2-3 days, but will quickly overripen—turning soft and sugary on the inside, while teh skin gradually blackens. Keeping them in the fridge will slow the process slightly—the sjin will still blacken, but the ripening of the fruit slows.

 PRESERVING
Ripe and browning bananas can be stored in a freezer to be used later. They can be frozen whole, with their skins removed, sliced, or as a mush.

 USES
Bananas are delicious enjoyed fresh as a snacking fruit. They can be eaten whole, by peeling down part of the peel to create an easy-to-hold snack. They can also be cut into slices and added to fruit salads, or on top of breakfast cereals or yoghurt. Bananas are a hugely popular smoothie ingredient, adding a deliciously creamy texture. Fresh bananas can be turned into a puree which is a popular baby food.

Sliced bananas can also be used in many baking recipes. Some popular "no-bake" desserts include layers of freshly-sliced bananas along with a sweet base and creamy custard. Bananas can also be pureed and baked into bread or muffins.

IN THE GARDEN

Banana trees are tropical, and can grow to 23-feet tall ; they also grow best in large groups, making them unsuitable for most backyards, and better suited to commercial growers.

 CLIMATE
Banana trees like warm, humid conditions without extreme shifts in either hot or cold spells. They like to be sheltered from wind, and grow well surrounded by other banana trees.

 PLANTING
Banana trees should be planted in an area of full sun, but which is sheltered from strong winds. They like to be planted together, to provide shelter and share moisture.

 MEDICINAL USES

Bananas have mild laxative properties, and can be used to treat constipation. However they also are recommended for to treat diarrhea and promote overall digestive health. Bananas are part of an approach known as the BRAT diet, which emphasizes bland foods during periods of stomach irregularities.

NUTRITIONAL VALUE

1 serving = 140
Potassium = 500 mg/serving
Vitamin C = (15% DV) Intake
Fibre = 3 g/serving
Sodium-free = 0 mg/serving
Fat-free = 0 g/serving

HEALTH BENEFITS

Maintains Healthy Blood Sugar
Digestive Health
Weight Loss
Heart Health
Appetite Suppressant

BLACKBERRY

Rubus

Blackberriesare low in calories while extremely high in antioxidants, fiber, and a variety of other healthynutrients. They are native to Europe, where they grow largely wild, have been consumed for centuries. They are now also cultivated on commercial farms in North American and other parts of the world.

VARIETIES

NAVAHO Nahavo have an unusually long harvest season, making them a top choice for commercial berry growers. The plants are thornless,producing especially sweet fruit.This blackberry stores well also.

NATCHEZ Natchez Thornless is the earliest ripening thornless variety with very high production. Large good tasting berries can be harvested during a 3-5 week season. performs best with a trellis.

PRIME ARK FREEDOM This rthornless blackberry fruits very early in the season, and where the climate is suitable, fruits again in the fall. It has large fruit and good flavor.

 FUN FACT

In the United Kingdom, folklore says that blackberries should not be picked after Old Michaelmas Day (11 October) as the devil has made them unfit to eat thereafter. There is value in this legend, as the fallweather often allows the fruit to become infected by various molds and may be toxic.

IN THE KITCHEN

Fresh blackberries are a top-choice sweet-treat for almost every form of dieting, since they are so low in natural sugars.

 SELECTING
Look for plump, firm berries which are a deep, almost black. Avoid berries which are still green or broken.

 PREPARING
Blackberries require little preparation beyond a quick, gentle rinse, before being patted dry.

STORING
Blackberries are highly perishable and will last only a couple days once harvested, even when refrigerated. Blackberries can be frozen in order to be enjoyed year-round. They can also be stored longer by canning or preserving into jams.

PRESERVING
Blackberries make a very popular preserve in the form of jams and jellies. The berries can be boiled with sugar to create a sweet stew, which can either be strained to make jelly, or left seeded and fleshy to make jam. Blackberries contain some natural pectin, though some should be added.

 USES
All varieties of blackberries can be eaten immediately off the bush as a snacking fruit, when ripe. Fresh blackberries can also be eaten on top of breakfast cereal, yoghurt, or ice cream, as well as added to smoothies for an extra healthy boost.

Fresh blackberries are often used as ingredients in popular summer desserts, such as pies, tarts, and crumbles. They berries can also be cooked into a stew, which is then added as a dessert ingredient in much the same manner. Blackberries can also be added to savory sauces and other dishes, as a sweet counterbalancing ingredient.

Blackberries can be fermented into a wine, as well as distilled into a sweet liquor. Blackberry juice can also be used in candy.

IN THE GARDEN

Blackberry brambles do grow wild in some parts of the world, and collecting them this way is a special treat. However, they can also be grown in the garden with relative ease.

 CLIMATE
Blackberry plants grow well in many temperate climates. They are winter-hardy.

 SOIL
Bushes like soil which is rich and fertile. They prefer a slightly acidic soil, and plenty of moisture.

 PLANTING
Blackberry bushes should be planted when dormant, in the early spring, though they can be planted in late fall in warmer areas. For best fruit yield, choose an area with full sun and good drainage.

 GROWING
Blackberry plants will need water in dry spells. They will benefit from annual pruning and fertilizing..

 HARVESTING
When harvesting, look for shiny, fully black fruits. Mature berries will be plump and slightly firm, and pull easily off the plant. Berries do not ripen after being picked, so avoid picking green, unripe fruits..

BLUEBERRY

Cyanococcus

Fresh blueberries are a popular early-summer treat. They have a mild, sweet flavor, and are succulent and nutritious. Blueberries can be eaten freshly picked or incorporated into a variety of recipes. Commercially offered blueberries are usually from species that naturally occur only in eastern and north-central North America.

VARIETIES

LOWBUSH Lowbush varieties grow generally no more than two feet high. They are used for ornamental landscaping as well as container growing.

NORTHERN HIGHBUSH This variety is native to the northeastern United States, and grows between 5-9 feet tall. They require the most consistent pruning in order to yield the maximum fruit harvest. .

SOUTHERN HIGHBUSH These highbush blueberry varieties are hybrids, designed for mild winter regions, requiring less chilling time to break bud and flower. The bushes blossom in the late winter.

RABBITEYE This bush grows between 6-10 ft tall. It thrives in areas with long, hot summers.. Skins are thick with more obvious seeds, making them less popular for commercial growing.

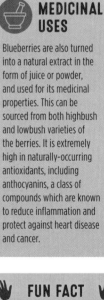

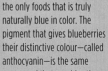

MEDICINAL USES

Blueberries are also turned into a natural extract in the form of juice or powder, and used for its medicinal properties. This can be sourced from both highbush and lowbush varieties of the berries. It is extremely high in naturally-occurring antioxidants, including anthocyanins, a class of compounds which are known to reduce inflammation and protect against heart disease and cancer.

FUN FACT

The blueberry is one of the only foods that is truly naturally blue in color. The pigment that gives blueberries their distinctive colour—called anthocyanin—is the same compound that provides the blueberry's amazing health benefits.

IN THE KITCHEN

Blueberries are an antioxidant rich fruit, that provides many unique health benefits. Not to mention they're delicious.

 SELECTING
Look for blueberries that are plump, and firm with a deep blue skin. Avoid berries with wrinkled or broken skin.

 PREPARING
All blueberries should be washed before eating. Place the berries in a colander before submerging it into a bowl of cold water. Gently swish the berries in the water and then allow them to drain. Carefully spread out the berries in a single layer and gently pat them dry. When the blueberries are completely dry they can be eaten fresh or added to other meals. t them into bite-size pieces.

 STORING
Arrange berries unwashed on a paper towel, in shallow pan or container. Cover, and berries should keep refrigerated for up to ten days. For longer storage, blueberries can be frozen for up to one year.

 PRESERVING
To freeze the leaves, boil them for three minutes, cool them in ice water, and strain the water before placing them in an airtight containers.

 USES
Blueberries are delicious enjoyed fresh as a snacking fruit. They can also be added fresh on top of yoghurt, breakfast cereals, and ice cream. Fresh blueberries are often added to healthy smoothies. They also make a great ingredient for baking and cooking. Fresh berries can be baked into muffins and breads, and also as the base of many popular pies and tarts.
Blueberries can also be cooked down into a stew, which can then be added to yoghurt or ice cream, or used as a baking ingredient. The stew can also be turned into a jelly or jam, though pectin must be added.

IN THE GARDEN

New varieties of blueberries have been bred to adapt to an enormous range of growing conditions. See if there's a type that will grow in your region!

 CLIMATE
Blueberries traditionally grow in humid, northern climates that have winter chills, mild summers and low-pH or acidic soils, conditions that limit their range. New varieties are bred for lower chill areas, very warm areas, and coastal areas.

 SOIL
The blueberry is a very resilient plant and can withstand temperatures from -5 °F to -13°F without any damage, so long as the roots are protected with some sort of winter cover.. During the growing season, blueberry plants require a lot of moisture, but don't like soggy soil.

 PLANTING
Blueberry plants should be planted as early in the spring as possible. The hole should be twice as wide and deep as the young plant's roots.

 GROWING
Blueberry plants will need to be watered during dry spells. They will benefit from a generous layer of mulch before winter frosts.

 HARVESTING
The blueberry fruits usually reach maturity between June and August. Once ripe, the berries will begin to fall off the bush on their own.

NUTRITIONAL VALUE

1 serving = 80 g
Vitamin C = 10% Recommended Daily Intake
Fber = 2g/serving
Fat-free = 0g/serving

HEALTH BENEFITS

Reduced risk of cancer
Increased insulin response
Reversal in age-related memory loss
Lowered blood pressure

BREADFRUIT

Artocarpus altilis

This prickly fruit is very popular throughout Southeast Asia and the Pacific Islands, and when cooked, it tastes similar to—you guessed it!—freshly baked bread. The fruit can be eaten ripe, but it is preferred parboiled or fried, prepared in the same way as vegetables such as potatoes or yams. Breadfruit seeds are eaten like chestnuts: fried, toasted, or boiled.

VARIETIES

ARAVALI This plant produces especially large fruits, between 8 -12" long.. The skin is spiky, but the spikes drop as it ripens. The flavor is considered among the best.

MAOHI
Maohi grows in Tahiti; its fruit is smaller than other varieties, but produces large quantities of fruit. The flavor is good and the texture very smooth. They cook slowly.

HAVANA Havanas are a seeded variety and have a sweeter flavor than most, but are more perishable than others. Once picked, they must be eaten within two or three days. They cook quickly and are considered a desirable variety. In Cuba, this fruit is very commonly eaten in western provinces, especially in rural areas, but increasingly few people are aware of the fruit's significant potential. Cuban recipes include a breadfruit stew made with coconut milk. Nowadays, breadfruit is mainly found in backyards and it is both produced and distributed on a small scale. The ripe fruit is used in salads or fried as a side dish.

IN THE KITCHEN

Breadfruit is used abundantly in many South-East Asian countries, where it takes the place of the given starch in most meals. It also can be enjoyed sweet, once ripe.

 **SELECTING**
When selecting a ripe breadfruit look for a slightly soft fruit with an even color and small globules of latex on the surface. Ripe breadfruit has creamy to yellow flesh, is slightly pasty in texture and is sweet to the taste. Unripe varieties are firm and evenly green.

PREPARING
The immature green fruit can be cooked whole, or cut into thin slices or chunks and boiled until tender. Once boiled, they can be eaten plain, marinated, or pickled. .

STORING
The breadfruit should be used quickly after being brought home. Breadfruit does not handle refrigeration well and should be kept in a thick bag to prevent from cold damage.

PRESERVING
Ripe breadfruit can be pureed into a mash, which can be frozen in a sealed container for up to a year for future use.

 USES
Breadfruit can be used at all stages of development and prepared many ways. It is typically eaten at the mature, starchy stage, when it is often used as a potato substitute in many dishes.

When breadfruit ripens it becomes soft, creamy and sweet. At this stage it can be eaten raw straight from the fruit. It can also be used fresh to make beverages, baked goods, desserts like flan, and other sweet dishes.

Mature breadfruit can steamed, boiled, fried, baked, or cooked in traditional ways in a fire. The flavor of breadfruit is relatively bland, making it a versatile base or accompaniment in many dishes.

The flesh of the breadfruit can be cooked down into a mash, and then can then be used in f dishes such as casseroles, fritters, pancakes, breads, curries, stews, chowders, and more. Breadfruit can be sliced into strips or wedges, oiled, and roast or fried, much like a potato. It can be mashed and made into cold dips, like hummus, or into into a pâté.

IN THE GARDEN

Whether planted in a pot or outdoors, under the right conditions the fast-growing breadfruit tree will thrive with little care.

 CLIMATE
Breadfruit trees are grown widely in tropical regions.. They prefer warm, ultra-tropical conditions with a temperature range of 61–100 °F and an annual rainfall of 80–100 in. The trees prefer deep, fertile, well-drained soils.

 SOIL
The right soil or growing media is extremely important for growing a successful breadfruit plantlets into a fruiting tree. A well-drained and light nursery mix should be chosen, which is composed of composted bark, peat moss or coconut coir and perlite. It should be light and airy but heavy enough to weigh the plants down.

 **PLANTING**
Breadfruits are most easily planted from seedlings or shoots. Allow the seedling to grow roots in a container for 3-5 months before planting.

 GROWING
The trees prefer deep, fertile, well-drained light-and-airy soils.

 HARVESTING
The or pick young leaves as needed. Removing the terminal bud encourages branching of young shoots. Harvest young leaves as needed. Removing the terminal bud encourages young shoots.

NUTRITIONAL VALUE

1 serving = 96 g (1/4 fruit)
Vitamin C = 46% Recommended Daily Intake
Magnesium = 10% Recommended Daily Intake
Vitamin B1 = 8% Recommended Daily Intake
Fiber 5g/serving
Sodium-free 2 mg/serving
Fat-free 0.2g/serving

HEALTH BENEFITS

Supports Digestive Health
Stabilize Blood Sugars
Maintain Healthy Blood Sugar
Defend from Infections
Heart Health
Aid from Insomnia

CANTALOUPE

Cucumis melo var. cantalupensis

Fresh, sweet canteloupe are a quintessential part of summer, and a much-appreciated addition to any picnic or backyard barbecue. Beyond being deliciously refreshing, cantaloupe provides a wide spectrum of different nutrients while remaining quite low in calories.

VARIETIES

The European cantaloupe, *Cantaloupe melo var. cantalupensis,* is lightly ribbed with a sweet and flavorful flesh and a gray-green skin that has quite a different appearence to that of the North American cantaloupe. *Cantaloupe melo var. reticulatus,* common in the United States, Mexico, and some parts of Canada, is a muskmelon that has a "net-like" (reticulated) peel. It is a round melon with firm, orange, moderately sweet flesh.

BUENA VISTA This honeydew melon (below) features flesh of a pale-salmon color. It is a mid-size melon, and relatively firm. They are harvestable in 60-90 days, depending on regional temperatures.

INFINITE GOLD Bred for its long shelf-life and ability to travel, Infinite Gold (below) maintains excellent taste and quality. The plant produces a high yield of uniform, round fruit with dark orange flesh.

GOLDEN HAMI This oblong melon variety weighs between 3-4 lbs and comes from a resilient, disease-resistant plant. It produces a high yield of fruit which will take 90 days to mature.

SNOW LEOPARDV These unusual looking cantaloupe are immediately recognizable by their albino, green-streaked skin and white flesh. The fruits are smaller, weighing 2-3 lbs.

IN THE KITCHEN

A fresh juicy cantaloupe is so delicious raw, that it hardly seems necessary to enjoy them any other way. Thankfully these fruits are so big that if you have a couple in the kitchen, you can try enjoying them fresh, frozen, and more!

 SELECTING
When selecting a canteloupe, look for a deeply textured, yellow-gold rind. A ripe melon will be fragrant and yield slightly to pressure, but should not feel overly soft or hard.

 PREPARING
Rinse the outer skin of your melon. Slice the melon in two halves and scoop out the seeds. The halves can be cut into long slices, or the flesh can be cut from the skin in small bite-size cubes.

 STORING
A whole, ripe cantaloupe will keep for 2-3 days at room temperature or 4-5 days in the fridge. Already cut fruit will keep for 4-5 days in a sealed container in the fridge.

 PRESERVING
Fresh cantaloupe can be preserved for year-round use by storing in the freezer. Prepare your melon as you would to eat fresh, then lay the cubed or balled fruit in a single layer on a baking tray, and leave in the freezer until fully frozen. Once frozen, transfer the pieces into a ziplock bag, and use for up to a year.

 USES
Fresh melon is delicious when eaten raw, as a snacking fruit. Fresh cantaloupe also makes a great addition to fruit salads, on top of yoghurt or granola, or skewered as a fun fruit-kebab.

Canteloupe are sometimes used as an addition to summer salsas, combined with red onion, cilantro and lime juice. Prosciutto-wrapped melon bites, makes a surprising and fun barbecue snack. Canteloupe can even be marinated and thrown on the grill for an unusual, richly satisfying variation of the fruit.

Fresh and frozen cantaloupe make a great blended addition to health-promoting smoothies. Fresh and frozen cantaloupe can also be blended and used in cold summer soups. Throw a handful of fresh or frozen melon pieces in a jug of water, and let sit for a fruit-infused water.

IN THE GARDEN

Sweet, juicy backyard-grown cantaloupe can be yours if you have the right combination of sun and soil, as well as some visiting pollinators.

 CLIMATE
Canteloupe plants like warmth and plenty of sun. Ground temperatures should be at least 70 degrees before planting seeds. In colder regions, seeds can be started in doors, but you will want to get them in the ground before they get too big.

 SOIL
Most of all, melons like to be in warm soil. In addition, they prefer a loamy, well-draining soil, that is rich in organic matter. Growing in raised hills helps to ensure better drainage and warmth-retention.

 PLANTING
Melon vines like plenty of room to grow, and should be planted 36" apart, or 12" apart if using a trellis. Put mulch down to keep the plant warm.

 **GROWING**
Young melon plants need a constant supply of moisture in order to grow. A drip-irrigation system is best, as well as special care during dry-spells.

 HARVESTING
Melon flowers are not self-pollinating, so having plenty of pollinator-attracting plants in your backyard is helpful to induce fruiting. Cantaloupes will take at least 45-days to mature, and should pull easily from the vine once ripe.

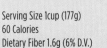

CARAMBOLA

Averrhoa carambola

Carambola, or starfruit, is the fruit of *Averrhoa carambola*, a species of tree native to Indonesia, the Philippines, and throughout Malaysia. This sweet and sour fruit grows in the shape of a five-pointed star. The skin is edible and the flesh has a mild, sour flavor that makes it popular in a number of dishes. The fruit is popular throughout Southeast Asia and the South Pacific.

VARIETIES

ARKIN Arkin are the leading commercial cultivar, with highly uniform fruit, between 4-5" long. They are very sweet, juicy, and have firm flesh with few seeds. They keep and ship well.

GOLDEN STAR The Golden Star produces large, deeply winged fruit. The skin is golden yellow and very waxy. The flesh of the is juicy, crisp and mildly subacid to sweet in flavor.

MAHA The Maha variety originated in Hawaii. It produces slightly larger, roundish fruit with light yellowish-white skin. The fruit is sweet and crunchy. It has white flesh with low acid content.

WHEELER This variety produces medium-large, elongated fruit. The skin and flesh of these starfruit are bright orange. They have a mildly sweet flavor. The Wheeler Tree a heavy bearer.

IN THE KITCHEN

Ripe carambolas can be used in cooking. In Southeast Asia, they are often stewed with apples in cloves and sugar. In China they are cooked with fish. Australians often cook them as a vegetable.

SELECTING
When selecting a perfect, ready-to-eat Carambola, look for firm, glossy unbruised fruit. Browning on the tips of the ridges is a sign of ripeness.

PREPARING
Wash, dry and cut crosswise into thin slices. The sliced fruits have an aesthetically pleasing appearance and are often used as garnish for salads or drinks.

STORING
Cover and refrigerate unwashed ripe carambola for up to 2 days. Ripen the fruit at room temperature until the skin is golden and its ribs are tinged slightly brown. A ripe carambola will have a noticeably sweet smell.

PRESERVING
Carambola become quickly perishable once harvested, but thankfully lend themselves to a variety of preserving methods for later use. Fresh carambola can be sliced and frozen for up to 6 months. The fruit can also be canned and preserved, in the form of a savory chutney or sweet jam. Make sure to research safe canning methods before attempting to preserve starfruit at home.

USES
Carambolas are most commonly eaten fresh, sliced into stars. These can be eaten on their own as a snacking fruit, or added to breakfast cereal, yoghurt, or as a salad garnish.

Fresh carambola can also be juiced into a delicious tropical beverage. Carambola juice can be blended with other tropical fruit juices or used for making cocktails and sangria.

The fruit can also be baked in pies, pastries, tarts and cakes. This can be done either with fresh fruit or fruit that has been cooked down into a stew. Sour or slightly under-ripe Carambolas are often used for making jams and candying, or are salted and pickled. Young, green fruits are used to make relishes or chutneys.

IN THE GARDEN

Carambola is a fairly easy plant to grow from seed under the right conditions. However these trees are slow-growing and will not produce fruit for some time.

CLIMATE
Carambolas do best in a frost-free location. They are tolerant of wind but need full sun. The carambola is not too particular as to soil, but will grow faster and bear more heavily in rich loam..

SOIL
The carambola will grow faster and bear more heavily in rich loam. It prefers a moderate pH.

PLANTING
In the tropics, carambola should be planted any season except summer. In cooler regions, plant in summer months in an area with plenty of sun.

GROWING
The tree should be regularly watered when young, but only needs to be watered during dry spells once established. It can be fertilized once a year.

HARVESTING
Carambolas are available year-round in tropical regions, and in the late summer through early winter in subtropical areas.

CHERRY

Prunus avium / Prunus cerasus

These small but juicy fruits are in season for only a short window in early summer, but are considered among our most beloved fruits. There are two distinct kinds of cherries: the sweet *prunus avium*, which can be eaten fresh; and the sour *prunus cerasus*, which are often dried for use in cooking, including soups, pork dishes, cakes, tarts, and pies.

VARIETIES

BING Bing are the most widely produced cherry. They are sweetest and juiciest by June and July. The fruits are heart-shaped and deep red to purple... They keep very well in cold-storage.

RAINIER Ranier are among the most popular in commercial growing. They are recognizable by their yellow-to-red skin. Deliciously sweet with a thin skin and creamy yellow flesh.

CHELAN These sweet cherries are much smaller and darker than other more well-known varieties. They grow abundantly in the Pacific Northwest, available early in the season.They are very sweet.

ROYAL ANNE Royal-Annes are most well-known as jarred Maraschino Cherries, which are heavily sweetened and dyed a bright red. A fresh Royal Anne is incredibly sour and tart when picked.

IN THE KITCHEN

When they are in season, look for plump, bright-colored market fruit. In general, the deeper the color of the fruit the sweeter it will be.

SELECTING

In stores or at the market look for plump, bright-colored fruit. In general, the deeper the color of the fruit the sweeter it will be. Avoid very soft or shriveled looking cherries.

PREPARING

All cherries should be properly rinsed in a colander to remove any lingering pesticides or harmful bacteria. Once rinsed, remove the pits and stems and enjoy.

STORING

Arrange cherries unwashed on paper towel in a shallow pan or ventilated container. Cover and refrigerate for up to three days.

PRESERVING

To freeze the leaves, boil them for three minutes, cool them in ice water, and strain the water before placing them in an airtight containers.

USES

Both sweet and sour cherries lend themselves to a variety of different uses. Sweet cherries can be eaten straight off the tree. They can also be stemmed and pitted, and then the flesh can be chopped up and added to cereal, yoghurt, or ice cream, as well as incorporated into some sweet baked recipes such as caked, breads, and pies. Fresh cherries can also be juiced. Fresh cherries can be cooked down into a soft stew, once pitted. Stewed cherries make a wonderful addition to yoghurt or ice cream, and can also be added to both sweet and savory sauces. Stewed cherries may be turned into jam, or into jelly by straining through a cheesecloth.

Cherries can also be dried, frozen, or even pickled. Dried cherries are delicious in granola and other breakfast cereals. Frozen cherries, once thawed, can be enjoyed much like stewed cherries.

Sour cherries are rarely available fresh; most are processed. When sour cherries are at their peak, they are picked and pitted, then immediately frozen, canned, or dried. Sour cherry juice is a popular health-food beverage. Sour cherries are often jarred in a sweet liquid then sold as a garnish for ice creams or cocktails.

IN THE GARDEN

In terms of care, there are no major differences between sweet and sour cherry trees. Both would make a great addition to your home garden!

CLIMATE

Sweet cherries are best suited where temperatures are mild and humidity is low while tart cherries grow in cooler climates and need about two months of winter temperatures below 45° F.

SOIL

Cherry trees like deep, rich soil which drains well. They prefer soil which is in the acidic range.

PLANTING

Trees should be planted in full sun, with good air circulation and well-drained soil. Plant seedling when they are at minimum 2" tall.

GROWING

A tree will do best if it is consistently watered, but not soaked. A thick layer of mulch will keep the roots of the tree moist and cool.

HARVESTING

Cherries are harvestable in late spring or early summer, depending on the region.. Full size varieties can produce up to 50 quarts of fruit.

NUTRITIONAL VALUE

1 serving = 140 g
Potassium = 350 mg/serving
Vitamin C = 15% Recommended Daily Intake
Sodium-free = 0 mg/serving
Fat-free = 0 g/serving

HEALTH BENEFITS

Helps With Arthritis And Inflammatory Conditions
Helps Lower Blood Pressure
Reduced Risk of Heart Disease
Reduced Risk of Colon Cancer
Improves Memory
Prevents from Insomnia

COCONUT

Cocos nucifera

The coconut is one of the most useful plants in existence, every part of which has some value. As a result, coconuts are called the "Tree of Life" and can produce drink, fiber, food, fuel, utensils, musical instruments, and much more.

VARIETIES

MALAYAN YELLOW DWARF These trees are extremely high yielding, producing an oblong, medium-sized fruit. The fruit turns pale-yellow throughout when ripe.

DWARF ORANGE COCONUT Dwarf Orange treed live 40 years, and will grow to 5 meters tall. They produce round, reddish yellow colored nuts. The fruit has sweet water and high meat content.

KING COCONUT
Native to Sri Lanka and India these are slightly shorter than other palms. The fruits are an elongated oval shape with bright orange skin. They produce a sweet, flavorful liquid.

WEST COAST TALL COCONUT
Also known as the Common Tall Coconut, these grow easily in all soils. They yield about 80 nuts per year. These yield a significant amount of coconut water.

IN THE KITCHEN

Coconuts are one of the most versatile fruits, when it comes to their culinary uses. There is almost no part of the fruit which is not delicious and healthy.

 SELECTING
Shake the nut up and down a little, if you do not hear anything, the coconut is too ripe and may taste soapy.

 PREPARING
Cracking open a raw coconut seems daunting, but with the right technique its fairly straightforward and worth the trouble. Its helpful to first heat the coconut up in a hot oven. Use a screwdriver to drill into the softest of the coconut's three "eyes". Create a small hole from which you can drain the water of the coconut. Next use a hammer, and hit the coconut firmly at the point which you created your drainage hole. After a few whacks your coconut should crack in two.

 STORING
Store a whole coconut in the fridge for up to two months. Once opened, the coconut meat can be kept covered in the fridge for up to 7 days.

 PRESERVING
Coconut flesh can be shaved and dried or frozen for future use.

 USES
The milk of the young nut is a highly nutritious drink. Coconut milk can be drank as-is, added to other nutritious beverages, or used in cooking, particularly in curries and south-east asian cuisine.

Commercially the greatest value of the coconut lies in the oil, which is extracted from the dried kernels of the fruit. This oil has a wide multitude of uses in cooking, and many other uses, includings beauty products.

Shredded coconut flesh is used chiefly in making cakes, desserts, and confectionery. The flesh can also be processed into a flour, which makes a versatile gluten-free alternative to traditional wheat flour.

IN THE GARDEN

To grow a coconut, begin with a fresh unopened coconut that still has its husk and water. Soak it in water for two to three days, then place it in a container filled with well-draining potting soil.

 **CLIMATE**
Coconut trees prosper is tropical areas that receive 47-94" of rainfall per year and stay between 71 and 93 degrees F.

SOIL
Coconut trees will tolerate a wide range of soil conditions and pH levels, provided there is plenty of drainage.

PLANTING
Coconut trees can be planted in the ground at any point of the year.

 GROWING
A coconut seed will take around 9 months to germinate, but after is an extremely fast-growing tree. Keep the soil of your tree consistently moist, especially during dry spells.

HARVESTING
Trees will live between 60-80 years, but will take at least 8 years to bear their first fruit. A mature tree will produce 50 fruits or more in a year, and will keep producing fruits until it dies.

NUTRITIONAL VALUE

1 serving = 100 g
Manganese = 75% Recommended Daily Intake
Copper = 22% Recommended Daily Intake
Selenium = 20% Recommended Daily Intake
Iron = 17% Recommended Daily Intake

HEALTH BENEFITS

Bone Health
Healthy Metabolism
Heart Health
Regulate Blood Sugars
Reduced Risk of Heart Disease

CRANBERRY

Oxycoccus

The cranberry has become a staple of American culture for its place in the Thanksgiving meal. Cranberries are marketed as superfruit due to their antioxidant and nutrient qualities, making them a must-eat food all season. Given their very sour taste, cranberries are rarely eaten raw. 98% of world production of cranberries results from the USA, Canada, and Chile.

VARIETIES

STEVENS These plants yield a slightly lower but very reliable crop of berries. They are easily managed, and keep and travel well - making them a commercial growing favorite.

GH1 This variety will produce berries for several decades if kept under healthy conditions. The berries are highly uniform in color and size. They are very winter-hardy.

VALLEY KING Valley King produce a high yield of fruit, with extremely large berries. The berries are very firm and a mottled red color. They are harvestable from September through October.

GRANITE RED This variety of cranberry yields an extremely firm, mid-size fruit. The fresh fruits have an excellent keeping quality, compared to other varieties. They produce fruits with very uniform color.

IN THE KITCHEN

In cooking, cranberries have a wide variety of uses both fresh and dried. Cooking with fresh cranberries always beats the taste of those in a can.

 SELECTING
Fresh cranberries are harvested in September and October, so fall is the best time to get them in season. Look for firm, dry berries with a clear pink or bright red color. Cranberries should be firm to the touch and unwrinkled.

PREPARING
Cranberries require little preparation, beyond a thorough rinse in a bowl of cool water, then drain the berries and gently pat dry.

STORING
Fresh cranberries will keep in the fridge for up to 8 weeks, if kept in a ventilated container with very little moisture. They can also be kept frozen for up to a year for later use.

 PRESERVING
To freeze the leaves, boil them for three minutes, cool them in ice water, and

USES
Due to the sour taste of fresh cranberries, they are rarely consumed without some preparation. Typically some type of sweetener is added, and cranberries are then incorporated into a filling for pies and other sweet desserts and sauces. Fresh cranberries can be baked into breads and muffins, so long as the batter is sweet enough to combat their naturally sour bite.

Cranberries are also available dried or in a can, but may contain added sugars. Check the ingredient label and make sure that the product contains cranberries only. Dried cranberries make a great addition to granolas, salads, and to certain baked treats. Cranberry juice is often mixed with other fruits and added sweeteners. Look for juice with cranberries as the first ingredient.

Cooking your fresh cranberries into a homemade sauce is a much healthier, and tastier, alternative to canned cranberries. Rinse your cranberries off and add them to a pan with a 1/2 cup of water and 1/4 cup of sugar. Bring the mix to a boil for 4-5 minutes, then cover and turn down as low as your stove will go and slowly cook the cranberries until they are a desirable sauce consistency.

NUTRITIONAL VALUE
1 serving = 100g
Protein = 0.4g/serving
Vitamin C = 24% Recommended Daily Intake
Fiber = 4.6g/serving

HEALTH BENEFITS
Prevention from Urinary-Tract Infections
Heart Health
Prevention from Stomach Ulcers and Cancers
Lowered Blood Pressure

IN THE GARDEN

The cranberry is one of only a three fruits native to North America, the other two being the blueberry and concord grape. Their growing conditions are very specific.

CLIMATE
98% of global cranberry production comes from Northern United States, Canada and Chile. Parts of Eastern Europe are slowly emerging as cranberry-growing regions, though on a much smaller scale.

SOIL
Cranberries grow on low-lying vines, in moist sandy soil. In the wild they would grow in bogs or marshes, created by glacial deposits. They prefer only rainwater, and will tolerate extreme cold in the winter.

PLANTING
Cranberry plants can be grown from seed, but must be watered in every day after planting. Plant after the last major frost in your area.

 GROWING
Frequent fertilizing and generous mulch in the winter will help a young cranberry plant to survive.

HARVESTING
A healthy cranberry plant should begin producing fruit in its second year.

CURRANTS

Ribes

The genus *Ribes* includes the edible currants (blackcurrant, redcurrant, white currant), the gooseberry, and several hybrid varieties. It should not be confused with the dried currant used in cakes and puddings, which is a small-fruited cultivar of grape (Zante currant). Harvested in summer months, these berries pack a healthy punch of nutrients in a tiny package.

VARIETIES

BALDWIN For years this was the favorite commercial variety of blackcurrant, grown for its large, mild, juicy berries, which ripen simultaneously for easier picking. Growers now prefer higher-cropping varieties.

BEN CONNAN The Ben Connan is a small-bush blackcurrant variety with a surprisingly heavy yield. The fruits are large, glossy and almost-black. In one season it produces over 7lbs of fruit. cropping varieties.

ROVADA Many growers consider 'Rovada' the best redcurrant cultivar. Plants are dependable, vigorous, late ripening, and very productive, bearing long-stemmed clusters of large easy-to-pick red berries.

BLANKA This is the commonly available variety of white currant fruit. The berries are large and an almost-translucent pale yellow color. They are fairly mild in their flavor.

HEALTH BENEFITS

Boosting immune system
Cardiovascular system health
Controlling high blood pressure
Controlling diabetes,
Relief from insomnia
Anti-viral benefits
Strengthened bones and teeth

IN THE KITCHEN

Punnets of fresh currants at the market are a rare treat. Buy them up, as they have a wide varieties of uses and means of preserving.

SELECTING
Look for firm, round berries with a consistent color throughout. Avoid buying punnets of currants, in which some of the berries look overripe or damaged. Underripe currants of all kinds will appear still slightly green.ave a slightly bitter taste.

PREPARING
In order to avoid damaging these very delicate fruits, the best way to clean them is to submerge the berries in a bowl of cool water, one cluster at a time. Lay the berries on a clean towel to dry.

STORING
Avoid keeping fruits piled tightly on top of each other. Refrigerate fresh currants this way for up to ten days. For longer storage, you can freeze them for up to one year.

PRESERVING
In order to get the most out of your fresh currants, year-round, the berries can be frozen whole and will keep this way for up to a year. Fresh currants are not usually canned without cooking down.

USES
The fruit of black, red, and white currants can be eaten raw, but they have a strong, tart flavor. They are more often added to a granola, yoghurt, or fruit salad to add a small, sour surprise. Fresh currants can be cooked into fruit breads, alongside meat and fish, or in pies and tarts.

Currants are more often cooked down with some sugar added. This stew can be strained in order to make a jelly, or left seeded and fleshy in order to make a jam. The cooked currant puree can also be used to create a delicious sauce which pairs well with many savory dishes and meats. In the U.K. redcurrant sauce is a common pairing with lamb. The stewed currants can also be used in baking, such as pies, cheesecakes, and other treats. It can be used to flavor ice cream and sorbet.

Once cooked and sweetened, currants, particularly black-currants, are often processed into a juice or concentrate.

NUTRITIONAL VALUE

100 g of berries
63 Calories
Protein 1.4g
Vitamin C 301% D.V.
Iron 9% D.V.
Potassium 9% D.V.
Calcium 6% D.V.
Vitamin A 5% D.V.

IN THE GARDEN

Currant Bushes are a great venture for an aspiring home fruit grower, as they thrive quite easily.

CLIMATE
Currant bushes are very easy growers, and will crop fruit under most circumstances. They like a sunny spot, but also tolerate light shade. During a dry spell, they appreciate being watered, as well as Occasional feeding.

SOIL
Currant bushes prefer well-drained, slightly acidic soil, rich in organic matter. If your soil contains more clay or sand, work in lots of organic matter.

PLANTING
Currant bushes need plenty of room and should be planted no closer than 4 feet apart.

HARVESTING
Pick only berries which are fully ripe. Avoiding picking underripe berries as they will not continue to ripen once picked.

MEDICINAL USES

Many health foods and drinks worldwide include different varieties of currants, particularly blackcurrants, among their ingredients. People use the whole plant, from the leaves to the seeds, for treating many conditions. The most common form is seed oil, but you can also make infusions and teas out of the plant's leaves, fresh or dried.

CUSTARD APPLE

Annona squamosa

Custard apple, sugar-apple, or sweetsop, is a delicious, fragrant fruit, popular for its sweet, slightly tangy, creamy-textured flesh. Custard apples originated in South America and the West Indies, though are now grown in Asia, Australia, and other tropical countries. It is high in energy, an excellent source of vitamin C and manganese, a good source of thiamine and vitamin B$_6$.

VARIETIES

PINK MAMMOTH Pink Mammoth custard fruits, as the name might suggest, are one of the much larger of the varieties of custard apples. Though the tree takes longer that others to produce fruit, it is the top choice of commercial custard apple growers. The fruit is sweet with a delicious flavor and melting texture. It has less seeds than other varieties.

AFRICAN PRIDE This variety of custard apple comes from a much smaller tree, and produces generally smaller fruits which contain numerous seeds. It produces heart-shaped fruit, with a slightly thicker skin which makes it easier to slice open and eat. The fruit of this tree can be enjoyed at a younger stage, and are still quite flavorful. African Pride is best for cooking.

IN THE KITCHEN

In the tropical regions where they are grown, custard apples are available year-round. This makes them a hugely popular choice in many dishes.

NUTRITIONAL VALUE

1 serving = 120 g
Vitamin C = 38% Recommended Daily Intake
Magnesium = 22% Recommended Daily Intake
Vitamin B6 = 15% Recommended Daily Intake
Iron = 6% Recommended Daily Intake

HEALTH BENEFITS

Hair and Skin Health
Healthy Weight
Prevents Asthma
Prevents from Heart Attack
Digestive Aid
Aid for Diabetics
Regulates Blood Pressure
Reduces Cholesterol

SELECTING
Look for even-colored fruits which yield slightly when pressed. The ridges of the fruit may be tinged with brown, but the fruit should not appear black, pulpy or withered. Avoid small or dark green fruits.

PREPARING
Custard-apples are soft when ripe and easily cut open and enjoyed. Wash the fruits to remove dirt, then pat dry. Slice the fruit in two and gently pull apart the fruit.You can use a spoon to scoop edible flesh.

STORING
A ripe custard apple will keep in the fridge, uncut, for up to five days. To ripen an unripe custard apple, leave it out at room temperature..

PRESERVING
They can be pureed and frozen in a sealed container for up to a year.

USES
Fresh ripe fruits can be eaten on their own without any additions and seasoning, as a snacking fruit.

In cooking, it is more common to use the flesh of a not-yet-ripened fruit. Underripe breadfruit can be used more like a vegetable for cooking with. The flesh, when mature but not yet ripe, is very starchy and can be used much like a potato. Though it cannot be enjoyed raw in this form, it can be steamed, boiled, roasted or fried. The flesh can be mashed and added to curries, or sautéed with garlic and oil and eaten as is. It can also be cut up and picked or candied, in order to preserve and enjoy.

Once ripe, the fruit can also be cooked down into a sweet puree which can be added to sorbet, yoghurt, or baked into muffins and cakes.

IN THE GARDEN

Custard Apples grow best at low altitudes, in arid or semi-tropical conditions.

CLIMATE
The majority of custard apples are produced in Central and South America, They are also grown in India, Sri Lanka, Malaysia, Viet Nam, the Philippines, and Taiwan, and on a smaller scale in southern Florida, Australia, tropical Africa, and Egypt. Exportation of these fruits is fairly limited.

SOIL
This tree needs tropical conditions, but can withstand some cooler winter temperatures. This species prospers in a consistently humid atmosphere. It does best in low-lying, deep, rich soil with good drainage.

CAUTION!
Never ingest the seed of the fruit as they are toxic!

PLANTING
It is possible to grow these trees from seed, though they are more typically grafted. Multiple trees should be grown 10-15ft apart.

GROWING
Regular pruning will be required for a healthy Custard Apple tree, though they can withstand fairly long periods of drought.

HARVESTING
Pick when they begin to turn from green to their ripened color.

DATE FRUIT

Phoenix dactylifera

Dates have been a staple food of the Middle East and the Indus Valley for thousands of years. There is archaeological evidence of date cultivation in Arabia from the 6th millennium BCE. Dates are high in natural sugar, so many people think they may not be a healthy choice food, these sweet fruits are packed with plenty of nutrients, making them an excellent snack.

VARIETIES

MEDJOOL This is the most widespread commercially-grown date fruit. The fruits are very large, and ripen early. They are deliciously sweet, moist, and flavorful, and cook well.

DEGLET NOOR This tree produces a fruit which is drier, firmer, and more elongated. This variety keeps its shape when cooked, and also are often found pitted and dried in supermarkets.

BARHI The Barhi is sweetest of dates, syrupy-rich and very soft. They can be eaten underripe or ripe. Barhi do not ship well, therefore are rarely found outside of their native areas.

KHADRAWY Khadrawy are rich and soft, not overly sweet. Khadrawy are considered some of the best in flavor and texture.. They do not keep long so must be enjoyed quickly.

IN THE KITCHEN

Dates are a versatile fruit for eating fresh, cooking with, and preserving. Though they are only fresh during the summer months, they are enjoyed dried year-round.

 SELECTING
Look for dates that are shiny and unbroken. Do not eat dates that have a sour smell, are very hard, or have crystallized sugar on their surface.

 PREPARING
Fresh dates should be rinsed gently, and then can be eaten whole, around the pit. You can also slice the flesh in two and pull the segments from the pit. Dried dates which still contain pits are fairly easy to cut into and pull the pit out before consuming. Dried dates do not require rinsing.

STORING
Fresh dates will last about a week in the refridgerator. However, most people eat dried dates, which will last up to a year in the fridge or at room temperature a few months.

PRESERVING
Dates can be frozen for up to three years.They can also be canned or pickled.

 USES
Fresh dates can be eaten straight off the plant, or sliced into segments. They are delicious on their own, or can be added to breakfast cereals, yoghurts, or as a salad garnish. Fresh dates can also be blended into smoothies, stuffed with cheese or nuts, or chopped and added into fruitcakes and other sweet baked goods.
Fresh dates can also be cooked down to a stewed fruit which is delicious as

is, but can also be used in a variety of ways. Stewed dates can be added on top of various breakfast items like oatmeal or yoghurt, as well as on ice cream.
Cooked dates make a great jam, jelly, or chutney, preserving them for later use. Dates can be boiled with sugar and strained into a sweet date syrup, which is a popular alternative to other sweeteners. Stewed dates are also great as filling in baking recipes, such as pies and tarts. Cooked dates are used in some savory dishes as well. Dried dates can be chopped and added to a variety of meals, including on top of breakfast cereals, yoghurt and granola, as well as in a salad.

IN THE GARDEN

Dates are the fruit of the date palm tree, which is grown in many tropical regions of the world.

 CLIMATE
Date fruits are grown commercially largely in the Middle East and parts of Africa. They will also grow on many subtropical islands as well as in parts of the United States.

 SOIL
Date trees do best in areas of full sun where soil is well draining. They are fairly adaptable and can grow in soil which is sandy, loamy, or clay-rich. The tree is drought-tolerant but will need plenty of water in order to flower and produce fruit.

 **PLANTING**
Date trees are not self-pollinating, so a male and female tree should be planted side-by-side. Young seedling trees will usually be labeled as males or females, when purchased.

 GROWING
The date tree is drought-tolerant but will need plenty of water in order to flower and produce fruit, especially during long dry spells.

 HARVESTING
Date trees usually begin to fruit in April or May and become harvestable in early-September. They ripen off the tree, so can be picked at various stages of ripeness.

HEALTH BENEFITS

Reduced risk of Disease
Brain Health
Promotes Natural Labor
Bone Health
Low Glycemic-Index

NUTRITIONAL VALUE

1 serving = 3.5 ounces
Fiber = 7g/serving
Protein = 2g/serving
Potassium = 20% Recommended Daily Value
Magnesium = 14% Recommended Daily Value
Copper = 18% Recommended Daily Value
Manganese = 15% Recommended Daily Value
Iron = 5% Recommended Daily Value
Vitamin B6 =12% o Recommended Daily Value

DRAGON FRUIT

Hylocereus undatus

Dragon fruit grows on the Hylocereus cactus, also known as the Honolulu Queen, whose flowers only open at night. The plant is native to southern Mexico and Central America. The brightly-colored fruit is sure to catch your eye, should it appear in your local grocery store or market. In addition to its visual wow-factor, this unusual fruit has a winning flavor and health-profile.

VARIETIES

H. POLYRHIZUS These pitaya roja, or red-skinned dragonfruit are perhaps the most eye-catching, with a bright red skin and flesh. These tend to mature in the late summer or fall.

H. UNDATUS These are the most commonly seen variety of dragonfruit, particularly in non-native areas. They typically have a pink or white skin and white inner flesh.

SELENICEREUS MEGALANTHUS
These yellow-skinned fruits are much smaller but also sweeter than other dragonfruit varieties. The plants prefer warmer climate and are not frost-tolerant.

HYLOCEREUS MONACANTHUS
This variety has dark pink skin, and vivid red flesh with black seeds. The fruit has spines and sharp edges; use extreme caution when handling

IN THE KITCHEN

Though they may appear intimidating, cutting, preparing, and eating this exotic fruit is as easy as it is delicious.

SELECTING
When looking for a ripe dragonfruit, seek out fruits with bright, evenly-colored skin. Some blemishes are okay, but lots of bruising is a sign of over-ripe fruit. A ripe fruit should yield slightly to pressure but not be overly soft or hard.

PREPARING
Dragonfruits should be rinsed just as a precaution. The fruit will cut easily in two, after-which the flesh can be easily scooped from the skin of the fruit. The seeds are edible, though the skin is not. The flesh can then be balled or cubed.

STORING
A ripe, uncut dragonfruit will keep on the counter for 2-3 days. For longer storage, place the fruit in a sealed bag in the fridge. Once cut, a dragonfruit should be quickly enjoyed, as it will not keep.

PRESERVING
In order to use these tasty-fruits year-round, dragonfruits can be cut and frozen for up to one year. Simply lay the cubed fruit pieces out on a baking tray in the freezer, until solid. Then transfer the frozen fruit to a sealed bag or container. Dragonfruit readily absorbs scents and odors, so a well-sealed container is necessary.

USES
Most commonly, dragonfruits are enjoyed fresh, with very little preparation at all. Once cut into bite-size segments, dragonfruits make a great snacking fruit, or addition to a fruit salad, breakfast yoghurt, or overnight breakfast bowl. The fruit can also be used fresh or frozen as an addition to health-promoting smoothies.

Fresh dragonfruit pairs well with many fish dishes. It can be served as-is or prepared into a more savory salsa, with red onion and lime juice. Dragonfruits are also sometimes used to make a flavorful vinaigrette dressing, simply by blending the raw fruit with oil, salt, and vinegar.

Dragonfruits are not usually cooked, as they don't tend to keep their color or flavor very well. Dragonfruit can be cooked down into a fruity stew, which can be used as a topping or flavoring in other dishes. To revive their vibrant pink color, powdered dragonfruit can be added to the stewed fresh fruit.

IN THE GARDEN

Dragonfruits are actually a cactus plant, meaning they love lots of sun and heat. However, they will adapt well to container growing, if you live in a cooler or urban area.

CLIMATE
Dragonfruit do not like cooler weather, nor do they like excessive heat. In regions where temperatures exceed 100 F the plant will need afternoon shade. Dragonfruits will not survive in regions where temperatures fall to freezing.

SOIL
This plant prefers a sandy, very well-draining soil. It is forgiving of poor-quality soil, lacking in nutrients. For container growing, make sure there are plenty of drain-holes.

PLANTING
Dragonfruit is a vining-cactus and will need a support. Dragonfruits can be grown from seed, but are more easily grown from cuttings.

GROWING
Water plants twice a week. Fertilize only very poor soil.

HARVESTING
A dragonfruit usually takes at least 30 days to mature. The longer fruits are left on the plant, the sweeter they will get.

DURIAN

Durio

Known colloquially in South-East Asia as the "king of fruits", the durian is easily recognized by its large size, unpleasant smell, and thorny rind. Despite the unusual, intense odor of the durian fruit, the inner flesh is sweet and custard-like with complex, robust flavors. The durian is the fruit of several tree species belonging to the genus Durio.

VARIETIES

MUSANG KING This variety of Durian fruit is often hailed as the richest and best tasting ever bred. Its rich and creamy texture, coupled with a bittersweet and complex layer of tastes has earned its reputation.

RED PRAWN The red prawn is distinctive from other varieties, by its orange to red flesh. Younger trees produce much sweeter fruits while older trees produce increasingly bitter durian fruits.

BLACK THORN The black thorn durian tree grows predominantly in Penang. It has a black, thorny outer skin, distinctive from others. The flesh is a deep yellow, with a rich, custardy flavor.

The flesh is rounded and mounded and very thick. Black Thorns vary a lot in size, but can be recognized by their perfectly plump pumpkin shape and squat little stems, about as long as a thumb.

IN THE KITCHEN

The flesh can be eaten at various stages of ripeness, and it is used to flavour a wide variety of savoury and sweet desserts in southeast Asian cuisines. The seeds are toxic when raw.

 SELECTING
Choose crisp bunches with small leaves and thin, tender stems for the freshest flavor. Avoid those with obvious insect damage or budding flowers. Thick, more mature stems may have a slightly bitter taste.

 PREPARING
Opening a durian's hard, spiky shell often requires gloves or mitts to protect your hands. You need to cut the shell with a knife and pry it open with your hands before gently removing the durian flesh.

 STORING
Store durian fruits in the refrigerator for up to five days. Store the whole durian in an air-tight container in order to preserve its taste and natural aroma, as well as to avoid it contaminating other food items in the fridge.

 PRESERVING
To freeze the leaves, boil them for three minutes, cool them in ice water, and strain the water before placing them in an airtight containers.

 USES
Durian is commonly eaten fresh, out the fruit, on its own. It is also frequently turned into a sweet dessert, steamed with sticky rice and sweet coconut milk. Another popular dessert combines fresh durian fruit with coconut milk, red bean paste, and palm sugar. Fresh durian fruit can be added to smoothies. In Southeast Asia, where these fruits are widely available, they are incorporated into a variety of sweet foods, such as cheesecakes, pies, and sweet breads. They are also used to flavor ice cream, sorbets, and candies.

IN THE GARDEN

As a backyard fruiting tree, the durian tree will grow and produce well with relative ease, so long as local conditions are right.

 **CLIMATE**
Durian are cultivated widely in parts of Southeast Asia where temperatures average between 75-86 F, and never fall near freezing. These trees are extremely sensitive to cold temperatures, and will drop their leaves and die should temperatures fall below 46 F.?

SOIL
Durian trees like conditions that are both hot and extremely humid. Durian trees prefer loamy, well-draining soil, preferably on slightly sloping land such as a hillside.mal pH range is 5.5 to 7.0.

 PLANTING
Wait for the hottest rainiest time of year to plant your durian tree. A fully grown tree can grow up to 150ft tall, so will need plenty of room to grow.

 GROWING
The plant should be kept in the shade for the first two weeks after planting, and water well.

HARVESTING
Harvesting is best done on sunny days, once the fruit has fully matured and a strong odor is noticeable.

NUTRITIONAL VALUE

1 serving = 243 grams
Fiber = 9g/serving
Protein = 4g/serving
Vitamin C = 80% Recommended Daily Value
Thiamine = 61% Recommended Daily Value
Potassium = 30% Recommended Daily Value

HEALTH BENEFITS

Reduced risk of Cancer
Prevents Heart Disease
Fights Infection
Lowers Blood Sugar
Used in Traditional Medicine to treat various illnesses

ELDERBERRY

Sambucus nigra

Throughout Europe, Western Asia, North America, and North Africa; elder bushes are commonplace in woodlands and hedgerow. Black Elderberries are one of the most commonly used medicinal plants in the world. Elderberry fruit or flowers are used as dietary supplements for minor diseases such as colds, constipation, and other conditions, often as a tea, extract, or in a capsule

VARIETIES

ADAMS Adams are native to North America, and very similar to wild varities. The most common commercial-grown bushes,they produce small white flowers and large clusters of deeply colored berries.

BLUE This bush produces large dusty-blue berries which are often confused with blueberries. The fruits on this bush have a rich, intense flavor.

MEDICINAL USES

Elderberry leaves, bark and fruit are all commonly found in homeopathic remedies for a variety of ailments, particularly in those which boost the immune system, reduce cold or flu symptoms, treat bladder infections, and improve digestive health.

YORK York is an old-style cultivar, and produces by far the largest berries, and a very considerable yield.. Many use it as'fencing' as it grows up to 12ft tall.

IN THE KITCHEN

Black ederberries can be eaten raw, blue varieties should be cooked before eating, and red elderberries should be deseeded and cooked before eating.

 SELECTING
Look for firm berries, of an almost-black color. Avoid fruits which look mushy or bruised. Under ripe berries can cause mild to severe stomach problems.

PREPARING
Clean elderberries while still attached to their branch. Submerge the whole cluster in a bowl of water, swishing around to remove any unwanted insects or debris. Gently pat the berries dry before pulling them from the stem.

 STORING
Elderberries have a very short "shelf-life" and should be enjoyed quickly. They may store fresh in the refrigerator for up to five days, or frozen and enjoyed for up to a year

 PRESERVING
Elderberries can be frozen, dried, or canned for later use.

USES
Black elderberries can be eaten fresh, though they are often quite sour. More commonly they are stewed with sugar into a sauce which can be enjoyed in both savory and sweet recipes. Sweetened, stewed elderberries can be eaten as is, on top of yoghurt, granola, or ice cream. The stewed berries can also be turned into jam or jelly. It can also be used in a variety of baked goods, such as pies, tarts, and crumbles.

Fresh elderberries can be turned into a wine, with only about six months of fermentation. Elderberries can be fairly easily turned into a juice. In this form they are cooked with sugar, then strained to obtain the sweet concentrated juice. This can be turned into a jelly or syrup for later use. As a syrup, or cordial, has become an extremely popular way to enjoy the delicious flavor of the elderberry. The cordial can be added to water for a sweet drink, or used in cocktails.

IN THE GARDEN

Once planted, these bushes are quite straightforward to maintain, and if they survive their first year, you can almost count that they will survive for years to come.

 CLIMATE
Elderberry bushes prefer partial to full-sun, but would rather be cool and moist than hot and dry. They are fairly adaptable to a variety of regions and growing conditions.

SOIL
Elderberry bushes prefer moist, well-drained soil with a fairly neutral pH, though they are fairly adaptable to a variety of different soil-types. They prefer partial to full-sun, but would rather be cool and moist than hot and dry.

PLANTING
Elderberry bushes should be planted in the spring, once the risk of frost has passed. A single bush will grow up to 12ft tall and 6ft across, so be sure to give them plenty of room to grow.

GROWING
Once planted, these bushes are quite straightforward to maintain, and if they survive their first year, you can almost count that they will survive for years to come. They will benefit from yearly pruning.

FEIJOA

Acca sellowiana

The Feijoa fruit, or guava pear, is an egg-shaped fruit. Most varieties are similar in color to a lime, with a soft, succulent flesh which likens in texture to a pear, though with a slightly more tart and tropical flavor. Native to South America, this fruit is now also grown widely in New Zealand and California.

VARIETIES

STRAWBERRY FEIJOA
Strawberry feijoa can grow up to 10 feet , although they can grow taller. As the name suggests, this tree usually produces a red fruit, but yellow fruits are also possible.

COOLIDGE These are the most widely cultivated variety in California.The trees grow upright and strong, while bearing many fruits. The fruits are slightly smaller with wrinkled skin and mild flavor.

MAMMOTH The Mammoth feijoa variety produce large, round or oval fruits, with slightly thicker, wrinkled skin, and a gritty, but delicious flesh. They are soft and do not ship well.

OPAL STAR This is a classic, smooth, darker skinned feijoya, medium in size. The flesh is juicy and very fragrant. The trees are strong and compact, and produce a fairly heavy crop. which stores well

IN THE KITCHEN

Fresh feijoa fruits are deliciously sweet and fragrant, and are a pleasure to keep in the fruit bowl, while they are in season.

 **SELECTING**
A ripe fruit will be noticeable fragrant, and will yield slightly when pressed. If they are hard, leave the fruits at room temperature for a couple days to ripen.

PREPARING
In order to enjoy a fresh feijoa, peel off the bitter skin and slice the flesh into bite-size segments. In most varieties the seeds will be unnoticeable and are fine to ingest.

STORING
Feijoa will store for up to a week in the refrigerator. At room temperature they ripen very quickly.

PRESERVING
Feijoa do not keep well, and therefore preserving techniques are a useful way of prolonging their delicious flavor. TThey can be jarred skinned or unskinned in a preserving liquid of your choice.

USES
Feijoa are delicious as a fresh snacking fruit. Fresh feijoas can be chopped and added on top of breakfast cereals, yoghurt, or as a salad garnish. They can also be chopped and turned into a fresh salsa. Fresh feijoa can be incorporated into muffins, pies and fruit breads. Feijoas are delicious poached whole, and enjoyed with cream or on their own. They can also be cooked down into a stewed fruit with a wide variety of uses. Once stewed, feijoas can be easily processed into chutney, jam, jelly, or a sweet cordial. The stewed fruit can also be used in a variety of baking and cooking recipes, as either a sauce or filling.

IN THE GARDEN

If you live in a climate to which feijoa are partial, they are a great backyard fruit tree for their adaptable growing tendencies.

 CLIMATE
Feijoa trees like mild, sub-tropical climates. Feijoa are fairly drought-resistant, but will need both adequate water and drainage.

SOIL
Feijoya are quite adaptable and can be grown in a wide range of soil types. It does best in rich soil which is slightly acidic, but is not limited by these factors.

PLANTING
Feijoya seeds will germinate in three weeks, in proper growing soil. The seedlings can be transplanted into pots once they have grown their second leaf, and then can be transferred into the ground fairly easily.

GROWING
Feijoa's are slow-growing trees and will benefit from plenty of water and bi-monthly fertilizing in their first year. Pruning is not necessary.

 HARVESTING
Once ripe, fruits will begin to fall from the tree, a sign to get picking!

FIGS

Ficus

The fig tree is one of the oldest cultivated fruit trees in the world, growing indigenously from asiatic Turkey to Northern India. Particularly, in the Mediterranean figs are a staple of the diet, known as the "poor man's fruit". Figs can be eaten fresh or dried, and used in jam-making. Most commercial production is in dried forms, since the ripe fruit does not transport well.

VARIETIES

BLACK MISSION This is a staple of commercial fig growers worldwide. The fruits are smaller, with a soft, pink flesh and many seeds which provide a pleasant bite.

BROWN TURKEY These figs are also hugely popular and grown worldwide. The fruits are pear-shaped, with maple-brown skin. Look for slightly soft fruits, as they are often picked underripe.

CALIMYRNA This Turkish fig is often dried, though still tasty fresh. The fruits often split when ripe, because they are so plump with sweet juice. They retain this moisture when dried.

KADOTA These are the most common green figs, believed to be thousands of years old. The skin is yellowish green, and the flesh smooth and silky. They are common in California.

IN THE GARDEN

Fig trees are extremely easy to harvest and will produce an abundant yield of fruit, under the right conditions. Be sure to handle the figs as little as possible while harvesting.

 CLIMATE
Figs require lots of sunlight and warmth, and enjoy a dry climate.They prefer only light spring rains, and require soil with food drainage.

 GROWING
Fig trees need plenty of water in the first weeks after planting. Overwatering ruins the flavor of the fruits, and over-fertilizing lowers fruit yield.

SOIL
Fig trees are fairly adaptable when it comes to soil type. They will be happiest in slightly acidic, very well-draining soils.

HARVESTING
Fig trees are one of the rare trees that can be harvested multiple times in a season, particularly in warmer areas. The harvest periods will be first in June and then again in late summer. In cooler areas, a single harvest is more likely, in late summer or early fall. To detect ripe figs look for signs of the stems wilting, or fruits which droop down from the tree.

PLANTING
Fig trees will be happiest planted in spring, before the warmest season. They are self-pollinating and do not need to be planted in pairs.

IN THE KITCHEN

Fresh figs used in cooking should be plump and soft, without bruising or splits. If they smell sour, the figs have become over-ripe. Figs are most flavorful at room temperature.

 SELECTING
Look for a soft, sweet-smelling fruit. Avoid figs with wrinkled skin, or which are split or oozing.

 PREPARING
Figs can be eaten whole, skin and all, needing only a gentle rinse. The seeds provide a pleasantly crunchy texture, and are safe to ingest. When cooking with figs, there is no need to remove the skin.

 STORING
Figs can be stored, unwashed, in a plastic bag in the fridge for 2-3 days. They will overripen very quickly if left at room temperature. If frozen, figs will keep for up to one year.

 PRESERVING
Fresh figs are delicious but ripen quickly and have a very short shelf-life. Thankfully there are a variety of ways to preserve figs. They pickle well, and pickled figs will keep in the fridge for up to three months.

 USES
Fresh figs can be sliced for a delicious topping on breakfast cereal, yoghurt or as a salad topping. Whole or halved figs are great roasted in the oven. Roast figs can be enjoyed on their own, on a pizza, or in a salad, among other dishes. Fresh figs are sometimes sliced and baked into sweet cakes and other batters, or on top of savory dishes

Figs can be cooked down into a fruity stew, which has a wide variety of uses. The stewed fruits can be enjoyed as is, on top of yoghurt, or ice cream. The fruity stew can also be processed into a chutney, jam, or jelly. Fig preserves are delicious paired with cheese and crackers. This can also be strained into a juice, consumed in smoothies and other beverages. The stewed fruits can be added to a variety of sweet and savory recipes, as both a sauce or filling.

 NUTRITIONAL VALUE

1 serving = 100 g (2 medium)
Magnesium = 7% Recommended Daily Intake
Vitamin K = 6% Recommended Daily Intake
Vitamin B6 = 6% Recommended Daily Intake

 HEALTH BENEFITS

Regulates Blood Sugars
Prevents from Infections
Stimulated Metabolism
Regulates Blood Pressure

GOJI BERRY

Lycium barbarum

Goji berries have exploded in popularity recently, gaining a reputation as a leading super-fruit. They are believed to have innumerable health benefits, and are uniquely rich in amino-acids. While they can be found as a powder or supplement, they are also great in dried or fresh fruit-form. In Asia young shoots and leaves are harvested commercially as a leaf vegetable.

VARIETIES

CRIMSON STAR This is a self-pollinating variety which can fruit as a single plant. They yield a large amount of fruit as early as their first year. They will reach 6-8ft tall. .

PHEONIX TEARS This goji berry bush has a long harvest of over four weeks. It will yield a very large crop of bright orange, jelly-bean shaped berries. The fruit has a sweet flavor and medium acidity.

IN THE KITCHEN

While they are all the rage in the health food world, not everyone knows the wide variety of ways to use goji berries in home cooking and eating.

 SELECTING
Because of their varying forms in grocery stores and health food shops, it is best to think about what your intended usage is for the goji berries before you buy them. Powdered goji berries will pack the most nutritional value, while dried berries retain the greatest flavor.

 PREPARING
Goji berries are most commonly purchased in dried form. While the dried berries can be used straight from the bag in granolas and smoothies, they can also be rehydrated for different preparations. In order to rehydrate goji berries, simply soak berries in just-boiled water for a few minutes.

 STORING
Both dried and powdered goji berries will keep for a long time in the cupboard, though they will begin to lose their nutritional value after a year of storage.

 USES
Goji berries are rarely eaten fresh outside of the Himalayan mountain region, where they are native. Fresh berries grow on vines and are similar to tomatoes in appearance. The fresh berries are very tart, and are commonly dried for consumption. Once dry they lose much of their tartness and resemble a cranberry, cherry and tomato mix in flavor.

The dried berries can be used in many ways, such as in salads, granolas, yoghurt, or baked into cookies, cakes and fruit breads—they can be used in any way that a raisin might be used.

Dried goji berries can also be rehydrated and then used moist. The rehydrated berries can be folded into rice pudding, savory pilafs, salsas, chili, or a variety of other dishes that will benefit from their sweet, bite-size surprise. The hydrated berries can be blended and added to sauces, smoothies, and ice creams.

IN THE GARDEN

Goji berry plants are in the nightshade family, relatives of tomatoes and peppers. However they will typically require hotter temperatures.

 CLIMATE
Goji plants prefer to be grown in full-fun, and can handle fairly extreme conditions where many other plants might not survive. They require plenty of room in order to reach full-size, though pruning will keep them in check.

SOIL
Goji plants like a loamy, slightly alkaline soil, but can adapt to other soil types. If planting in clay-rich soil, make sure that irrigation is monitored to avoid waterlogged soil. If growing in more sandy soil, water your plant often.

PLANTING
Goji plants can be grown from seed or from a young seedling, and will usually be ready for proper transplanting in their second year. They should be planted in the spring, after the risk of frost.

 GROWING
Keep the soil surrounding your bush moist for the first few months after planting. Generous mulch will help retain moisture. After this allow the soil to dry out between watering.

 HARVESTING
Goji plants will bloom in late spring, and their fruit will be mature by mid-summer. Harvest is quite labor intensive, as the fruits must be hand-picked and are very susceptible to damage.

NUTRITIONAL VALUE

1 serving - 1/4 cup of berries
90 Calories
Protein 4g
Dietary Fiber 4g
Vitamin A 180% D.V.
Vitamin B2 63% D.V.
Vitamin C 30% D.V.

HEALTH BENEFITS

Boosts Immune System
Eye Health
Skin Health
Reduces Blood Pressure
Heart Health
Protects from some Chronic Diseases
Anti-Diabetic

GOOSEBERRY

Ribes grossularia

Much more common in European growing and cooking, gooseberries remain largely unknown in the United States and other parts of the world. This is a shame, as these small berries are both delicious and packed with healthy benefits. Their culinary uses are many, as they can be enjoyed both ripe and underripe.

VARIETIES

BLACK VELVET These plants are used widely in commercial growing as a dessert berry. The fruits are small, deep red, and sweet with a flavor which like a blueberry. The plant is hardy and very cold-tolerant.

CAPTIVATOR These thorn-free bushes are a top choice for home-growers. The pinkish-red fruits are sweet and mild. They do not yield huge amounts of fruits, and will drop them when ripe.green leaves.

HINNOMAKI YELLOW This hybrid plant produces a large yield with great flavor. The bush is fairly disease-resistant. The fruits are large and sweet, with a yellow skin and a good flavor.

POORMAN This bush produces large, flavorful fruits, enjoyable fresh and cooked. The berries are pear-shaped and reddish. The yield of fruit is smaller than most, making is best for home-growing.

IN THE KITCHEN

These lesser-known fruit gems have a wide variety of kitchen uses, both in their sweet and sour varieties.

 **SELECTING**
Look for brightly colored fruits with plump skins, and without mold or soft spots.

PREPARING
Rinse berries only immediately before consumption. In order to avoid damaging these delicate berries, submerge them in a bowl of water, swish around, then gently pat dry. Remove any small segments of stem that might be still attached.

STORING
Unwashed berries will last from 5-7 days in a ventilated tub in the fridge.

PRESERVING
TGooseberries can be preserved whole in a canning liquid of your choice. They can also be frozen whole or as a puree.

 USES
Gooseberries come in two major varieties: sweet, eating berries and sour, cooking berries. The sweet berries really are best eaten fresh. When cooked, they do not tend to keep their flavor. Gooseberries are often used fresh in a popular English summer dessert called a "fool", in which the berries are gently folded in with cream and meringue. Sweet gooseberries can be frozen and eaten later, so long as they are defrosted immediately before use.

Gooseberries have a wide variety of culinary uses. They can be added whole into sweet batters and breads, though they are normally cooked down into a sweet stew before use. This stew is delicious as is, on top of yoghurt or ice cream. The stewed berries can also be processed into chutneys, jams, jellies, or a concentrated juice.

MEDICINAL USES

Gooseberries have long been used for their medicinal properties in natural remedies. The fruit of the gooseberry plant can be turned into a healthy juice which is drank on its own, or added to smoothies and other beverages. The fruits can also be dried and turned to a powder, which can be incorporated to your diet in a variety of ways.

IN THE GARDEN

Gooseberries are less finicky than most other small fruits about soil acidity and tolerate a wide range of soil types, making them a great choice for gardeners.

 CLIMATEE
Gooseberries are not picky about soil, but prefer lots of morning sun and afternoon shade, as well as rich soil. They are very winter hardy, but fruit well in warmer climates.

 SOIL
Gooseberry bushes are fairly lenient when it comes to soil type, but will do best in a rich, and well-draining soil.

 PLANTING
Plant gooseberry bushes in late fall or early spring. Be sure to dig a whole with plenty of room for bushy root growth.

 GROWING
In, moisture-retaining soil gooseberries need little water, unless during a long, dry spell. Regular pruning will promote fruiting.

 HARVESTING
Gooseberries are ready to pick from early summer onwards. Pick only the plump, fully ripe berries and handle them extremely gently. Refrigerate quickly.

GRAPE

Vitis vinifera

The grape is an ancient fruit, and some of today's grapes are directly descended from ancient varieties. They are grown worldwide, on incredibly large scales, as a major export both for eating fresh as table grapes or they can be used for making wine, jam, juice, jelly, grape seed extract, raisins, vinegar, and grape seed oil.

VARIETIES

PINOT NOIR This is a popular wine-making grape, originating in Northern France but now grown worldwide. The fruits are thin skinned and deep purple when ripe.

CRIMSON SEEDLESS Crimson seedless are found widely in supermarkets, referred to usually just as 'Red Grapes'. They are very firm, with a slightly thicker skin which gives them a pleasant bite.

COTTON CANDY These pleasant green grapes are grown widely in California and really do taste like cotton candy! They are larger fruits with a soft green skin, and undetectable seeds.

REISLING Reisling grapes grow best in slightly cooler climates. It is an incredibly versatile fruit, lending itself to wines which are bone-dry to very sweet, desert-wines.

IN THE KITCHEN

Fresh grapes off the vine make a truly perfect bite-size treat. But just how else can you use these kitchen gems?

 SELECTING
Choose crisp bunches with small leaves and thin, tender stems for the freshest flavor. Avoid those with obvious insect damage or budding flowers. Thick, more mature stems may have a slightly bitter taste.

 PREPARING
Grapes require little preparation beyond a good rinse in cold water. They can be enjoyed right off the stem.

 STORING
Grapes stored in a perforated bag in the fridge will keep for up to a week. Left at room temperature they will ripen quickly.

 PRESERVING
Grapes freeze extremely well, and will keep in the freezer for up to a year. Simply wash and remove stems, then lay out on a baking tray in the freezer. Once fully frozen, they can be transferred to a ziplock bag.

USES
In the summer months, fresh grapes are a perfect refreshing, and sweet bite-sized snacking fruit. Many people also enjoy eating frozen grapes straight out the freezer. Fresh grapes can also be sliced and added to fruit salads, on top of breakfast cereal or yoghurt, or as a garnish to chicken salads. Unripe, sour grapes are used in some cooking, particularly in the middle east. Ripe grapes are also used in cooking, especially pairing with savory meats. They can also be roast whole on their own, producing an intense and sweet flavored dish, which can be enjoyed on its own, or as a topping for ice cream or toast.

Fresh grapes can be juiced, or turned into syrup to be bottled. In order to make a grape syrup, fresh grapes are cooked down into a thick, dark, molasses-like substance. It can be added to a variety of recipes, or used in the place of other sweeteners. Sweet, stewed grapes can also be turned into a jelly or jam.

Grape wines can be used in a wide variety of ways in the kitchen, for cooking into sauces and gravies, as well as in many popular desserts.

IN THE GARDEN

Grapes are one of the worlds oldest cultivated fruits, and still the most widely grown in the world.

 CLIMATE
There are many different varieties of grape vines, meaning they can be grown in fairly wide-ranging conditions. Almost all grape vines require 6-8 hours of sun daily. They prefer soil which is sandy or rocky and well-draining.

 SOIL
Grape vines prefer soil which is sandy or rocky and well-draining.

 PLANTING
Plant dormant, bare-root grape seedlings in the spring. Select an area with full sun in well-draining soil. They will need a trellis or support system.

 GROWING
In the first few years, a yearly, vigorous pruning is necessary to promote future fruiting.

 HARVESTING
A grape vine will take 1-3 years before producing its first sweet fruits. Taste the grapes before harvesting to ensure that they are ripe and ready. Avoid picking grapes prematurely, as they will not continue to ripen once picked.

GRAPEFRUIT

Citrus paradisi

The modern grapefruit was first bred in the 18th century as a hybrid of an orange and pomelo. They were given their name because of their growing in clusters similar to grapes. They are both delicious and packed with health-boosting nutrients.

VARIETIES

STAR RUBY Both sweet and tart, the Star Ruby is recognized by its soft pink, blushed looking skin, and deep-red flesh. In general, the deeper red the grapefruit flesh, the sweeter the fruit will be.

MARSH SEEDLESS The White Marsh grapefruit is the most widely grown worldwide. It is both sweet, acidic, and very juicy. Ruby Red and Pink Marsh varieties are also grown.

FLAME The Flame Grapefruit is even more richly-colored than a Ruby Red, and considerable sweeter as well. It is known for being particularly juicy.

DUNCAN This type of grapefruit is grown largely in Florida. It is larger, yellow-skinned, juicy, and extremely flavorful. Because it is heavily seeded, it is mostly used for juicing.

IN THE KITCHEN

Grapefruits have long been lauded as a healthy and invigorating breakfast food. However their healthy uses go way beyond breakfast!

 SELECTING
Look for a firm, rounded fruit that feels heavy when lifted. Avoid bruised or wrinkled fruits.

PREPARING
Grapefruits should be washed and cut in two around the width of the fruit. Use a serrated knife to separate the flesh from the skin, and you should be able to scoop out bite-sized segments.

STORING
Stored in a plastic bag in the refridgerator, grapefruit will keep for up to six weeks. Before eating, take the grapefruit out and allow to sit at room-temperature, to ensure it will be at its juiciest. .

PRESERVING
Grapefruits can be preserved by either canning or pickling. They also can sliced into rounds, and frozen for up to a year.

USES
Grapefruits are delicious and at their healthiest when enjoyed fresh and as is. They can also be sliced and used on top of yoghurt or salads. Grapefruits are incredibly juicy and will yield a considerable amount of fresh juice. This can be drank alone, or with other fruit and vegetable juices to neutralize the sourness.

Though healthiest left as is, grapefruits are highly acidic, and can lend themselves to a variety of other uses with a little sweetening. They are delicious when left to marinate in a little sugar or maple syrup, then used. Grapefruit can also be roast in the oven, and used as a dessert, breakfast, or snack.

Grapefruits can be cooked down with some sugar into a sweet and sour stew, which is easy to eat on its own, or added to yoghurt or ice cream. The fruity stew can also be strained and used to make a delicious glaze for cooking or for topping desserts.

IN THE GARDEN

The grapefruit is an evergreen tree that can grow up to 15 meters tall. This makes it more suited for commercial growing, unless you have a very tall ladder.

CLIMATE
Grapefruits are a warm-weather fruit, requiring lots of sun and a well-draining, loamy soil. A well-established tree can endure quite cold dips in temperature.

SOIL
Grapefruit trees need a well-draining, loamy soil. They are not particular about pH, though they do well in slight-alkaline.

PLANTING
Choose a spot for your tree with full sun, and which is protected from strong winds or run-off flooding.

GROWING
Water your tree everyday for the first few weeks, then just a week. There is no need to prune.

HARVESTING
Most grafted grapefruit trees will begin bearing fruit as soon as two years after planting. They should be harvested in the fall, and fruits should be left on the tree as long as possible for maximum sweetness.

NUTRITIONAL VALUE

1 Serving = 128 g
41 Calories
Vitamin C = 59% Recommended Daily Intake
Pantothenic Acid = 7% Recommended Daily Intake
Copper = 7% Recommended Daily Intake

HEALTH BENEFITS

Boosted Immune System
Curbed Appetite
Aids in Weight Loss
Regulates Insulin Levels
Heart Health
Reduced Risk of Kidney Stones

GUAVA

Psidium guajava

Guava trees are found widely in most warm, tropical climates where they thrive. They are one of the richest fruits in antioxidants and vitamin C, as well as extraordinarily sweet and delicious. They have a pronounced and typical fragrance, similar to lemon rind but less sharp. The outer skin may be rough, often with a bitter taste, or soft and sweet.

VARIETIES

BEAUMONT This variety, native to Hawaii, is very vigorous, producing fruits which are perfect for processing into juice. The fruits are large, mildly acidic and full of seeds.

RUBY SUPREME This tree is drought tolerant but will produce more fruit if watered regularly. It will easily adapt to most soil conditions and enjoys full sunlight. All guava trees love organic fertilizer.

MEXICAN CREAM These small, red-blushed guavas make excellent dessert fruits. Their flesh is creamy, white and very sweet. The seeds are relatively small and unnoticeable.

SWEET WHITE INDONESIAN This tree produces a large, round fruit with a thin, pale yellow skin. The flesh is thick white, meltingly juicy and sweet. The seeds are small and edible.

IN THE KITCHEN

If you've seen these exotic, green fruits in your grocery store but haven't known how you would use it at home, fear not! Guava fruits lend themselves to a wide variety of delicious kitchen uses.

 SELECTING
Look for firm, brightly colored fruit which are free of bruising or blemishing

 PREPARING
Wash the outer skin of your guava just before eating. Some guavas can be bitten straight into. Otherwise, cut the fruit in half and scoop out the flesh, or skin and then slice.

 STORING
Ripe guavas will keep covered in the refrigerator for 2-3 days. Leave an unripe guava at room temperature until it yields to slight pressure.

 PRESERVING
Guavas can be cut up and frozen for up to a year. They will discolor in the freezer, but adding lime juice or freezing them in a simple syrup will help keep their color. Guavas can also be cut in two and canned in a preserving liquid for up to a year.

 USES
Guava is delicious enjoyed fresh, as a snacking fruit. In many parts of the world, guava is served topped with honey, salt, or coated in a spice mix Fresh guavas can be added to smoothies, or juiced. Guava juice is hugely popular around the world, though most store-bought varieties have been sweetened. Underripe guavas can be turned into a salsa.

Guavas can be sliced fresh and roast with meats in some savory dishes, or used as a filling in pies and tarts. Guava is also often cooked with sugar until it reduces down to a thick, sweet fruity stew. The stewed guavas are high in natural pectin and can be turned into a jam, jelly, or syrup. They can also be eaten as a topping on yoghurt, ice cream, or other desserts. Stewed guavas make a delicious filling for many baked treats and regional desserts.

IN THE GARDEN

A healthy backyard guava tree will live for up to 40 years, and will provide you with harvestable fruit twice a year.

 PLANTING
Plant your guava tree in the spring, in a hole which is at least two feet deep. Water it in well.

 GROWING
Guava trees should be watered every day for the first couple weeks, then 2-3 times monthly.

 HARVESTING
In certain, warmer regions guavas will ripen year-round, with the heaviest bloom at the onset of spring. They are sweetest left on the tree to ripen, but will continue to ripen once picked.

CLIMATE
Guava trees grow widely and easily in subtropical areas. They will tolerate either humid or dry conditions, but will not survive a sudden frost. They need full sun, but are not fussy about soil type so long as it is draining.

SOIL
Guavas need full sun, but are not fussy about soil type so long as it is draining. Beyond this they are not picky about soil.

NUTRITIONAL VALUE

100g
68 Calories
Vitamin C 228mg (381% D.V.)
Dietary Fiber 5.4g (22% D.V.)
Potassium 417mg (12% D.V.)
Vitamin A 624IU (12% D.V.)

HEALTH BENEFITS

Improved Blood Sugars
Heart Health
Relieved Menstrual Symptoms
Improved Digestion
Aid in Weight Loss
Immune Boost
Skin Health

HONEYDEW

Cucumis melo L. (Inodorus Group) 'Honey Dew'

The honeydew melon, also known as a honeymelon, is the fruit of one cultivar group of the muskmelon, *Cucumis melo* in the gourd family. They are closely related to cantaloupes, though they ripen slightly later. Of the two, honeydew melons are sweeter, juicier and have a melting texture which makes them very popular summer fruits.

VARIETIES

SUPER DEW This is a 'standard' variety of honeydew, with a large, 6-lb fruit. The skin turns to creamy yellow as the fruit ripens, containing light green flesh which is juicy, aromatic and very sweet.

CRENSHAW This is another standard, green-skinned melon. It is more pear-shaped, with a sweet, pink inner flesh. It is a favorite of backyard gardeners in warm, dry climates.

ORANGE SORBET Though green-fleshed honeydews are much more common, this orange-fleshed variety can also sometimes be found in fruit markets. They are slightly smaller, and mature more quickly.

MARYGOLD This is another lesser-found honeydew variety, which is recognizable by its wrinkly-yellow skin once ripe. The fruit has a short maturation period and flesh is white and crisp.

IN THE GARDEN

Sweet, juicy backyard-grown honeydews can be yours if you have the right combination of sun and soil, as well as some visiting pollinators.

 CLIMATE
Melon plants like warmth and plenty of sun. Ground temperatures should be at least 70 degrees before planting seeds. In colder regions, seeds can be started in doors, but you will want to get them in the ground before they get too big.

SOIL
Most of all, melons like to be in warm soil. In addition, they prefer a loamy, well-draining soil, that is rich in organic matter. Growing in raised hills helps to ensure better drainage.

PLANTING
Melon vines like plenty of room to grow, and should be planted 36" apart, or 12" apart if using a trellis. Put mulch down to keep the young plant warm.

GROWING
Young melon plants need a constant supply of moisture in order to grow. A drip-irrigation system is best, as well as special care during dry-spells.

HARVESTING
CMelon flowers are not self-pollinating, so having plenty of pollinator-attracting plants in your backyard is helpful to induce fruiting. Honeydews will take at least 75-days to mature, must be allowed to fully ripen before picking.

IN THE KITCHEN

A fresh, ripe, refreshing cantaloupe is a real summer treat - and one that will do you nothing by good to have in the kitchen!

 SELECTING
When selecting a honeydew, look for a heavy fruit, free of soft spots of bruising. A ripe melon will be fragrant with a creamy-colored skin.

 PREPARING
Rinse the outer skin of your melon. Slice the melon in two halves and scoop out the seeds. The halves can be cut into long slices, or the flesh can be cut from the skin in small bite-size cubes.

STORING
A whole, ripe honeydew will keep for 2-3 days at room temperature or 4-5 days in the fridge. Already cut fruit will keep for 4-5 days in a sealed container in the fridge.

 PRESERVING
Fresh honeydew can be preserved for year-round use by storing in the freezer. Prepare your melon as you would to eat fresh, then lay the cubed or balled fruit in a single layer on a baking tray, and leave in the freezer until fully frozen. Once frozen, transfer the pieces into a ziplock bag, and use for up to a year.

 USES
Fresh melon is delicious when eaten raw, as a refreshing snacking fruit. Fresh honeydew also makes a great addition to fruit salads, on top of yoghurt or granola, or skewered as a fun fruit-kebab. Honeydew melons are sometimes served alongside cottage cheese, as a great hot-weather pairing.

Honeydew are sometimes combined with peppers, cucumber and mint to make a refreshing, cold, summer soup. Prosciutto-wrapped melon bites, makes a surprising and fun barbecue snack. They can also be added to spicy, savory salsas for a surprising bite of sweetness.

Fresh and frozen honeydews make a great blended addition to health-promoting smoothies. They can also be blended and used as a base for ice cream and frozen fruit pops. Throw a handful of fresh or frozen melon pieces in a jug of water, and let sit for a fruit-infused water.

NUTRITIONAL VALUE

1 serving - 1 cup, diced
61 Calories
Protein .92g
Dietary Fiber 1.4g (5% D.V.)
Vitamin C 51% D.V.
Potassium 11% D.V.
Vitamin B6 8% D.V.

HEALTH BENEFITS

Reduces Blood Sugar
Bone Health
Reduces Risk of Heart Disease
Replenishes Electrolytes
Digestive Aid
Improves Hydration
Skin Health

HUCKLEBERRY

Vaccinium / Gaylussacia

Huckleberries have a sweet spot in American heritage, where they grow wild. These bite-size berries might be small, but they are certainly not unimportant, both in their regional significance and their wealth of healthy flavor. Huckleberries were traditionally collected by Native Americans for use as food or traditional medicine.

VARIETIES

DWARF HUCKLEBERRY Native across America, this plant will grow up to 2ft tall, and yield bright blue berries with delicious flavor. They are not grown commercially because berries are too small.

CASCADE HUCKLEBERRY This popular plant produces large, bright-blue berries with outstanding flavor and aroma. They grow best at higher altitudes, forming wide-spreading heaths.

MOUNTAIN HUCKLEBERRY The fruits of this species vary widely, from red, blue, black, purple and sometimes white. Though they only grow wild, they are the most widely harvested variety of huckleberry.

RED HUCKLEBERRY These red huckleberries grow in an around clearings, particularly in America's coastal areas. They berries are quite sour, but are popular in jams and other preserves

IN THE KITCHEN

While these small, blue berries are often confused for blueberries, they certainly deserve their own place in any home kitchen, when available. Their taste is much different to a blueberry, sharper and more expansive.

SELECTING
Ripe huckleberries can be found in blue, red, purple and even black. A ripe berry will have a deep, all-over color. Avoid berries which look damaged, squished, or shriveled.

PREPARING
Huckleberries require little preparation beyond a thorough rinse of their outer skin. They are delicate berries, so the best way to rinse them is by submerging the berries in a bowl of cold water, then gently laying out to dry.

STORING
Huckleberrries can stored in the fridge for up to one week, in a ventilated container. Avoid purchasing unripe berries, as they will not ripen after picking.

PRESERVING
In order to enjoy your fresh huckleberries all year round, they can be laid in a single on a baking sheet and frozen. Once solid, transfer the berries to a sealed ziplock bag, and enjoy for up to a year.

USES
Huckleberries are the sweetheart of many mid-western U.S. states for a reason. They have a variety of uses, and a unique taste from other, more popular berries. They can be enjoyed raw, off the bush as a delicious snacking fruit. They will have noticeable seeds, though these can be swallowed or spit out. They can also be used fresh in fruit salads, on top of breakfast foods, or in smoothies. They can be baked fresh into muffins, pies, or fruit tarts. They can also be frozen when fresh, and will keep for up to a year. More or less, they can be used anywhere a blueberry would be, but provide a richer, more aromatic flavor.

Huckleberries can also be cooked down into a fruity stew, with or without added sugar. This can then be processed into a jam, jelly, or sweet syrup. The huckleberry stew can be enjoyed on top of yoghurt or ice cream, or eaten on its own.

IN THE GARDEN

Huckleberries are more or less intolerant of both commercial and home-growing. Seek out these bushes in the wild, to pick the fruits yourself.

CLIMATE

Most huckleberry varieties enjoy plenty of afternoon shade, and moisture. They grow in rocky hills and boggy, cypress swamp margins, but also can thrive in dry woods and sandy pinelands where they have full sunlight in the morning and partial shade in the afternoon.

SOIL

Huckleberries tend to prefer moist, but well-draining soils, which are slightly acidic. Most of all they like an abundance of decomposed plant matter and organic material within their surrounding soil.

HARVESTING

Expect Huckleberry bushes to flower between April and May. Most huckleberries are at peak harvesting season in August. They will not continue to ripen once picked, so avoid picking underripe berries.

JACKFRUIT

Artocarpus heterophyllus

While the spiky, green jackfruit skin gives it a dauntingly inedible appearance, this couldn't be further from the truth. Inside the jackfruits thick skin is a highly versatile and nutritious flesh, that has recently become hugely popular as a meat-alternative protein. Its native range is unknown but it is thought to originate in the region between southern India and the rainforests of Borneo.

VARIETIES

BLACK GOLD This Australian jackfruit tree is a vigorous fruit producer, and easily maintained. The flesh of these fruits is more easily removed from the fruit and provides a sweet, aromatic flavor.

DANG RASIMI From Thailand, this jackfruit tree is one of the most prolific fruiters and fastest-growing, if unpruned. The fruits are pale yellow-green and fairly uniform in size, with flavorful flesh.

GOLDEN PILLOW This variety has a reputation for especially beautiful, flavorful fruit. The flavor is mild and sweet, with no musky aftertaste. The tree is a manageable size and bears fruit very young.

TABOUEY An Indonesian Jackfruit variety with particularly irregularly, misshapen fruits. The flesh is firm, pale yellow and has almost no aroma. The flavor is very mild.

IN THE KITCHEN

Jackfruits are a tropical fruit, which have gained popularity worldwide in recent years, due to their unique ability to provide a meat-like substitute in plant-based cooking.

 SELECTING
A ripe fruit will range in color from yellow to green, making it hard to ascertain ripeness just by looking. It should be noticeably fragrant, and the flesh bright yellow.

PREPARING
Many suggest oiling your hands and cutting knife before slicing into this sticky fruit. It is best to use a serrated knife to cut the skin from the flesh. Pull out the flesh from the outer skin and remove the core and seeds, as they are inedible. cut them into bite-size pieces.

 STORING
A whole jackfruit will keep at room temperature for up to five days, or in the refrigerator for 6 weeks.

 PRESERVING
Both the flesh and rind of the jackfruit can be canned in a brining liquid or syrup, depending on how you intend to use it later. The flesh of the jackfruit can also be laid out in a warm oven and dried into jerky-like strips.

USES
The fresh, ripe flesh of jackfruit is sweet and can be eaten straight out the fruit. It can also be used in smoothies, or as a fresh ingredient in muffins, cakes, and ice cream. It can be pureed and enjoyed with yoghurt or added to sticky rice for a delicious, tropical rice pudding.

Jackfruit has become hugely popular as a plant-based alternative to meat. In this case the flesh of a young, unripe jackfruit is used for cooking. Like tofu, jackfruit absorbs flavors incredibly well, without adding much flavor of its own. The flesh can be shredded, and cooked much in the way meat might be, in the oven, on the stovetop, or in a slow cooker. Jackfruit lends itself well as a "pulled pork", in sliders, sandwiches, and lettuce wraps.

IN THE GARDEN

A single jackfruit tree is a highly efficient and productive food source, yielding 100-200 fruits per year.

 CLIMATE
Jackfruit trees enjoy full sun and a climate which is hot, humid, and receives plenty of rainfall.

 SOIL
Jackfruit prefer deep, rich soil that is loamy and well-draining, with a pH of 6.0-7.5. They will not tolerate wet roots.

PLANTING
Jackfruit do not transplant well from cuttings, and will grow more successfully from seed. Germination takes 3-8 weeks and your seedling should be planted when no more than 4 leaves have grown. s

 GROWING
Jackfruit trees should be fertilized twice yearly, and also pruned generously once a year.

 HARVESTING
Jackfruit trees are precocious fruiters, yielding fruit as early as their second year. The fruits mature 2-5 months after flowering. In native areas, trees yield fruits year-round, but most heavily in summer.

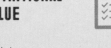 **NUTRITIONAL VALUE**

100 g
94 Calories
Vitamin C 6.7mg (11% D.V.)
Potassium 303mg (9% D.V.)
Dietary Fiber 1.6g (6% D.V.)
Vitamin A 297IU (6% D.V.)

HEALTH BENEFITS

Improved Blood Sugar Levels
Reduced Inflammation
Decreased Risk of Certain Diseases
Heart Health
Improved Immune System
Skin Health

JUJUBE FRUIT

Ziziphus jujuba

Jujube fruits have been grown in China for over 4,000 years, where over 400 known cultivars can be found. Beyond their regional importance, they are a delicious bite-sized treat that pack a healthy punch of vitamin C alongside many lesser-occurring nutrients and antioxidants.

VARIETIES

LI This Chinese Jujube produces loads of fruits at a very early age. The fruits (drupe) resemble a small egg in size and are green as they begin to mature in the fall. They are super sweet eaten fresh, or dried.

GOLA Gola jujube fruits and larger than average, and are the earliest variety to ripen. The golden-yellow fruits are jvery uicy and provide a good flavor.

KAITHLI This jujube tree produces an average yield of fruit, as well as medium-sized fruits. These jujubes are less sour than other varieties, with a pulp that id very soft and sweet.

KATHA PHAL These jujube fruits are on the small size that ripens later in the season than most. When ripe, the fruits will have a green blush on one side and a reddish-yellow on the other.

IN THE KITCHEN

In terms of culinary use, jujube is consumed as a fruit, dry candy or in the form of juice. They have a variety of other uses also.

SELECTING
Jujube fruits typically turn from a bright green, to a chocolate-brown as they ripen. Look for fruits which are fairly firm and free of bruising or other blemishes.

PREPARING
This fruit is mostly consumed raw, and can be eaten without needing and preparation beyond a quick rinse. For cooking, the jujube fruit can be sliced in two, in order to remove the pit, and then chopped or used as is.

STORING
A fully ripe jujube fruit can be stored at room temperature for up to five days, or in the fridge for much longer. Jarred, candied jujubes will last for about 3 months.

PRESERVING
Fresh jujube fruits can be preserved in a couple different ways, to prolong their enjoyment. They can be jarred in a simple syrup or other preserving liquid and will keep this way for up to three months. They also can be dried and enjoyed much like dates.

USES
Fresh jujube fruits can be enjoyed in their raw state, as a snacking fruit. The whole fruit can be pickled, or jarred for preservation. Fresh jujube can also be used in many recipes where an apple might otherwise be used, as they have a similar taste and consistency. This includes on salads, in smoothies, or in baking pies, tarts and more. In many regions they are baked into a fruit cake.

Fresh jujubes can be stewed down with sugar and then enjoyed as is, or used in a variety of ways. The stewed fruit might be used as an ingredient in cooking or baking, or may be processed into a jam, jelly or chutney.

Jujubes can be turned into a juice which is a popular Korean welcome drink.

IN THE GARDEN

Jujube, or the Chinese Date, is a great fruiting tree for beginner gardeners. It grows in a wide range of climates and requires very little pruning.

CLIMATE
Jujube trees do best in warm, dry climates but can tolerate extreme winter colds once well-established. They prefer to be in full-sun, for maximum fruit yield. ?

SOIL
Jujube trees like to be planted in well-draining, loamy soil, but are fairly lenient when it comes to pH and soil type. The tree is remarkable in its ability to tolerate water-logging as well as drought.

PLANTING
The jujube plant is readily grown from seed, which will germinate in just 7 days. Seeds should be sewn in the spring and should bud by four months. Seedlings should be given space of 30ft between.

GROWING
Water your jujube tree every few days until it seems like it has established healthy roots. Do not fertilize before this point.

HARVESTING
It is extremely easy when it comes times for harvesting jujube fruit. When jujube fruit has turned dark brown, it will be ready to harvest.

NUTRITIONAL VALUE

100g
79 Calories
Vitamin C 69mg (110% D.V.)
Copper .073mg (*% D.V.)
Iron .48mg (6% D.V.)
Pyridoxine .081mg (6% D.V.)
Niacin .900mg (5% D.V.)
Potassium 250mg (5% D.V.)

HEALTH BENEFITS

Sleep Aid
Regulate Circulation
Bone Strength
Aids in Weight Loss
Stress Reliefe
Boosts Immune System
Skin Health
Digestive Aid

KIWI FRUIT

Actinidia deliciosa

Kiwi fruit, or Chinese gooseberry, is the edible berry of several species of woody vines in the genus Actinidia. These once-exotic fruits are native to New Zealand and were nicknamed after the kiwi bird for their shared characteristics, both having a soft, fuzzy brown covering. Kiwis are nutrient-dense, providing a healthy dose of nutrients while containing few calories.

VARIETIES

HAWYARD This is the kiwi variety most commonly found in stores and supermarkets. They are larger in size, with a fuzzy brown skin and sweet juicy flesh. They prefer mild winters.

BRUNO Bruno fruits are a large cylindrical kiwi which is darker brown than the ubiquitous Hayward. They require lower winter chilling temperatures, but will be sensitive to a very sudden chill.

SAANICHTON 12 Saanchiton kiwis are large and rectangular shaped. That flavor is sweet and flavorful and the plant is hardier than others.

ANANASNAYA This is the most hardy, commercial variety of kiwifruit. They are very good quality with a good aroma and sweet, intense flavor. The skin tends to be tough.

IN THE KITCHEN

Kiwi fruit are much more than a tropical treat. These brightly colored green fruits contain numerous phytonutrients and vitamins that will do much more than brighten up your food salad.

SELECTING
Look for an every ripe fruit with no obvious bruising or discoloration, that yields slightly when pressed.

PREPARING
People often do not know that the skin of the kiwi is edible, and the fruit can be eaten much in the same way as a pear. The soft fuzz can be gently rubbed off, if the texture is unpleasant. Alternately the fruit can be sliced in half, and the flesh scooped out from the skin.

STORING
Unripe kiwis can be left to ripen at room temperature, out of full-sunlight. Then they will keep in the fridge for up to two weeks.tor for up to six months.

PRESERVING
Kiwi fruits can be preserved and enjoyed year round by freezing, drying, or canning. Freezing is the easiest way, and can by done by laying out sliced kiwi on a baking tray. Kiwis can be canned in a preserving liquid of your choice for us to 6 months. They can also be sun-dried, oven dried or dehydrated.

USES
Kiwi fruits are at their most delicious and nutritious eaten fresh, as is. They can be sliced in half in order to scoop the flesh straight from the fruit with a spoon, or sliced into refreshing, bite-size segments. The fruit is also sometimes coated in a drizzle of honey or salt before enjoying fresh. Kiwis can be added to blended smoothies, or juiced with other health-forward fruits and veggies. Kiwis make a great addition to fruit salads, yoghurt, or as a green salad garnish. Kiwis can be blended with other fruits or vegetables to make a sweet, refreshing cold summer soup.

Fresh kiwis can be processed into a delicious chutney by cooking down with garlic, onion, vinegar and various other chutney spices. Kiwis can also be cooked down and processed into a jam or jelly, though they contain very little natural pectin.

Kiwis do not cook well, losing much of their color and flavor, and breaking down in structure. They are sometimes used to top fruit tarts.

Dried kiwis make a great addition to breakfast granolas and other treats.

NUTRITIONAL VALUE

serving size 100g
61 Calories
Vitamin C 92.7mg (155% D.V.)
Dietary Fiber 3g (12% D.V)
Potassium 312mg (9% D.V.)
Calcium 34mg (3% D.V.)
Iron .31mg (2% D.V.)

HEALTH BENEFITS

Improves Asthma Symptoms
Digestive Aid
Immune System Support
Prevents from Health Conditions
Improved Blood Pressure
Reduced Risk of Blood Clot
Eye Health

IN THE GARDEN

Botanically kiwis are actually a berry, though one which grows on a vine. If you live in an area with mild winters and a long frost-free period, they make a great choice for backyard growing.

CLIMATE
Kiwi fruits require a well-draining soil and plenty of sunlight. In areas that are excessively hot, kiwi fruits will need to be in shade during the midday sun.

SOIL
Kiwis like a very fertile well-draining soil with plenty of well-rotted organic matter.

PLANTING
Kiwi vines spread up to 20ft and 40ft high and require lots of room for growing. Kiwis do not self produce, so there must be both a male and female plant close by in order to induce pollination.

GROWING
Water plants twice a week. Fertilize only very poor soil. More text to this point maybe? It seems rather short as it was.

HARVESTING
Kiwi fruits reach full size by August but become harvestable only by late-October. If kiwi fruits have not fully ripened before the risk of frost, it is best to pick them and let them ripen off the vine.

KUMQUAT

Citrus Japonica

Kumquat translates to "golden orange" in Chinese, the region where these fruits are native. Now they are grown in various countries worldwide. Kumquats are not much bigger than a grape, but they possess an incredible depth of sour, tart, and delicious flavor.

VARIETIES

HONG KONG This variety of kumquat is native to Hong Kong and the mountainous regions nearby. The fruit is almost-round and bright orange, with a thin skin and less flesh than other fruits.

MARUMI Marumi kumquats were introduced to Florida from Japan as a more cold-tolerant variety. The skin is golden-yellow and smooth, with a spicy, aromatic flavor. The seeds are very small.

MEIWA This hybrid kumquat is much larger than others, and more oblong than round. They peel is orange-yellow and thick, with a sweet, seedless pulp. They are best for eating fresh.

NAGAMI Nagami kumquats are the most commonly cultivated in the United States, from a tall-growing and prolific tree. The fruits are oblong and smaller, usually containing a small number of seeds.

IN THE KITCHEN

When you see fresh, brightly-colored kumquats at your local market, buy them up! They can be preserved in a variety of ways, therefor will make a great year-round option.

IN THE GARDEN

Kumquat trees are believed to be native to China, though now are grown world-wide, by commercial growers and home-gardeners alike.

CLIMATE
Kumquats enjoy hot summer weather, but also will withstand cooler temperatures than other citrus plants. They are cold-hardy, but grow better and produce larger and sweeter fruits in warmer regions.

SOIL
A kumquat tree will tolerate any soil pH and most soil types as long as the soil is well-draining. Soil should be kept moist, but not soaked or soggy.

PLANTING
Kumquats are rarely grown from seed as they do not do well on their own roots. They do not do well being root-bound, and potted kumquat trees must be dwarfed.

GROWING
Water plants twice a week. Fertilize only very poor soil. More text to this point maybe? It seems rather short as it was.

HARVESTING
Kumquats usually begin to become harvestable in late January, and remain in-season as late as April. It is customary to clip 2-3 leaves along with each fruit.

SELECTING
When looking for a ripe kumquat, select fruits which have a glossy, brightly-colored rind and no cracks or bruises. Overly soft fruits will spoil quickly. Avoid fruits which are shriveled.

PREPARING
Kumquats are unique citrus fruits in that they can be eaten whole, skin included. Simply give the fruits a thorough wash under the tap before eating. They can also be sliced in two, for other preparations.

STORING
Kumquats will keep for several days at room temperature, or can be kept in a sealed bag in the refrigerator for up to a month.

PRESERVING
There are a variety of ways to prolong the shelf-life of your kumquats, so they can be enjoyed year-round. The fruits will preserve very well in a simple syrup, either whole or sliced. Kumquats also are delicious pickled, in either a sweet or savoring pickling brine. They will keep this way for up to a year. Kumquats can be pureed and frozen.

USES
When in season, kumquats make a delicious, zappy snacking fruit straight out of hand. They can also be enjoyed sliced in half and added to fruit salads, yoghurts, and as a garnish on green dinner salads. Kumquats can be baked fresh into fruit breads and into pies and tarts.

Kumquats can also be cooked down with sugar into a fruity stew, which can be used in a variety of ways. The stewed fruits can be enjoyed on top of yoghurt or ice cream, or as an ingredient in cooking and baking. They are sometimes used in marinades for fish, chicken or meat. They can also be used as a filling in pies, cakes and other confectionaries.

The stewed kumquats can be processed and preserved into a chutney, jam, jello or marmalade. Kumquats are slightly sweeter than seville oranges, and make a delicious alternative in marmalades.

NUTRITIONAL VALUE

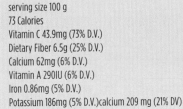

serving size 100 g
73 Calories
Vitamin C 43.9mg (73% D.V.)
Dietary Fiber 6.5g (25% D.V.)
Calcium 62mg (6% D.V.)
Vitamin A 290IU (6% D.V.)
Iron 0.86mg (5% D.V.)
Potassium 186mg (5% D.V.)calcium 209 mg (21% DV)

HEALTH BENEFITS

Lowers Cholesterol
Anti-Inflammatory
Supports Immune Health
Regulate Blood Sugar
Represses Appetite

LEMON

Citrus Limon

This sour citrus fruit is a mainstay in the home kitchen. The tree's yellow fruit is used for culinary and non-culinary purposes globally, primarily for its juice, which has both culinary and cleaning uses. The pulp and rind are also used in cooking and baking. The distinctive taste of its juice makes it a key ingredient in drinks and foods such as lemonade and lemon meringue pie.

VARIETIES

EUREKA This is the predominant lemon variety, grown most widely around the world. The tree is a thornless, year-round bearer making it hugely popular for commercial growing. It contains few seeds and highly acidic juice.

FINE The fine, or Primofiori, lemon is spherical with a smooth, thin skin. The flesh is very juicy and contains few seeds, though the tree is a thorny variety. This variety has highly acidic juice.

FINGER CITRON Also known as Buddha's Hand, these fruits are extremely fragrant and misshapen. In China, where they are native, they are a welcome offering. It is typically used for pith and rind, rather than its juice.

BUSH This Australian native is a hardy fruit, with thick bumpy skin. The flavor is strong and authentic. They are lower in juice but have a strong-tasting flesh. The bush lemon is self-seeding, and also good for grafting.

IN THE KITCHEN

Keeping a couple fresh lemons around is a must in all home kitchens. Not only is lemon juice a super versatile ingredient, but even the rind and skin of the lemon can open up a world of culinary possibilities.

 SELECTING
Select a fruit with bright, shiny skin and a saturated yellow color throughout. A ripe lemon will be noticeably fragrant. Avoid fruits with obvious bruising or shriveled skin.

 PREPARING
Fresh lemons can be cut lengthwise into smaller wedges, or cut around the width in order to juice. To use the rind, rinse, dry, and finely grate the outer skin.

STORING
Fresh lemons will keep at room temperature for up to one week. They will also keep in the fridge for up to one month.

PRESERVING
Fresh lemons can be preserved whole or in slices, in a brine of salt and lemon juice. Once preserved, even the skin of the lemon becomes edible and delicious. Lemons can also be preserved by separately freezing the juice and the rind. First grate the rind of your lemon, then juice the grated halves. The juice can be frozen in cups, quarts, or in ice cubes. The rind can be kept frozen in a zip lock bag.

USES
Despite being too sour to enjoy completely raw, lemons lend themselves to an incredible variety of uses in the kitchen. Fresh lemons are often used as a garnish, served alongside fish, salads and drinks.

Most often, lemons are used for their plentiful, zippy juice. The juice of lemons can be used in a variety of beverages, like lemonade, tea, cocktails and many more. Lemon juice is used in salad dressings, sauces, and as a marinade. It can be added to cake batters, cookies, and muffins. Lemon juice can be used to flavor ice cream, frosting, icing, as well as many savory dips. Lemon juice is also often used to preserve other fruits and vegetables from losing their color and flavor.

The rind of the lemon is used for flavor in baking of cakes, sponges and biscuits, puddings like lemon meringue pie, rice pudding and many other confectionaries.

Once cooked or preserved even the skin of the lemon can be eaten. Lemons can be cooked down and turned into a marmalade or chutney, or turned into a lemon curd. These are all delicious over toast.

IN THE GARDEN

Lemon plants are becoming an incredibly popular indoor citrus tree. Not only are they beautiful in appearance, but you can be harvesting homegrown lemons in no time.

CLIMATE
Lemons are among the least cold-tolerant of citrus trees. They like full-sun and temperatures around 70 F. They will go dormant in temperatures below 50 F.

SOIL
Lemon trees are not picky when it comes to soil, and will do fine even in poor soils. They like well-draining , slightly acidic soil. They are intolerant of wet feet.

PLANTING
While an outdoor lemon tree will need a good 12ft of room, a young citrus tree will do just fine in a container, so long as it is transplanted to a larger pot when needed. Both should be planted in the spring, and potted lemons trees should be moved outdoors in the summer.

GROWING
Water plants twice a week. Fertilize only very poor soil.

HARVESTING
A lemon will take 6-8 months to mature, though once ripe it can be left for a long time on the tree without over-ripening. Avoid picking unready fruits, as they will not further ripen once picked.

LIME

Citrus aurantifolia

There are several species of citrus trees whose fruits are known as limes, but they have diverse origins. Wild limes are believed to have originated in Indonesia or Southeast Asia, and arrived in the Mediterranean region around 1,000 CE. In cooking, lime is valued for the acidity of its juice and the floral aroma of its zest.

VARIETIES

KEY LIME The Key lime is named after the Florida Keys, where it was naturalized. It is valued for its unique flavor, higher acidity, stronger aroma, and thinner rind than most limes.

KAFFIR The flesh of Kaffir lime, Citrus hystrix, is not commonly eaten. The leaves are the most frequently used part of the plant, and are popular in Thai and Vietnamese cooking.

RED RANGPUR The Rangpur lime is a cross between mandarin orange and citron. About the size of a lemon, it is a warm orange color, but the aroma and flavor are like a sweet lime.

PERSIAN Also known as Bearss lime, the Persian lime, *Citrus × latifolia*, is the most widely cultivated lime species. The fruit is often sold while still green but turns yellow as it ripens.

IN THE KITCHEN

Lime is valued both for the acidity of its juice and the floral aroma of its zest. It is also used for pickling in ceviche. Dried limes are a common ingredient in Middle Eastern cuisine.

 SELECTING
Look for limes that are brightly colored, have smooth skin and are heavy for their size. Avoid any that are soft, have blemishes or are shriveled. Fruit with thinner, smoother skin is easier to juice, while unwaxed fruit with thicker, rougher skin is best for zesting.

PREPARING
Wash limes before slicing. If they have been waxed, scrub away the shiny coating with plenty of hot water and a stiff brush. If using the zest, remove it first with a very fine grater, then cut in half and squeeze the juice.

 STORING
Citrus fruits, including limes, keep well at room temperature for a week or more, as long as they are whole and not cut. Refrigerate limes for up to 2 weeks, unwrapped. Lime wedges or slices can be wrapped in plastic and refrigerated for up to 5 days.

PRESERVING
Whole fruit is not well suited for freezing, but lime juice can be frozen for up to 4 months

 USES
It's worth knowing that the average lime will yield around 1 tablespoon of juice, especially when a recipe calls for a large quantity. Lemon is the go-to citrus for squeezing over fish, but lime works just as well and is also good on spicy grilled chicken, or added to salad dressing and vinaigrette. It combines well with oriental flavors in recipes such as stir-fried pork with scallion, ginger and lime, lime-glazed shrimp with garlic and chili, or coconut-lime soup with chicken and rice noodles. Mexican food also relies on limes for many dishes, not least sopa de lima – lime soup – a light, refreshing and spicy chicken soup.

IN THE GARDEN

Limes are small trees that are ideal for home gardeners, given the right climate. Flowering isn't seasonal, but occurs with warm weather and regular rainfall, so flowers and fruits may coincide.

 **CLIMATE**
Lime trees grow best outside in zones 8 through 11.

SOIL
Lime trees enjoy well-draining, rich soil, pH level between 5.5 and 6.5.

PLANTING
To grow a lime tree from seed, soak overnight in water and plant ½ inch deep in moist compost. Cover with a plastic bag sit in a warm, sunny spot until germination, then uncover and grow on. Plant outside in a sunny and wind-protected area; in cold areas, grow in containers and bring indoors during the winter.

GROWING
Water when the soil is dry to about 6 inches and fertilize every couple of months.

HARVESTING
Limes turn yellow when completely ripe, but are most flavorful while still green and just developing a yellowish tint to the skinwords to fill this line.

NUTRITIONAL VALUE

Serving size 100 g, raw juice
25 calories
Dietary fiber 0.4 g (2% DV)
Vitamin C 30.0 mg (50% DV)
Vitamin B6 0.038 mg (2% DV)
Thiamin 0.025 mg (2% DV)
Magnesium 8.00 mg (2% DV)

HEALTH BENEFITS

antioxidant
aids weight loss
improves digestion,
reduces respiratory disorders
enhances immunity
helps relieve constipation

LOQUAT

Eriobotrya japonica

The loquat tree is native to the hilly regions of southeast China, where it still grows wild. Loquat fruit, sometimes known as nispero, is round to pear-shaped, grows in clusters and has an edible yellow, orange or blushed skin. It is sweetest when soft and orange in color, with a mango-peach-citrus flavor.

VARIETIES

VISTA WHITE Vista White is a small to medium sized, round loquat. The skin is light yellow with pure white flesh. The flavor is very sweet and high in sugar content.

Champagne is a dependable variety, with very fragrant flowers and large clusters of fruit. The large, yellow-skinned fruit has very juicy white flesh, and a sweet-tart flavor.

BIG JIM Big Jim originated in Southern California and bears large, pale orange skinned fruits up to 1 ½ inches in diameter. The sweet orange flesh is very juicy with just enough acidity.

GOLD NUGGET A popular, late-season variety, the Gold Nugget loquat produces abundant, medium-sized orange fruit that is sweet and juicy, with a flavor resembling that of an apricot.

IN THE KITCHEN

The loquat fruit has a high sugar, acid and pectin content, so it makes excellent jam, jelly and chutney. It is most commonly eaten fresh, and mixes well with other fruits in fresh fruit salads or fruit cups.

 SELECTING
Loquats are not widely sold commercially, since they don't travel well, but if you find some for sale, look for bright, yellow or orange, smooth, firm fruit that feels heavy for its size.

 PREPARING
To prepare a fresh loquat, remove the stem, cut the fruit in half and remove the seeds, the interior pithy membrane and the calyx. Remove the skin if preferred, as it can be leathery and becomes tough when cooked.

 STORING
Keep loquats at cool room temperature for one week or refrigerate for up to one month. Remove from the fridge before use, as the fruit has a better flavor when eaten at room temperature.

 PRESERVING
Wash firm, ripe loquats. Remove the stem, blossom end and seeds, pack into airtight containers and cover the fruit with syrup (made with 1 ¾ cup sugar to 4 cups water), seal and freeze. Loquats may also be canned.

 USES
Fresh loquats make a tasty dessert, an unusual sauce or dessert topping and add variety and color to fruit salads. Although the peel is edible, it should be removed if the fruit is to be cooked. Loquats can be used in many sweet recipes, such as pies, tarts, cobblers, breads and compotes, and makes excellent ice cream, either alone or combined with other flavors such as coconut, mint, or rum liqueur.

In Italy nespolino liqueur is made from loquat seeds, reminiscent of nocino and amaretto, which are prepared from nuts and apricot kernels. Both the loquat seeds and the apricot kernels contain cyanide compounds, but the drinks are prepared from varieties that contain only small quantities, so there is no risk of poisoning.

In Japan, the loquat leaves are used to make tea which high in antioxidants, and is thought to be beneficial to combat diabetes, liver disease, and cancer.

IN THE GARDEN

Loquats are unusual among fruit trees in that the flowers appear in the autumn or early winter, and the fruits are ripe at any time from early spring to early summer.

 CLIMATE
The loquat tree does best in zones 8 to 10.

 SOIL
Most soils, except those that are very alkaline, are suitable for loquats.

 PLANTING
Some varieties of loquat are bred for backyard production, meaning they fruit gradually over time, rather than producing hundreds of fruits all at once. Loquats prefer full sun and are drought-tolerant, but produce more fruit if kept watered.

 GROWING
Water regularly and apply fertilizer three times during the growing season.

 HARVESTING
The fruit is ready to pick when it turns a golden color. Cut fruit clusters from the branches with clippers. Loquats are quite sensitive so they must be handpicked with care.

 ## NUTRITIONAL VALUE

Serving size 100 g, raw
47 calories
Dietary fiber 1.7 g (7% DV)
Vitamin A 1528.00 IU (31% DV)
Vitamin B6 0.100 mg (5% DV)
Manganese 0.148 mg (7% DV)
Potassium 266.00 mg (6% DV)

 ## HEALTH BENEFITS

Antioxidant
Helps prevent diabetes
Lowers cholesterol levels
Helps improve gastrointestinal health
Strengthens the immune system
Soothes the respiratory tract
Boosts circulation

LYCHEE

Litchi chinensis

The lychee bears small fruit encased in a thin, brittle, pink-red, roughly textured skin. The translucent white flesh has a floral smell and a fragrant, sweet flavor. Some varieties produce a high percentage of fruits with shriveled seeds known as "chicken tongues", due to their shape. These fruits are often more expensive because they contain more edible flesh.

VARIETIES

KWAI MAI PINK
Kwai Mai Pink produces small-medium lychee fruits with small seeds and excellent flavor. This variety is popular with growers due to its consistent cropping.

HAK IP Hak Ip - "black leaf" in Chinese – is a superb variety with large, sweet fruits, which always have chicken-tongue seeds. It is one of the preferred varieties for the home garden.

MAURITIUS Mauritius is a medium-sized, easy-to-peel lychee with a wonderful perfumed, exotic flavor, and high levels of sweetness and juice. It has a high proportion of chicken-tongue seeded fruits.

SWEET HEART
Sweetheart consistently produces large, heart shaped fruit with chicken-tongue seeds. It is a popular choice with home growers for its reliability and superior quality.

IN THE KITCHEN

Lychees are one of the most popular and flavorsome fruits of Southeast Asia. Since the distinctive, perfume-like flavor is lost in the process of canning, the fruit is best eaten fresh.

SELECTING
Lychees should look fresh and plump, without signs of bruising, softness, or mold. Skin color does not indicate eating quality, with some varieties having a light pink or red hue, while others retain a greenish peel.

PREPARING
Peel off the skin leaving the juicy, white, slightly translucent fruit and nibble or suck the flesh from the seed. To prepare for a recipe, score in half and open up the two halves of the fruit, then use your finger and thumb to pinch and remove the seed.

STORING
Once picked, lychees stop ripening. Store ripe lychees in the refrigerator for 2-3 days, but return them to room temperature before eating. The red rind may darken when the fruit is chilled, but the flavor is not affected.

PRESERVING
Unpeeled lychees can be frozen whole, in an airtight container or freeze bag, for up to 12 months. Alternatively, freeze lychee juice in ice-cube trays and use as required.

USES
Serve fresh, pitted lychees in a bowl as a refreshing summer snack, or add them to a fruit salad - lychee pairs particularly well with tropical fruit like mango, coconut, banana, passion fruit, and pineapple. Lychees can be cooked gently with sugar and water, plus complementary flavors such as vanilla or ginger, to create a simple dessert to eat with ice cream or yogurt. Lychee sorbet is also a popular and fragrant dessert option. sweet, gluten-free flour that can be used for baked goods. The exotic, sweet taste of lychee works well in Oriental sweet-and-sour dishes, and in sticky-sweet glaze for grilled chicken and fish. The flavor of lychee is also very popular in cocktails, adding a floral note as well as tangy sweetness. Peeled lychee is the perfect garnish for your cocktail glass, too.

IN THE GARDEN

The evergreen lychee tree is often grown as an ornamental specimen, bearing clusters of small white, yellow, or green flowers that are distinctively fragrant.

CLIMATE
Lychees can be grown in zones 10-11 only.

SOIL
Well-drained loam is best, but amaranth tolerates poor soil. The optimal pH range is 5.5 to 7.0.

PLANTING
Lychees can be grown from seed, and germination is usually reliable, but it could take as long as 20 years to produce fruit, if it ever does. To grow a fruit bearing tree, buy one from a nursery and plant in an area protected from strong winds, since their dense canopy can cause them to be blown over.

GROWING
Water regularly and fertilize twice a year with an organic fertilizer. While lychee trees will tolerate slightly water logged soil for short periods, avoid continual standing water.

HARVESTING
Allow the fruits to turn red, since unripe lychees will not ripen further.

MANDARIN, ETC
Citrus reticulata

Collectively termed "easy peelers", confusion surrounds the small, sweet, orange-colored citrus fruits known as mandarin, clementine, tangerine and satsuma. The mandarin was one of the original citrus species, from Southeast Asia. Tangerines are mandarins – but not all mandarins are tangerines. Clementines are sweet and easy to peel, while satsumas peel easiest of all.

VARIETIES

RUBY TANGO MANDARIN This is a cross between blood orange and clementine. It has deep orange, smooth rind that peels easily, and seedless, dark maroon flesh with a full-bodied, sweet flavor.

CLEMENULES CLEMENTINE This is a tangor, a cross between a willowleaf mandarin orange and a sweet orange. Clemenules is a popular, seedless variety with a very pleasing sweet flavor.

MURCOTT Widely grown in Florida, the Murcott, or honey tangerine, is also a tangor, or mandarin–sweet orange hybrid. The flesh is richly orange with an intense sweetness and flavor.

DOBASHI BENI SATSUMA The satsuma, Citrus unshiu, is a sweet, seedless and easy-peeling citrus species. Dobashi Beni is an early to mid-season satsuma with deep orange-red coloration.

IN THE GARDEN

Because of their small size and compact growth habits, dwarf mandarin orange trees readily adapt to growing indoors, but will thrive outdoors in the right climate.

 **CLIMATE**
All varieties grow best in plant hardiness zones 9 to 11.

 **SOIL**
Mandarin trees prefer well-drained, sandy loam with added organic material and pH 5.5 to 6.5.

PLANTING
Mandarins can be grown from seed or cultivated root stock. Seeds should be started indoors and, once germinated, transplanted into a large pot for indoor growing, or outdoors where suitable. When planting out, choose a site with full sun exposure. Water regularly until well established.

GROWING
Apply citrus fertilizer in early spring, summer or fall.

HARVESTING
Pick mandarins as soon as they start to ripen, or the flavor will begin to decline. Once the fruit has turned from green to orange, it is ready to harvest.

IN THE KITCHEN

Any of the "easy peelers" makes a great snack fruit, since they are small, sweet and easier to peel than regular oranges (and many are seedless), making them more suitable for children.

 SELECTING
For the sweetest and tastiest fruit, choose mandarins that have a nice, bright orange tone and feel heavy for their size, and avoid any that have soft spots, blemishes, or mold.

 PREPARING
Wipe or wash fruits, then peel and eat out of hand. To prepare for salads, peel off the white membrane with a sharp knife, and cut away individual segments or cut into slices crosswise, removing any seeds.

STORING
Mandarins, tangerines, clementines and satsumas can be used interchangeably in place of oranges in most recipes, though they are often sweeter than their citrus cousins, so may need less sugar or the addition of extra sharpness such as lime or lemon juice.

 PRESERVING
Freeze mandarins either whole or in sections and use within 10 months. Mandarins are commonly canned or preserved in light sugar syrup, too.

 USES
Mandarins, tangerines, clementines and satsumas can be used interchangeably in place of oranges in most recipes, though they are often sweeter than their citrus cousins, so may need less sugar or the addition of extra sharpness such as lime or lemon juice.

Mandarins are generally peeled and eaten fresh or used in salads, desserts and main dishes, or drunk as fresh juice. They can be used to make preserves such as marmalade or tangerine-lemon curd, or baked into a clementine and date cake. For an impressive seasonal treat, bake a whole mandarin inside a traditional, steamed Christmas pudding – when cut open, a tender fruit center and oozing citrus syrup is revealed.

 NUTRITIONAL VALUE

Serving size 100 g, raw
53 calories
Dietary fiber 1.8 g (7% DV)
Vitamin C 26.7 mg (44% DV)
Vitamin A 681.00 IU (14% DV)
Vitamin B6 0.078 mg (4% DV)
Thiamin 0.058 mg (4% DV)

 HEALTH BENEFITS

Antioxidant
Reduces the risk of cancer
Boosts immune system
Maintains healthy skin
Helps reduce bad cholesterol
Maintains healthy blood pressure

MANGO

Mangifera indica

Mangoes are native to South Asia, but have spread worldwide to become one of the most widely cultivated fruits in the tropics. The ripe fruit varies in size, shape, sweetness and color, being variously yellow, orange, red, or green. Each mango contains a single flat, oblong pit that does not separate easily from the pulp.

VARIETIES

ALPHONSO Originating in India, the Alphonso has been called the King of Mangoes. Sunshine-yellow skin surrounds succulent, saffron-colored flesh prized worldwide for its sweetness, richness and flavor.

TOMMY ATKINS Although generally not considered the best for sweetness and flavor, the large Tommy Atkins mango is valued for its long shelf life and tolerance of handling and transportation.

ATAULFO Originating from Mexico, Ataúlfo, or honey mango, is a somewhat oblong shape with a gold-blushed yellow skin. The buttery flesh is not fibrous, and is high in sugar with a rich, sweet flavor.

KEITT The Keitt mango is a late-season variety that originated in south Florida, where it is still widely planted. The large fruit has green skin with some light red blush, and has a tangy sweet flesh.

IN THE KITCHEN

The color of a mango varies according to its position on the tree. Sunshine causes a red blush on the skin, but mangos from within the tree can taste just as delicious, even with less red coloring.

 SELECTING Color is not the best indicator of ripeness. Squeeze the mango gently; a ripe mango will give slightly, but a firmer mango would be a good choice if you don't plan to eat it for several days.

 PREPARING Wash mangos before cutting. Slice down the fruit each side of the flat seed, or use a mango splitter to remove the seed. Cut long slices into the flesh without breaking the skin, then scoop out slices with a spoon.

 STORING Keep unripe mangos at room temperature until they ripen. They will become sweeter and softer over several days. Once ripe, whole fruits will keep in the refrigerator for up to five days. Alternatively, peel, cube and place in an airtight container in the refrigerator for several days. .

 **PRESERVING** Freeze peeled, cubed mango, or pureed mango flesh, in an airtight container or freezer bag for up to 12 months.

USES Given its Indian origins, it is unsurprising that mango features heavily in the cooking of South Asia. Sour, unripe mangoes are used in chutneys, pickles and side dishes, or may be eaten raw with salt, chili, or soy sauce. One typical pickle is made from raw, unripe, sour mango, mixed with chili powder, fenugreek seeds, mustard powder, salt, and groundnut oil. Mango lassi is a popular drink throughout the region, and is easily made by mixing ripe mangoes or mango pulp with buttermilk and sugar.

With their intense sweetness and melting texture, mangoes are especially well suited to blended drinks and creamy desserts, and are often used to make juices, smoothies, milkshakes, ice cream, sorbet, aguas frescas and pies – or even mango upside-down cake.

IN THE GARDEN

Mangos are an attractive shade tree and can grow to 115 feet tall. Although they prefer a tropical climate, they will grow elsewhere if protected from frost when young.

 CLIMATE Best in zones 10b through 11 but mature trees will survive in cooler climates.

 SOIL Mango trees can thrive in almost any soil but it must be well-drained.

 PLANTING SPlant mango trees in late winter to early spring, in an open, sunny position protected from winds. Mangos also grow easily from seed. Slit the husk of a fresh mango pit, remove the seed inside and plant in seed compost with ¼-inch protruding above the soil surface. Germination may take up to three weeks.

 GROWING Water frequently until well established and apply nitrogen fertilizer three times per year.

 HARVESTING For sweetest results let the fruit ripen on the tree. Pick fruit with a 2-inch stem so the sap doesn't burn the skin of the mango.

MELON

Cucumis

Melons originated in Africa and the hot valleys of Southwest Asia, especially Iran and India. They are known to have been grown by the ancient Egyptians, and were among the first crop species brought by westerners to the New Worlds. The edible flesh can be used both as a sweet fruit and cooked as a vegetable.

VARIETIES

CHARENTAIS The Charentais is a small variety of cantaloupe melon with a fragrant aroma, which developed in western France around 1920 as a more refined cantaloupe

CANARY The bright-yellow Canary melon is large with pale green to white flesh like that of a soft pear. It has a distinctively sweet flavor, a little tangier than a honeydew melon

WINTER MELON This Benincasa hispida, the wax gourd or winter melon, is grown for its very large fruit. The immature melon has thick, sweet, white flesh, but it is eaten as a vegetable when mature.

PIEL DE SAPO The Spanish piel de sapo (toadskin), also known as Santa Claus melon, has a thick, green-striped rind and pale green to white flesh with a mild melon flavor similar to honeydew melons.

IN THE KITCHEN

Due to its high water content, melon is valued as a refreshing snack to keep you hydrated. Winter melon is often cooked in soup or stew, while sweet varieties have a wide range of culinary uses.

SELECTING
Choose a melon that's heavy for its size, and free of bruises, soft spots, moldy patches and cracks. A ripe melon should sound hollow when tapped, and should smell fresh and fragrant with a hint of sweetness.

PREPARING
Wipe the skin clean, cut into halves or wedges, and scoop out the seeds. Slice the flesh away from the thick rind and cut into chunks. The seeds can be saved and roasted to eat as a snack.

STORING
Store a whole melon at room temperature to soften and become juicier. If already quite ripe or once cut, it will keep in the refrigerator for up to 3 days. Cut melon absorbs odors from other foods easily, so use an airtight container or wrap tightly before storing it in the fridge..

PRESERVING
Melon chunks and puréed flesh can be frozen. Add a little sugar and lime juice, pour into popsicle molds, and freeze for a healthy treat.

USES
The sweetness of melon pairs very well with other fruits including citrus, kiwi and watermelon and makes a good addition to fruit salads. It has a special affinity with cheeses such as feta, burrata, ricotta and brie and can be used in savory salads alongside crunchy fennel or cucumber, for a texture contrast, or with capers or olives for a salt-sweet combination.

Prosciutto with melon is a classic appetizer, making the most of the sweet fruit against the savory cured ham – give it a twist by serving chilled, pureed melon "gazpacho" soup garnished with grilled crispy prosciutto. Melon is also a great partner for herbs and spicy flavors, such as in chili-spiked melon, feta and basil salad with spicy lemongrass vinaigrette.

Melon's high water content also makes it perfect for soft drinks and cocktails, such as melon and mint smoothie, melon and coconut agua fresca, and fresh melon margarita.

IN THE GARDEN

Melons require plenty of moisture, sunlight, and two to three months of heat. Some gardeners plant melons atop their compost piles to ensure sufficient warmth and plentiful nitrogen.

CLIMATE
Melon varieties can be successfully grown in zones 3 to 10.

SOIL
The ideal soil will have plenty of phosphorus and potassium, and a pH of 6.0-6.8

PLANTING
Melons thrive in warm soil, so don't plant until the ground temperature is above 70 degrees Fahrenheit. Prepare the planting bed well by adding several inches of compost or well-rotted manure. Space plants 36 to 42 inches apart, or grow vertically up a trellis.

GROWING
Keep soil consistently moist but not waterlogged and feed regularly through the growing season.

HARVESTING
Place ripening fruit on mulch, upturned coffee cans, or flower pots to prevent direct contact with the soil. Harvest when ripe, leaving about an inch of stem attached to keep the melon from rotting.

MULBERRY

Morus

The three main species of mulberry - black, red, and white - are widespread throughout many parts of the world. The color of the fruit does not identify the mulberry species; for example, white mulberries can produce white, purple or black fruit. Mulberry fruits taste sweet to very sweet, and are reminiscent of blackberries.

VARIETIES

RIVIERA Riviera is a variety of white mulberry - Morus alba, originally from China - with large, purple black fruits that ripen over an extended season.

ILLINOIS EVERBEARING This red mulberry variety, Morus rubra, is an American native tree that originated in Illinois in 1958. The tree is vigorous and produces large, reddish-black, very sweet fruit.

PAKISTAN MULBERRY This variety comes from Islamabad, and has sweet, firm fleshed fruit. It is sometimes called the 'King of Mulberries' for its very large fruit, which can be up to 3 1/2 inches in length.

NOIR DE SPAIN The Asian native black mulberry is generally considered to have the tastiest fruit. Noir de Spain was introduced by Felix Gillet, a French nurseryman, in California around 1880.

IN THE KITCHEN

White mulberry fruits are largely very sweet but lack tartness. Red mulberry - deep red to almost black – has a flavor that almost equals the black mulberry. Black mulberry fruits are large and juicy, with a good balance of sweetness and tartness.

 **SELECTING**
Mulberries should be plump, fragrant, and deeply colored red, purple or black fruits. White, green or pale yellow fruits are not mature - unless you're buying white-fruited mulberries, of course. Avoid mulberries that are soft and bleeding as they spoil easily.

PREPARING
Wash the mulberries gently. Stemming is not necessary if cooking or making juices, jellies or syrup but, in dishes where presentation is important, it's best to remove the stems even though it's a time-consuming task.

STORING
Mulberries deteriorate quickly after harvesting, but will keep for a couple of days at room temperature, or up to a week, unwashed, in the refrigerator.

PRESERVING
Mulberries don't freeze particularly well, but can be dehydrated, canned or made into jam.

USES
Although not quite as sweet, mulberries can be substituted for blackberries in many recipes. Mulberry pie, mulberry cobbler and mulberry pancakes all work well, as do breakfast dishes such as mulberry granola, oatmeal with mulberries, or mulberry smoothie. They make excellent fools, jellies and jams, and homemade mulberry ice cream is a real treat, especially topped with fresh berries.

Mulberry leaves are high in vitamins and antioxidants, and can be used fresh or dried to make tea. Simply crumble a few leaves into a cup and pour on hot water.

To make mulberry gin or vodka, add a pound of fruit to 1 ½ pints of vodka or gin and 5 ounces of sugar in a sterilized jar. Put in a dark place for 2-3 months, turning every few days. Strain the liqueur and bottle. The leftover fruit is delicious on top of ice-cream or yogurt, or used as a pie filling.

IN THE GARDEN

The large leaves and dense foliage of mulberry trees offer excellent shade. In North America, however, the white mulberry is considered an invasive exotic, so plant with caution.

 CLIMATE
White and red mulberries will grow in zones 4 -8, black mulberries in zones 5 – 9.

SOIL
Mulberries grow well in most soils, rich to poor, acidic to alkaline, sandy, clay or even rocky soils.

PLANTING
Mulberries can be grown from seed, and are generally of better shape and health, but are more often planted from large cuttings, which root readily.

Mulberries have shallow, aggressively spreading root systems, so plant the trees away from sidewalks, driveways and buildings.

 GROWING
Water well, as all varieties tend to drop their fruit if the tree becomes too dry.

 HARVESTING
Wear old clothing because mulberry juice stains. Put a sheet on the ground below the canopy and shake the branches. Pick the ripe fruit that falls.

OLIVE

Olea europaea

Olives are some of the oldest trees ever harvested by humans, and have been a part of the human diet for thousands of years - long before the advent of the canning industry and grocery stores - but until recently only a few varieties were commonly consumed in the United States. The olive is of major agricultural importance in the Mediterranean region as the source of olive oil.

VARIETIES

MISSION The Mission olive is a heritage variety developed in California by Spanish missions in the late 18th century, and remains one of the more common cultivars in the state.

ALFONSO Originating in Chile and Peru, the huge, deep purple Alfonso olives are brine-cured and macerated in red wine. They are supple, juicy and fleshy, with a hint of sour bitterness.

CASTELVETRANO
One of Italy's most popular table olives, this bright green fruit comes from Castelvetrano, Sicily, and is also known as nocellara del belice. They have meaty flesh, and a mild flavor.

KALAMATA
The popular Kalamata olives are almond shaped with deep purple, shiny skin. They're typically preserved in red wine vinegar, red wine, and/or olive oil for a distinctive rich, fruity flavor.

IN THE GARDEN

Amaranth is a low-maintenance plant that is tolerant of summer heat and periodic drought. Transplant with care, as its roots are sensitive. Amaranth is a low-maintenance plant that is 30

 CLIMATE
Amaranth grows best in zones 5 to 9 in full sun. Please add more text to this point. More text here?

 SOIL
Well-drained loam is best, but amaranth tolerates poor soil. The optimal pH range is 5.5 to 7.0.

PLANTING
Sow seeds indoors 6 to 8 weeks before the last frost, or outdoors after the last frost. Sow at a depth of ¼ inch (1 cm) in groups of 3 every 6 inches (15 cm).

Space rows 12 to 18 inches (30 to 46 cm) apart. Seeds germinate in 5 to 10 days

 GROWING
Water plants twice a week. Fertilize only very poor soil. More text to this point maybe? It seems rather short as it was.

 HARVESTING
Cut or pick young leaves as needed. Removing the terminal bud encourages branching of young shoots. Harvest seeds on a dry day just after the first frost. Few words to fill this line.

IN THE KITCHEN

Raw olives are bitter and rarely eaten fresh. They are cured and fermented to remove bitter compounds. It's the cure that imparts the characteristic saltiness, tender texture, and flavor.

 SELECTING
In general, the darker the olive, the riper it was when harvested. Green olives ripen, through light brown, to vibrant reds and purples, to eventually become black olives. When buying prepared olives, they should be relatively firm, never mushy or bruised. Look for olives dressed in brine, which helps them retain their moisture and flavor.

 PREPARING
Shop-bought olives normally need no further preparation, but can be pitted, if necessary, using a cherry or olive pitter.

 STORING
Store olives in the refrigerator in the liquid they came in, loosely covered with plastic wrap, for up to 10 days. If there's no brine, make your own—simply add a teaspoon of salt to a cup and a half of water.

 PRESERVING
Freshly picked olives may be preserved at home by brine-curing in salt water for up to a year, to produce a juicy, flavorful olive. To dry-cure, pack olives in salt for a month or longer for a deeply concentrated flavor, and a wrinkly, prune-like appearance.

 USES
Olives are hugely diverse and very versatile, whether eaten as a snack, ground to make a savory spread, tossed into salads, simmered in stews and sauces, or even popped into a martini. Their sweet, sour, salty, bitter and pungent flavors make them an essential item in any home cook's larder.

Olive bread makes a great accompaniment to any Mediterranean-inspired meal, and is just as good on its own. Black, purple and green olives feature heavily in many Italian recipes, including tomato-based pasta sauces and, of course, pizza toppings, as well as one-pot casseroles, savory tray bakes and roasts.

Olives are popular in the cuisine of other regions too, appearing in fragrant North African lamb tagines, Provencal tapenade, and Nicoise salad. For an irresistible appetizer, try deep fried olives stuffed with cheese, cured meats and anchovies, served with garlic and saffron mayo goods.

 NUTRITIONAL VALUE

Serving size 100 g, canned
115 calories
Dietary fiber 3.2 g (13% DV)
Sodium 735mg (32% DV)
Calcium 88.00 mg (9% DV)
Iron 3.30 mg (18%)
Vitamin A 403.00 IU (8% DV)

 HEALTH BENEFITS

Anti-inflammatory
Antioxidant
Improves heart health
Supports healthy bone, muscle, and nerve function
Helps lower blood pressure
Helps prevent liver damage

ORANGE

Citrus x sinensis

Orange trees are widely grown in tropical and subtropical climates for their sweet fruit. Also called sweet orange, to distinguish it from the related *Citrus × aurantium*, or bitter orange, the earliest mention of the sweet orange was in Ancient Chinese literature in 314 BC, and it has since become one of the most cultivated fruit trees in the world.

VARIETIES

There is now a wide range of cultivars and varieties, but around two-thirds of all orange production is made up of so-called common oranges - also called white, round, or blond oranges – including the Valencia orange. Though mostly grown for processing and orange juice production, the Valencia orange is also a desirable fresh fruit and is prized as the only variety in season during summer.

MIDKNIGHT VALENCIA This is a South African variety of the standard Valencia orange, with larger, juicier fruit and fewer seeds, good juicing quality, and earlier ripening than other Valencia types.

MORO BLOOD ORANGE High amounts of anthocyanin give the rind, flesh, and juice of the blood oranges their dark red color. Originally from Sicily, Moro is a medium-sized fruit with a long harvest.

CARA CARA ORANGE Cara cara oranges, also called red navel, are sweet and comparatively low in acid, with a bright orange rind similar to that of other navels, but distinctively pinkish red flesh.

SEVILLE ORANGE This is a bitter orange, which has a thick, dimpled skin, and is higher in pectin than the sweet orange. It is prized for making marmalade, giving a better set and also allowing a higher yield.

LIMA ORANGE An acidless orange - a fruit with very low levels of acid, also called "sweet" oranges in the USA. The lack of acid, which protects orange juice against spoilage, makes them unsuitable for export.

CALAMONDIN Calamondin, or calamansi, is a hybrid of the kumquat and mandarin orange. The fruit resembles a small, round lime, and the sour flesh is often used for preserves or cooking and eating.

NUTRITIONAL VALUE

Serving size 100 g, raw
47 calories
Dietary fiber 2.4 g (10% DV)
Vitamin C 53.2 mg (89% DV)
Potassium 181 mg (4% DV)
Thiamin 0.087 mg (6% DV)

HEALTH BENEFITS

Antioxidant
Reduces risk of colon cancer
Promotes healthy immune system
Prevents skin damage
Reduces blood pressure
lowers cholesterol

JAFFA Jaffa oranges are virtually seedless, with a sweet, fine flavor. Developed by Ottoman farmers in the mid-19th century, historically they were considered the most famous export in the early state of Israel.

PARSON BROWN
Once a widely grown juice orange, its popularity has declined, but it is still grown because it is the earliest maturing orange in the USA. The medium-large fruits have thick, pebbly peel.

FUKUMOTO NAVEL
Navel oranges are characterized by the growth of a second fruit at the apex, which protrudes slightly and resembles a human navel, and their thicker skin, which makes them easy to peel. Originally from Japan, the Fukumoto navel orange is favored for its rich, red-orange skin, large size, and seedless flesh. It is popular amongst home gardeners as it can be successfully grown in containers.

IN THE KITCHEN

The season for oranges varies by variety. Valencia oranges are in season from late spring to mid-summer, navels are best from mid-winter to early spring, and blood oranges are at their peak from early winter until spring. Sour oranges are harvested from fall through spring, depending upon the region.

 SELECTING
Choose a firm, smooth, thin-skinned orange that is heavy for its size. Color is not a good indicator as some oranges are dyed, and some fully ripened fruits are green. Avoid soft or moldy fruit.

 PREPARING
Wash and dry before use. To eat an orange out of hand, simply peel and break fruit into segments. To prepare for use in a salad, remove both the peel and the bitter white membrane beneath with a sharp knife – grate the zest before peeling, if needed. To juice an orange, roll the unpeeled fruit on a firm surface to soften the flesh, then cut in half and squeeze.

 STORING
Oranges will keep at room temperature for up to 1 week and in the refrigerator for up to 2 weeks.

 PRESERVING
Whole oranges are not recommended for freezing, but segments can be frozen in syrup or juice, and orange juice can be frozen in plastic containers for up to one year. Oranges can also be canned or bottled and the peel may be dried or candied.

 USES
There is a wealth of recipes ideas to help you include more oranges in your diet and boost your intake of vitamins and minerals. Oranges add a bold citrus flavor to drinks, salads, desserts, and main dishes, pairing as easily with chocolate as they do with salads, pork or salmon. Freshly squeezed orange juice or a simple fresh fruit salad require virtually no preparation, but are healthy and delicious.

For a zingy appetizer of light lunch, try a colorful spiced orange salad with onions, olives and fragrant vinaigrette made with cumin, curry, cilantro, and mint. Orange also matches especially well with sliced fennel – perhaps with a Dijon mustard dressing - or avocado, for a quick, tasty and nutritious salad.

An all-time favorite orange recipe is the classic duck a l'orange, which is an impressive dish well worth making for a dinner party or special occasion. Orange is a great partner for pork, too, in a casserole, in a sauce for chops, or even in a pork stir-fry.

Of course, oranges feature in very many drinks and desserts too. Satisfy your sweet tooth with chocolate-orange torte, orange sorbet, sticky orange cake with marmalade glaze, or simply slather homemade orange marmalade on toast. Orange juice is an essential ingredient in cocktails such as the screwdriver, mimosa, and tequila sunrise.

IN THE GARDEN

Although citrus trees are a subtropical fruit, in cooler climates they can be grown successfully in containers. Dwarf orange varieties may grow to just 8 to 12 feet tall, and can be overwintered indoors, and most are self-fertile so only one specimen is needed for fruiting.

 CLIMATE
Oranges grow best in zones 9 through 11, but some varieties are more cold-tolerant than others.

 SOIL
Orange trees need fast-draining, moist soil and plenty of nitrogen to promote growth.

 PLANTING
To grow oranges from seed, remove seeds from the desired fruit, soak overnight in water and plant them ½ inch deep in moist potting soil. Cover with a plastic bag and sit in a warm, sunny spot until the seeds germinate, then remove the plastic and grow on. Citrus trees should be planted out in a sunny and wind-protected area, spaced 12 to 25 feet apart, or 6 to 10 feet apart for dwarf varieties.

GROWING
Shortly after planting, and for the first few years before fruiting, feed with a balanced fertilizer. Once they begin to bear fruit, a citrus blend fertilizer is ideal.

HARVESTING
Citrus fruits will not ripen off the tree, so don't pick too early. The best indicator of ripeness is taste. Harvest the fruit by cutting them off or by pulling the fruit stalk from the tree. Fallen fruits can also be collected, but discard any that are bruised or have broken skin.

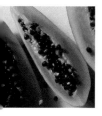

PAPAYA

Carica papaya

Papaya - also called pawpaw - is a tropical fruit native to Central and South America. The sweet-scented flowers open at night and are followed by amber-orange skinned fruit that ranges in length between 6 to 18 inches, with either sweet, red or orange flesh, or yellow flesh. Either kind, picked green, is called a "green papaya".

VARIETIES

SUNRISE SOLO This is a traditional variety, created in the early 1960s, with small 1 to 1 ½ pound fruits, perfect for the warm, sub-tropical home garden. The fruits have reddish- orange flesh that is sweet and tasty.

GOLDEN YELLOW Golden yellow is a palm-like tree that bears papaya fruit that is high in vitamin A and B, and whose enzyme is able to digest 35 times its weight in lean meat.

MOUNTAIN PAPAYA *Vasconcellea pubescens,* is native to the Andes. The fruit has five broad ribs from base to apex; its pulp is similar to papaya, and is usually cooked as a vegetable.

BELLA The Bella variety produces medium sized fruit, average 3 to 5 pounds, with red -pink flesh and good sweetness.

IN THE KITCHEN

Ripe papaya fruit is often eaten raw, but the unripe green fruit is also used as an ingredient in salads and stews. Green papaya fruit is rich in papain, which is useful for tenderizing meat.

 SELECTING
Ripe fruit should be firm yet yield to gentle pressure, feel heavy for its size and have smooth skin with no blemishes. When fully ripe, the skin is bright yellow and the papaya should have a sweet aroma. Unripe fruit will be an overall light yellowish-green, but not completely green. Avoid fruits that are overly soft unless you plan to puree them and use immediately.

 PREPARING
To prepare sweet or green papaya, peel, slice lengthwise and scoop out the seeds using a spoon.

 STORING
Papayas will ripen within a few days at room temperature. Once ripe, they can quickly turn to mush if not properly stored. Ripe papayas should be refrigerated to slow down the ripening process, and can be kept for a week.

 PRESERVING
To freeze, dice the prepared papaya and pack into containers or freezer bags. Cover with a 30 percent sugar solution and freeze up to 10 months.

USES
Because ripe papaya is very sweet, the addition of citrus or other tart ingredients helps to bring out its flavor. Ripe papaya is great in tropical fruit salads and puréed in smoothies, and is also a popular addition to salsas and savory salads, mixed with fresh coriander, mango, chili, fish, shrimp or grilled meat.

Use green papaya as a vegetable or turn it into pickle. It is particularly good raw in Thai salads such as the delicious som tam, or Thai green papaya salad, where it is paired with green beans, tomatoes, peanuts, and dried shrimp in a tangy, pungent chili lime dressing. Green papaya features in many savory salads, pickles and curries in Indonesian, Filipino and Thai cuisine.

IN THE GARDEN

Most papayas are grown from seed, which can be obtained from fruit purchased at the local market. It is a large herbaceous plant, usually with a single, straight trunk that can reach to 30 feet.

 CLIMATE
Papaya thrives best under warm, humid conditions in zones 10 and 11. It can be grown in a green house if pruned and trained.

 SOIL
A light sandy loam and well drained alkaline soil is ideal for growing papayas.

PLANTING
Extract seeds from fully ripe fruit, wash to remove gelatinous material and plant several per pot. Germination takes approximately two weeks under full sunlight.

The plants can be set out as soon as they are large enough - about 1 foot tall - spaced 8 to 10 feet apart.

 GROWING
Water to thoroughly wet the soil periodically as needed, and apply fertilizer monthly.

 HARVESTING
Papayas attain best quality if harvested when the fruit is completely yellow. Fruit can be ripened off the plant after it begins to get a yellow tinge.

 NUTRITIONAL VALUE

Serving size 100 g, raw
43 calories
Dietary fiber 1.7 g (7% DV)
Vitamin C 60.9 mg (102% DV)
Vitamin A 950.00 IU (19% DV)
Magnesium 21.00 mg (5% DV)
Potassium 182.00 mg (4% DV)

 HEALTH BENEFITS

Antioxidant
Lowers cholesterol
Improves heart health
Boosts immunity
Helps weight loss
Supports eye health

PASSION FRUIT

Passiflora edulis

Passionfruit grow on fast-growing, climbing vines with large, showy, flowers. The fruit is round or oval, yellow or dark purple, with a soft, juicy interior filled with seeds. The name comes from 16th century Jesuit missionaries, who saw the pattern of Christ's crown of thorns and other symbols of the Crucifixion, or passion, in the flowers.

VARIETIES

BLACK KNIGHT Ideal for home gardeners, this is a dwarf hybrid with beautiful, glossy green leaves and stunning flowers that give way to deep purple fruits, with a sour note to balance their sweetness.

SWEET SUNRISE The fruits of this Sweet Sunrise are yellow and baseball sized. This yellow passionfruit is mostly self-incompatible and needs to be cross pollinated with another cultivar.

SWEET GRANADILLA Sweet granadilla, *Passiflora ligularis*, is an orange to yellow fruit with light markings on its hard outer shell, and gelatinous, sweet pulp surrounding hard, black seeds.

BANANA PASSIONFRUIT *Passiflora mollissima* is an oval fruit around 4 inches long with yellow or red skin. The yellow or orange pulp has a sweet and slightly acid taste. especially tender.

IN THE KITCHEN

Purple fruit are more common in subtropical regions and preferred for fresh consumption; the tropical yellow variety is most often used for juice and preserves. Both yield delicious fruit and juice.

SELECTING
Select passionfruit that is plump and heavy for its size. Look for dark purple shells that are dimpled and shriveled, a sign the fruit is ripe. Smooth-skinned fruit will ripen at room temperature within 5 days.

PREPARING
Slice fresh passionfruit in half, and eat the pulp with a spoon. Alternatively, spoon out the pulp and remove the seeds by straining in a non-aluminum sieve, pressing with a wooden spoon to extract all the juice.

STORING
Ripen at room temperature, uncovered but out of direct sun, until the fruit's skin dimples and darkens. Refrigerate ripe passionfruit in a plastic or paper bag for up to 2 days.

PRESERVING
Passion fruit pulp and seeds can be frozen for up to 3 months. Scoop out pulp and seeds from halved fruit; transfer to containers and freeze.

USES
Passionfruit is usually served fresh, particularly as juice, although it may take more than 100 fruits to make one liter of juice! Seeded fruit pulp puréed in a blender is a popular flavor base for sorbets, ice cream, mousses, pies, and dessert sauces.

Passionfruit has a flavor affinity with other exotic fruits such as guava, mango, papaya, pineapple and star fruit, and also pairs well with ice cream, cream and yogurt. Confident cooks might like to try hot passionfruit soufflé, passionfruit and vanilla cheesecake or passionfruit ganache.

Although savory recipes for passionfruit are less common, the tangy flavor works well in tropical salad dressings or in a sauce for duck breast.

Perhaps the most popular way to enjoy passionfruit is in a cocktail, where the sweet-tart flavor lends itself well to tropical fruit blends and sweet rums. Add juice or puree to mojitos, martinis, Brazilian batidas, or punch.

IN THE GARDEN

Passionfruit can be grown from seed, but may not grow true to type – it may not be like the parent fruit and may not nice to eat. Named variety, nursery grown plants or seeds are more reliable.

CLIMATE
Passionfruit grows in zones 9b to 11, and can handle temperatures down to 32 degrees Fahrenheit.

SOIL
Passionfruit needs well-draining soil rich in organic matter, pH between 6.5 and 7.5.

PLANTING
A spot next to a south- or west-facing wall is ideal, with protection from strong winds, and sturdy support such as a trellis or arbor. Passionfruit may also be grown indoors near a sunny window although it can grow 15 to 20 feet per year once established.

GROWING
Water regularly especially when fruits are approaching maturity. If the soil is dry, fruits may shrivel and fall prematurely.

HARVESTING
Passionfruit quickly turns from green to deep purple (or yellow) when ripe and falls to the ground within a few days. Either pick when they change color or gather from the ground daily.

PEACH & NECTARINE

Prunus persica

Even though they are widely regarded as different fruits, peaches and nectarines are the same species. Whilst peaches are known for the characteristic velvety fuzz on their skin, nectarines are fuzz-free, with a smooth skin. It is thought that a mutation in a single gene is responsible for the difference between the two.

VARIETIES

Cultivated peaches are categorized as clingstones and freestones, depending on whether the flesh sticks to the stone; both types can have either white or yellow flesh. Peaches with white flesh are typically very sweet with little acidity, while yellow-fleshed peaches typically have an acidic tang, though this also varies greatly. White-fleshed peaches are most popular in Asian countries, while Europeans and North Americans favor the acidic, yellow-fleshed cultivars.

SATURN PEACH The small Saturn peach has a squat, flattened shape, with yellow and red skin that is less fuzzy than most. The flesh is pale yellow to white in appearance and usually sweeter than other peaches.

ELBERTA PEACH The Elberta peach is a large, attractive yellow freestone variety with a splash of crimson. The juicy, evenly yellow flesh is great for eating fresh and is highly recommended for canning.

RELIANCE PEACH The fruit of the Reliance tree is medium-to-large with a sweet flavor. It is one of the hardiest peach trees, and produces a heavy crop of fruit as far north as Canada, even after harsh winters.

GARDEN LADY PEACH A genetic dwarf peach that is superb for growing in containers on the patio. Beautiful pink flowers in spring are followed by sweet, juicy fruits with a fine yellow flesh.

CRIMSON SNOW NECTARINE This is a deep crimson nectarine with snowy white flesh that is sweet, juicy and firm. The attractive fruits are good for fresh eating, cooking and preserves.

RED GOLD NECTARINE One of the most widely planted nectarines in the USA, with stunning pink flowers in spring. It produces a large, yellow, freestone fruit with beautiful red blushed skin.

NUTRITIONAL VALUE

Serving size 100 g, raw yellow
39 calories
Dietary fiber 1.5 g (6% DV)
Vitamin C 6.6 mg (11% DV)
Vitamin A 326.00 IU (7% DV)
Niacin 0.806 mg (5% DV)

HEALTH BENEFITS

Antioxidant
Reduces inflammation
Improves immune function
Protects dna and controls cell growth
Helps reduce cancer risk
Improves cardiovascular and digestive health

FANTASIA NECTARINE
This tree has large, oval, red-blushed yellow fruit. The fruit is sweet-tart with a firm, smooth texture when picked early, becoming sweeter and juicier the later the fruit hangs on the tree.

JOHN RIVERS NECTARINE
Probably the earliest outdoor nectarine, it produces medium to large, golden yellow fruits with crimson flush and stripes. The flavor is very rich and juicy.

HEAVENLY WHITE NECTARINE
Heavenly White is a very large nectarine with creamy white skin that is heavily blushed red, white flesh and excellent flavor that is favored by connoisseurs.

FAIRHAVEN
This Medium-large freestone peach has yellow-red skin and yellow flesh. Fairhaven resists browning, and has a good flavor, traits that make it perfect for freezing and canning.

ARCTIC SUPREME PEACH
The Arctic Supreme peach is named for its white flesh rather than its hardiness. The fruits are large, with red over cream colored skin, a delicate, sweet and tangy flavor, and firm texture. The flavor of Arctic Supreme has won it quite a few awards in blind taste tests. The tree also produces an abundance of attractive pink flowers in mid-spring.

IN THE KITCHEN

Most peaches in the USA are yellow-fleshed and have a slightly acid tang. Favored in Asia and increasingly popular elsewhere, white-flesh peaches taste sweeter than yellow varieties due to their low acidity, and have a smooth, luscious texture. On the outside, they look similar until you cut into them.

 SELECTING
Choose fruits that feel heavy for their size, have a bit of give, and have an aromatic smell. The stem cavity of a ripe peach should be yellow or white - green means they're unripe.

 PREPARING
Fresh peaches and nectarines can be eaten out of hand – just rinse or wipe the skin. To remove the stone, or pit, slice lengthwise 360 degrees around the fruit and twist each half simultaneously in opposite directions. Freestone varieties should separate easily.

 **STORING**
Peaches and nectarines are highly perishable so, unless you plan to preserve them, buy only in small quantities. Fresh fruits can be kept at room temperature for three to four days, but leave space between them to allow air circulation. Refrigerate in a plastic bag and use within two days, and return to room temperature before eating.

 PRESERVING
Peel raw peaches and nectarines, and remove the stone before freezing or canning them, as it can impart a bitter flavor. If the fruit is over-ripe, puree or chop it, add an acidic juice to prevent the pulp from browning, and freeze in a tightly sealed container or freezer bag.

 USES
Peaches and nectarines can be used at every mealtime throughout the day, from breakfast through lunch, to dinner and dessert. The ripe fruits can be added to oatmeal, French toast, smoothies, or made into fruit butter to spread on toast, and are perfect in fruit salads.

To add a twist to the classic peaches and cream, whip the cream with a splash of almond essence or amaretto. Peaches and almonds are a natural flavor pairing, but other good matches include cinnamon, nutmeg, ginger, coriander, sherry, Marsala, and rum. Like other fruits, peaches and nectarines also work well with savory flavors, particularly in salads and appetizers such as grilled peach, goat cheese and pecan salad, peach and mozzarella crostini or peach and honey mustard chicken salad. Peach chutney or nectarine salsa makes a refreshing accompaniment to spicy grilled chicken dishes, or use to add tangy sweetness to stewed pork and veal dishes.

The classic use for these fruits is in desserts and baking. The famous Peach Melba, which combines peaches and raspberry sauce with vanilla ice cream, was invented by renowned French chef Auguste Escoffier to honor the Australian soprano Nellie Melba.

IN THE GARDEN

Peach and nectarine trees flower early in the spring and the flowers are easily damaged or killed by temperatures below about 28° Fahrenheit, so can't be grown in places where temperatures dip below freezing late into spring. Some varieties are more cold tolerant than others, so choose an appropriate tree for your conditions.

🌡 CLIMATE
Peaches and nectarines can be grown in zones 4 to 9, but do especially well in zones 6 to 8.

✂ SOIL
Peach trees prefer deep sandy, loamy ground with a soil pH of around 6.5.

🌱 PLANTING
Plant trees while they're dormant—typically in late winter or early spring - in an area that receives full sun all day long. Morning sun is especially important as it helps to dry morning dew off the fruit. Space them 15 to 20 feet apart, or 10 to 12 feet apart for dwarf trees.

🌱 GROWING
About 4 to 6 weeks after the tree blooms, thin the fruit so that they are 6 to 8 inches apart on the branch. If too much fruit is left on the tree, it is likely to be smaller and poor quality.

🍽 HARVESTING
The fruits found on the top and outside of the tree usually ripen first. When fully ripe, the color changes from green to completely yellow - no green should be left on the fruit, and they should come off the tree with only a slight twist.

🖐 **FUN FACT** 🖐

The inside of a peach stone tastes remarkably similar to almond, and peach stones are often used to make a cheap version of marzipan, known as persipan.

PEAR

Pyrus

There is evidence of the use of pears as a food source since prehistoric times. The pear was cultivated by the Romans, and a Roman cookbook has a recipe for a spiced, stewed-pear patina, or soufflé. Many species are valued for their edible fruit and juice, while others are cultivated as ornamental trees or to make perry, an alcoholic beverage made from fermented pears.

VARIETIES

Around 3,000 known varieties of pears are grown worldwide, with three main species accounting for the majority of edible fruit production. The European pear Pyrus communis is cultivated mainly in Europe and North America, while the Chinese white pear or bai li, Pyrus ×bretschneideri, and the Nashi pear Pyrus pyrifolia - also known as Asian pear or apple pear - both grow mainly in eastern Asia.

FORELLE Crisp, tangy and sweet, Forelle is a very old variety and produces some of the smallest fruits, which makes them a good choice for snacking. The symmetrical fruit is characterized by its red freckles.

BOSC This pear is a warm cinnamon brown color with russeting over the surface of the skin. The flesh is crisp and woodsy with a complex, honey sweetness. The curved stem and long neck creates a distinctive silhouette.

RED BARTLETT This is one of the first pears ready for harvest each season. The fruits change color while ripening, from striped dark red to a beautiful bright red. The flesh is sweet, soft and juicy when fully ripened.

TAYLOR'S GOLD This is a cinnamon-colored pear with a smooth, uniform russeted skin. It is grown in the cooler climate of the Northwest USA and has juicy, tender flesh with a delicate and delicious sweet flavor.

BEURRE D'ANJOU Cold-hardy and vigorous, this medium- large pear can be stored for seven months. It is bright green and firm at harvest, with a hint of yellow as it ripens, and fine-textured, subtly sweet flesh.

RED ANJOU PEAR This hardy, productive tree yields aromatic fruit. The fruit's smooth red skin houses soft, juicy flesh with a sweet, mild flavor. Flavor peaks 2 months after harvest. Pollinator required.

DOYENNE DU COMICE

A French variety from the region of Angers, this a short, irregular shaped pear with green-yellow skin, often blushed on the sunny side. It has fine, melting flesh, both sweet and tangy.

CONFERENCE

Conference can be enjoyed as a crisp, crunchy fruit, or at any stage of softening. When fully ripened, the soft flesh is quite smooth. It stores well for 10 to 12 months without deterioration.

SECKEL The Seckel is a tiny pear, with a chubby, round body and olive green skin, often with a dark maroon blush. An ideal snack-sized pear, the Seckel is also small enough to be canned whole.

CHINESE WHITE PEAR These very juicy, white to light yellow pears are shaped more like the European pear. Chinese white pears taste similar to Bosc pears, but are crisp, with a lower sugar content.

ASIAN PEAR

The nashi pear has a high water content and crisp, grainy texture that is quite different from the European varieties, and are commonly served raw. In East Asia, the nashi pear tree is a common sight in gardens and the countryside, and its flowers are a popular symbol of early spring. Nashi pears are often served to guests, given as gifts, or eaten together in a family setting, due to their relatively high price and the large size of the fruits.

IN THE KITCHEN

Unlike many fruits that may be picked and eaten immediately, most pears mature, but do not ripen on the tree. Before they can ripen, they must go through a period of cooling from one day to six weeks, depending upon the variety. The exception is the Asian pear, which does ripen on the tree.

 SELECTING
Natural blemishes and variations in skin color have no effect on flavor, but look for pears with no bruises or torn skin. Gently press your thumb against the upper neck - if it yields, it's ripe, but if it doesn't, it will need time to ripen at home. Most pears ripen in about a week.

 PREPARING
Rinse or wipe clean and eat out of hand, or peel, core and slice as needed. Drop peeled pears in cold, lightly salted water, so they won't turn brown.

 STORING
To avoid bruising and spoilage, do not stack pears. To ripen, simply leave on a plate on the kitchen counter, until the necks yield to gentle pressure. Wait to wash the fruit until you are ready to eat or cook with it. Store ripe pears in the refrigerator for up to five days in an airtight container or food storage bag, and return to room temperature before serving.

 PRESERVING
Pears are not the best fruit for freezing, as most types are quite soft when ripe. Firmer varieties like d'Anjou are the best choice. Pears can also be successfully bottled or canned.

 USES
There is little more luscious than biting into a sweet, ripe, juicy pear – no garnish needed. But pears are a versatile fruit that can match well with both sweet and savory flavors in salads, appetizers and meat dishes, as well as pies, tarts, bakes and desserts.

The salty tang of cheese works extremely well with soft, sweet pears. A leafy salad with pears and Manchego, or pears with blue cheese and walnuts would make a refined appetizer or light lunch dish. Pork and pears also have a natural affinity; try roasting peeled, cored and halved pears around a pork joint, in place of the more usual apples, or add chopped pears to the stuffing for a pork loin.

The list of sweet pear recipes is almost endless; pear cakes, pies and tarts, spiced poached pears, pear cobbler, pear bread, pear crumble and even pear upside-down cake.

One flavor combination that's tried and tested is pear and ginger. It appears in many recipes, such as ginger pear muffins, and ginger pear freezer jam, an easy-to-make preserve combining pears, lemon juice, lemon zest and ginger with sugar and vanilla. As it's not a true jam, it should be frozen if kept for longer than three weeks.

IN THE GARDEN

Pear trees are attractive and easy to fit into small yard spaces, and they require very little care once established as they have fewer pest and disease issues than apple trees. Most pear trees are not self-pollinating, so two compatible cultivars are generally needed for successful pollination and fruit set. Pears can take from 3 to 10 years to begin flowering and bear fruit, but once they start producing, they are prolific and long-lasting.

CLIMATE
Depending on the variety, pears can be grown in zones 3 to 10.

SOIL
Pears need well-drained soil, good air circulation and full sun for best fruit set.

PLANTING
Space standard-size trees 20 to 25 feet apart, and dwarf trees 12 to 15 feet apart. Pears can be grown in pots, but make sure to purchase trees specifically bred for containers.

GROWING
Water the young trees well during dry spells to help establish the roots and apply a small amount of fertilizer early in the year. Prune annually to keep the tree healthy. Thin out the young fruit, leaving about 6 inches between each cluster of fruit per branch.

HARVESTING
Mature pear trees produce a lot of fruit in a short window of time. Harvest pears when they are mature but still hard, and then ripen at room temperature for the best quality fruits. To store pears, pick them when they are fully grown but still very hard. Keep in containers in a dark, cool place - about 40°F - for 1 to 2 months.

FUN FACT
The pear tree was an object of particular veneration in the tree worship of the Nakh peoples of the North Caucasus.

PERSIMMON

Diospyros kaki

In Ozark folklore, the severity of the upcoming winter is predicted by slicing a persimmon seed and observing the cutlery-shaped formation inside. There are two main types of persimmon fruit: astringent, which contain very high levels of tannins and are unpalatable if eaten when not fully ripe; and non-astringent, which may be eaten when still very firm.

VARIETIES

SHARON FRUIT
Named after the Sharon plain in Israel, Sharon is the marketing name for the Israeli-bred cultivar, Triumph. The fruit has no core, is seedless and sweet, and can be eaten whole.

EARLY GOLDEN AMERICAN Considered one of the best American varieties, this cultivar is hardy to minus 25 F and bears very sweet, deep orange fruit, with a delicious taste quite similar to dates.

CHOCOLATE PERSIMMON
Also known as black sapote, or chocolate pudding fruit, the flesh of the chocolate persimmon has the taste and consistency of chocolate pudding when ripe.

FUYU ASIAN
One of the most widely grown persimmons, Fuyu's deep-orange fruit is medium-sized, with a consistently sweet taste, and stays firm even when ripe. especially tender.

IN THE KITCHEN

Fuyu and Hachiya are the two most popular types. Fuyu's firm, mildly sweet flesh is good raw or cooked, while hachiya's rich sweet flesh lends itself to baked goods, ice cream, and cocktails.

SELECTING
Avoid fruit with bruises or punctures, and try and pick the most symmetrical, since a lopsided persimmon might contain large seeds. Black spots on a persimmon's skin don't affect the fruit's quality one bit – simply peel if necessary.

PREPARING
Wash and pat dry. Fresh fuyus are firm enough to slice or eat like an apple - the skin is edible, but peel them if you prefer. Hachiyas are often too squishy to bite into so cut them in half and spoon out the flesh.

STORING
Non-astringent persimmons will be firm-ripe and ready to eat when you buy them, but will keep for weeks, if not months if refrigerated. Astringent fruits need several days on your counter to soften up. Once soft, move them to the fridge where they should keep for at least two or three more weeks.

PRESERVING
Persimmons are simple to freeze—simply spoon out the flesh from each one as it ripens, puree and store it in the freezer in an airtight container.

USES
Fresh or frozen ripe persimmon flesh is often used to make bread, muffins, cookies, cakes and pudding, as well as jam, ice cream and smoothies. For the simplest, no-sugar-added dessert, freeze ripe or overripe fuyu persimmons. To serve, cut off the tops with a serrated knife and eat the sweet, custard-like frozen fruit with a spoon.

Persimmons pair well with slightly salty, savory foods. Try wedges of sweet persimmon with paper-thin slices of prosciutto or bresaola, or serve alongside a cheese plate.

Steamed persimmon pudding, persimmon compote, and honey-drizzled broiled persimmons all make delicious sweet treats, but the fruit can also be cooked in savory dishes. A salad of endive with beet, persimmon and marinated feta, a winter version of tabbouleh with persimmons, or sweet persimmons and spicy mustard greens with a Marsala-glazed pork roast all demonstrate the versatility of this fruit.

NUTRITIONAL VALUE

Serving size 100 g, raw, Japanese
70 calories
Dietary fiber 3.6 g (14% DV)
Vitamin C 7.5 mg (12% DV)
Vitamin A 1627.00 IU (33% DV)
Manganese 0.355 mg (18% DV)

HEALTH BENEFITS

Anti-inflammatory
Antioxidant
Supports healthy vision
Reduces high blood sugar levels
Lowers high cholesterol levels
Decreases risk of chronic diseases

IN THE GARDEN

Persimmon trees are easy to grow, as they have few pests and require little care. They are also considered to be ornamental, as they are ablaze in the fall with orange and red foliage.

CLIMATE
Persimmons can be grown in zones 4 to 10, depending on the variety. Asian persimmons are not frost hardy.

SOIL
These trees are not picky about soil but do best with a pH of 6.5 to 7.5.

PLANTING
Plant grafted saplings in the spring. Although a single tree can self-pollinate, two will offer better pollination. Water potted saplings, and soak the roots of bare root saplings in a bucket of water, before planting.

GROWING
Water saplings deeply once a month from May to October.

HARVESTING
Persimmon trees may take up to six years to produce fruit. Pick persimmons when they are orange, but still firm. Snip the stem, leaving the calyx attached to each fruit. Handle carefully, as persimmons bruise easily.

PINEAPPLE

Ananas comosus

Due the cost of importing them – and the difficulty and expense of growing them in hothouses – pineapples were once a symbol of great wealth in Europe, and were displayed at dinner parties, rather than being eaten. Now grown and enjoyed worldwide, raw pineapple contains a powerful enzyme, bromelain, which can be used to marinade and tenderize meat.

VARIETIES

HILO Hilo is a compact variant of the 'smooth cayenne' pineapple, which makes up more than 70 percent of pineapples grown worldwide. The fruit is small and cylindrical with juicy, flavorful yellow flesh.

KONA SUGARLOAF
Kona Sugarloaf, sometimes called the Brazilian White, is an unusually sweet pineapple. Its white flesh has high sugar content and no woodiness in the center.

NATAL QUEEN
Natal Queen has golden yellow flesh, crisp texture and delicate, mild flavor. Popular for fresh consumption and the fruit keeps well after ripening.

RED SPANISH
Red Spanish is the most popular pineapple among growers in the West Indies, Venezuela and Mexico. The orange-red skin contains aromatic and flavorful, pale-yellow flesh.

IN THE KITCHEN

The tough and spiky exterior of a pineapple can be intimidating in the kitchen, but the juicy, aromatic flavor is worth the effort. Pineapple is indispensable in many Southeast Asian and Central American recipes.

SELECTING

Look for fruit that's firm but not hard, heavy for its size, with a rich, sweet fragrance. The leaves should be green and fresh-looking, and should pull easily from the center of the stem when Tthe fruit is ripe.

PREPARING

Trim off the top and base, and cut off the rind in strips. Slice straight down the middle, than in half again making four quarters. Taking each quarter in turn, cut away the core, then slice into bite-size chunks.

STORING

Whole pineapples can be stored for up to three days at room temperature, or up to a week in the refrigerator. Prepared chunks or slices can be kept in a container or tightly wrapped in plastic and refrigerated for two days.

PRESERVING

Pineapple freezes well. Place prepared chunks in a single layer on a cookie sheet and freeze. Transfer to a container or freezer bag.

USES

Fresh pineapple juice is great on its own, or added to smoothies, spritzes, mocktails and cocktails – including piña colada, a tropical blend of rich coconut cream, white rum and tangy pineapple. It is also the star of homemade desserts such as pineapple upside-down cake and caramelized grilled pineapple, delicious served with vanilla ice cream.

The sweet-sour flavor of pineapple lends itself well to savory dishes, too. Pineapple glazed ham delivers classic flavors, although the 'Hawaiian' pizza – with its combination of ham, pineapple and cheese toppings – divides opinion. Refreshing pineapple salsas and slaws are a great accompaniment for grilled meat and fish. Pineapple really comes into its own, though, in spicy and fragrant dishes such as pork and pineapple tacos, pineapple and ginger chicken stir-fry, Thai pineapple fried rice, Malaysian prawn and pineapple curry, and sweet-and-sour pork.

IN THE GARDEN

A pineapple can be grown by planting the top of a shop-bought fruit; however, tops take at least 24 months to flower, plus six months for the fruit to mature. Suckers produce fruit much sooner.

CLIMATE

Can be grown outdoors in zones 10-11. Pineapples enjoy full sun, but also do well in light shade.

SOIL

Pineapples don't need high quality soil. They prefer free draining, slightly acidic conditions.

PLANTING

Pineapples grow well in pots, and can be overwintered indoors in cooler climates. Plant in a large container and allow 3-4 feet in height and width to accommodate each plant. Protect from cold – anything below 60 degrees Fahrenheit slows growth and affects the flavor.

NUTRITIONAL VALUE

Serving size 100 g, raw
50 calories
Dietary fiber 1.4 g (6% DV)
Vitamin C 47.8 mg (80% DV)
Vitamin B6 0.112 mg (6% DV)
Manganese 0.927 mg (46% DV)
Copper 0.110 mg (6% DV)

HEALTH BENEFITS

Antioxidant
Anti-inflammatory
Reduces risk of heart disease, diabetes and cancers
Improves digestion
Boosts immunity
Maintains healthy metabolism

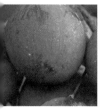

PLUM

Prunus domestica

Plums may have been one of the first fruits domesticated by humans, and traces have been found in Neolithic archaeological sites along with olives, grapes and figs. There is a diverse range of plum types but, when they flower in early spring, they are invariably covered in highly attractive blossoms.

VARIETIES

BAVAY'S GREEN GAGE
This small European tree bears attractive bright green fruit with amber, smooth-textured flesh. Is tart-sweet with a rich, candy-like flavor that is excellent fresh, dried and cooked.

BEACH PLUM Prunus maritima, the beach plum, is a species native to the East Coast of the United States. Although it is bitter or sour it can be eaten out of hand and is grown commercially to make jam.

PINK FLOWERED UME
Also called Chinese plum or Japanese apricot, Prunus mume is an Asian species whose yellow-fleshed fruit is used in juices, as a flavoring for alcohol, as a pickle and in sauces.

STANLEY
Very cold hardy and reliable, the European Stanley produces heavy crops of large, dark blue plums with meaty, green-yellow flesh, perfect for eating, canning or making jelly.

IN THE KITCHEN

Plums are a really versatile fruit to cook with. They are juicy and can be eaten fresh, or preserved in various ways – most popularly as prunes - which can then be used in recipes as an almost entirely different ingredient.

SELECTING
Choose unwrinkled, smooth-skinned fruits with no blemishes, free of soft spots or discolorations. The grayish sheen, or bloom, on plums is natural and does not affect quality.

PREPARING
Rinse leaves in cold water two to three times; pat dry. Cut off the roots and tough stalks, but retain the tender stems. You can use the leaves whole, or you can rip or cut them into bite-size pieces.

STORING
Plums that are slightly hard can be kept at room temperature for a few days to soften up, but they will not actually ripen further or become sweeter. Refrigerate ripe plums in a plastic bag and use within four days. Wash the fruit just before using.

PRESERVING
Both plums and prunes can be frozen, whole or sliced, for later use. Keep in an airtight container.

USES
Favorite plum recipes include crumbles, fruity bakes and pies. For a breakfast treat, top yogurt and granola with stewed plums, or make sweet plum jam or savory plum chutney.

In savory dishes, plums match particularly well with Asian spices and fatty meats like duck, lamb and pork belly, where the tart flavor of the fruit cuts through the richness of the meat. Roast duck with plums and star anise is a classic example.

Prunes are a type of dried or semi-dried plum. The plums are oval, black-skinned, loose-stoned and very sweet, and they add a sticky depth to puddings, stews or roasts. Typical dishes include prune and chocolate torte, and braised pork with prunes.

Homemade umeboshi – traditional Japanese preserved plums – are easy to make and worth trying if you have glut of ume plums. If stored well, umeboshi will keep indefinitely at room temperature.

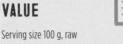

IN THE GARDEN

Plums are a great choice for beginner gardeners, as they are less demanding than most fruit trees. They are compact and prolific producers whose spring blossom adds beauty to any backyard.

CLIMATE
European plums grow in most regions across the U.S. The Japanese types flourish in warmer regions (where peach trees thrive, generally). American hybrids are the hardiest, with some varieties surviving as far north as zone 3.

SOIL
Plums prefer loamy, well-drained soil, and do not thrive in clay-heavy soils or where their roots will be constantly wet.

PLANTING
Choose bare-root rather than container-grown trees, as they usually establish better. Plant out in late winter or early spring, in a location that receives full sun - at least 6 to 8 hours of direct sunlight - 20 to 25 feet apart (or 10 to 15 feet apart for dwarf trees).

GROWING
Stake the tree for at least one year, until it is stable enough to stand on its own, and water well for the first few weeks.

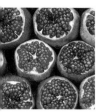

POMEGRANATE

Punica granatum

The pomegranate is a fruit-bearing deciduous shrub or small tree with multiple spiny branches. Its large, colorful blooms are so attractive that some pomegranate varieties are grown for the flowers alone. Pomegranates are a so-called superfood due to the high level of polyphenols, powerful antioxidants thought to offer heart health and anti-cancer benefits.

VARIETIES

AMBROSIA It bears a profusion of bright, orange blooms in spring and produces the largest fruit of all the pomegranates - up to three times the size of others - with pale pink skin and purple, sweet-tart juice.

With a name meaning 'Black Rose', this small pomegranate is very dark red, inside and out, with crunchy seeds and sweet-tart juice that is very high in vitamin C.

EARLY WONDERFUL
Early Wonderful are large, early harvest pomegranates, with bright to dark magenta skin, dark red seeds, and a sweet-tart flavor.

SALAVATSKI
Also known as 'Russian-Turk', Salavatski produces very large red fruit and is extremely cold hardy, having survived down to -6 degrees Fahrenheit.

IN THE KITCHEN

Due to its recently aquired superfood status, pomegranate juice is now consumed in large quantities, but the flavor and texture of fresh pomegranate lends itself to plenty more uses in the kitchen.

 SELECTING
Choose deeply colored purplish-red pomegranates that feel heavy for their size. Avoid any fruit that is cracked or has soft spots.

 PREPARING
Slice about half an inch from the top of the pomegranate and remove the lid. Slice down through each of the white membranes inside the fruit, pull the sections apart, turn the fruit inside out and pop the seeds out into a bowl.

 STORING
Whole pomegranates will keep for a month or more in an airtight bag in the refrigerator. Pomegranate seeds should be refrigerated and used within a few days.

 PRESERVING
To freeze pomegranate seeds, dry them and arrange in a single layer on a cookie sheet lined with wax paper. Once frozen, transfer into a freezer bag or container.

 USES
Add fresh pomegranate seeds to fruit salads, sprinkle over oatmeal, toss in green salads, blend in smoothies, stir into yogurt and mix into muffin and pancake batters.

Add fresh pomegranate juice to vinaigrette salad dressings or mix with honey to use as a glaze for chicken, turkey or lamb.

Pomegranate is popular in North African dishes, such as harissa lamb with pomegranate couscous. Try garnishing brown rice, quinoa or other whole grain pilafs with pomegranate seeds to add color, flavor and crunch.

Pomegranate molasses is an essential ingredient in Middle Eastern cooking, and is easy to make at home. Blend the seeds from about 8 large pomegranates, then strain through a fine mesh sieve. Heat the pomegranate juice, ½ cup of sugar and 2 tbsp of lemon juice in a pan and simmer for about an hour, until syrupy and reduced to 1 to 1 1/4 cups. When cool, store in a jar in the refrigerator.

IN THE GARDEN

The long-lived pomegranate makes a good garden specimen, with showy, red-orange flowers and a fairly compact habit. It grows between 15 and 30ft tall.

 **CLIMATE**
The ideal climate for pomegranates is zones 7 to 12, with short, mild winters and low humidity.

SOIL
Pomegranates grow best in well-drained, loamy soil, pH 5.5-7.0.

 PLANTING
Select a location in full sun, allowing a 20 foot diameter space for the tree to grow into. If planting as a hedge, you can plant them as close as 10 feet apart. Pomegranates may be grown in containers in colder places, and kept indoors or in a greenhouse over winter.

 GROWING
Pomegranates have low water requirements, and can survive drought conditions well.

HARVESTING
Pick as soon as they reach their mature color and sound metallic when tapped. If left on the tree too long, they will split. Fruit should be harvested with snips, and not pulled from the branch.

 NUTRITIONAL VALUE

Serving size 100 g, raw
83 calories
Dietary fiber 4.0 g (16% DV)
Vitamin C 10.2 mg (17% DV)
Vitamin K 16.4 mcg (20% DV)
Copper   0.158 mg (8% DV)
Manganese 0.119 mg (6% DV)

 HEALTH BENEFITS

Antioxidant
Improves blood flow
Lowers blood pressure
Delays oxidation of ldl cholesterol
Helps prevent plaque buildup
May slow the progression of prostate cancer

POMELO

Citrus maxima

The pomelo – also called pummelo or shaddock - is one of the original citrus species from which most cultivated citrus fruits have been hybridized. The fruit is similar in appearance to a large grapefruit, and is native to South and Southeast Asia where it is often featured in festive celebrations, or served after a meal in place of dessert.

VARIETIES

HONEY WHITE This is a crisp citrus fruit native to South Asia. It is usually pale green to yellow when ripe, with sweet white flesh and very thick pith. It is the largest citrus fruit, weighing up to 4.5 lbs.

TAHITIAN The Tahitian pomelo does exceptionally well in taste tests, with its flavor being described as outstanding, although it is somewhat seedy.

OROBLANCO This is another hybrid, a cross of pomelo and white grapefruit. The grapefruit-size fruits have an excellent, sweet flavor and tend to stay on the tree, getting sweeter into the summer.

VALENTINE The Valentine hybrid produces long fruits that resemble a heart when cut in half. This cross between a pomelo, mandarin and blood orange has sweet, dark-orange flesh.

IN THE KITCHEN

Pomelos are best eaten raw. Despite its size, a pomelo only yields enough flesh for one person if eaten plain for breakfast. The thick rind can be half an inch thick and must be removed, along with the white pith.

SELECTING
Choose fruit heavy for their size, with smooth skin. The bottom should be flat or have a dimple; if it is pointy, it is unripe. The flesh color may be pale lime, yellow, orange or dark pink depending on variety.

PREPARING
Cut away the thick rind and continue to peel away the soft white pith until you get to the fruit. Split from top to bottom, and pull out each segment. Cut the thick membrane open and gently peel off to leave only the flesh.

STORING
Pomelos can be kept at room temperature for up to a week. Refrigerate in an open bowl for longer, if necessary, but bring to room temperature before serving for the best flavor. Peeled segments can also be stored in a sealed container in the refrigerator.

PRESERVING
Freeze peeled segments in a single layer on parchment paper, and then put into freezer bags.

USES
Pomelos can be used in a similar way to other citrus fruits such as grapefruit and oranges: eaten fresh, juiced, in drinks and smoothies, or made into jam or marmalade. Pomelos also make an exotic, sweet fruit salad when combined with pomegranate seeds and lychees.

For a refreshing summer dish, enhance the delicate flavor of pomelo with chili, mint and lime in a savory, leafy salad and serve with shellfish such as shrimp, scallops or crab.

Yum som-o is a spicy Thai pomelo salad, which is a delicious fusion of fruity, salty, and sour flavors, spiced up with a kick of chili. Though traditionally served with prawns, vegan versions are every bit as good.

To make the most of pomelo fruit, even the peel can be used. Try making candied pomelo peel – the same way as candied orange peel – and then dipping in melted dark chocolate for a decadent sweet treat.

IN THE GARDEN

The pomelo tree is a compact evergreen with glossy leaves, and showy, aromatic white flowers in spring. The flowers are so fragrant that the scent is used in some perfumes.

CLIMATE
Pomelos enjoy full sun, especially in hot, rainy climates, and do not survive temperatures below 23°F. in a sheltered, sunny spot, or – if it freezes in your area – grow them in pots and bring indoors during the winter months.

SOIL
Pomelos will thrive equally in clay, loam or sand with an acidic or alkaline pH, but they do need good drainage.

PLANTING
Pomelo trees can be grown from seed, but will likely not fruit for at least eight years. Plant cultivated trees in spring

GROWING
Water at least once a week, and feed with citrus fertilizer according to the manufacturer's instructions.

HARVESTING
Ripe pomelos develop a nice yellow color and should easily detach from their stem. Fruits do not mature after picking.

PRICKLY PEAR

Opuntia

An unlikely-looking source of food, the prickly pear cactus is a native of Mexico and grows in arid and semi-arid climates. The fruit is also known as 'tuna ' – from the botanical name Opuntia - and the flesh of the plant pad, which is eaten as a vegetable, is known as 'nopal' or nopalitos.

VARIETIES

INDIAN FIG The spineless variety of prickly pear cactus, Opuntia ficus-indica, is now widely grown world-wide. This cactus goes by various names including Indian fig and Barbary fig.

SANTA RITA PURPLE Santa Rita is a colorful species with rich plum-purple coloring on young pads. Bright yellow flowers contrast against the purple pads, followed by small, edible purple fruit.leaves.

YELLOW PLATANERA The fruit of the Yellow Platanera has a tropical flavor like that of bananas. the fruit from which it takes its name.

XOCONOSTLE he wild Xoconostle is a sour prickly pear variety, botanically classified as Opuntia matudae, which has a sour, chewy peel that is used in savory stews.

IN THE KITCHEN

Prickly pear is a staple food of Mexico, eaten fresh and as a popular ingredient in candies, drinks, jams, and more. Nopalitos - small pads cut into bite-size pieces - are mucilaginous like okra, and good for thickening broths.

 SELECTING
Choose small, smooth, unblemished, deep-colored prickly pears that are firm but not hard, with shiny skin. The fruit will yield to gentle pressure when ripe. Avoid fruit that is moldy or damaged.

 PREPARING
Take care when preparing prickly pears! Wear gloves or use tongs to hold the fruit. Remove sharp spines with pliers, and then pass the fruit through an open flame to burn off the small, almost-invisible, stinging hairs. Cut off both ends, slice down the center and scoop out the fruit. Press the flesh through a sieve to remove the seeds.

STORING
Firm prickly pears will ripen and soften at room temperature in a few days. Ripe fruits can be refrigerated in a plastic bag for up to a week.

 PRESERVING
Whole fruits can be frozen for up to a year, and will be best used for juicing. Or juice the fresh pears, freeze in ice cube trays then transfer to freezer bags.

 USES
Prickly pear juice is celebrated for its vibrant magenta color, unique flavor, and its cooling properties. It can be diluted with water or lemonade or used to make syrup -, perfect on pancakes or ice cream, or in margaritas.

Xoconostle cactus fruit lends a sour flavor to sauces and salsas, as well as the traditional soup, mole de olla, in Mexico. Xoconostle are also sprinkled with chili powder and lemon juice and dehydrated for a snack, and the juice of the sour cactus is used to make traditional aguas frescas.

Huevos rancheros con nopales is a typical Mexican dish made with alternate layers of sliced, grilled prickly pear nopales, tomato sauce, fried eggs and more sauce, plus grated cotija cheese, lime, avocado and coriander.

Colonche is an alcoholic drink made in Mexico for thousands of years. Prickly pear juice is boiled for 2-3 hours and, after cooling, allowed to ferment for a few days to produce a red-hued, sweet, fizzy drink.

IN THE GARDEN

Prickly pears are drought-tolerant and easy to care for. They are, however, vigorous growers with detachable spines, so they may not be suitable for every garden.

 CLIMATE
Prickly pear is an arid garden specimen best suited to zones 9 to 11, but some varieties are hardy as far as zone 4.

SOIL
Plant in full sun in a sandy or gravely mix – good drainage is essential. Never let prickly pear cacti sit in waterlogged soil.

PLANTING
Wear thick gloves and handle carefully to avoid damage to the plant, and yourself.

 GROWING
For the first week, water once every 3-4 days; after that, water once every few weeks. Once established, it will require no additional water.

 HARVESTING
Look for fruits that are dark red or purple in color. Wear gloves to protect against the sharp spines and use tongs to pluck the fruit from the nopal pad - they should come off easily.

NUTRITIONAL VALUE

Serving size 100 g, raw fruit
41 calories
Dietary fiber 3.6 g (14% DV)
Vitamin C 14.0 mg (23% DV)
Magnesium 85.00 mg (21% DV)
Calcium 56.00 mg (6% DV)
Potassium 220.00 mg (5% DV)

HEALTH BENEFITS

Aantioxidant
Boosts the immune system
Improves digestion
Helps strengthen teeth and bones
Helps regulate cholesterol levels
Reduces high blood pressure

QUINCE

Cydonia oblonga

The fruit of the quince tree has been known throughout history, but the tree is also grown for its attractive blossoms and other ornamental qualities. Quince is a fragrant fruit, with a scent that has notes of pineapple, guava, pear, and vanilla, but it is seldom eaten raw, requiring cooking to transform both the taste and the texture.

VARIETIES

COOKE'S JUMBO
Cooke's Jumbo quince is one of the largest varieties of quince and can be more than double the size of common varieties, reaching 8 inches. The fruit is knobby and roughly pear-shaped.

ORANGE Orange quince bears attractive white blossoms in spring followed by large, golden-yellow fruit. A compact variety, it can be grown either as a tree or shrub, perfect for small spaces.

PINEAPPLE This quince is an American variety, with medium-sized, rounded fruits with a flat bottom and thick, raised neck, which ripen from green to a golden, lemon yellow.

RICH'S DWARF
Perfect for smaller gardens, Rich's Dwarf quince is a very hardy shrub that reaches just four to six feet in height. Fruits are fragrant with lemon-yellow skin.

IN THE KITCHEN

Though it may look like a juicy apple or pear, the quince in its raw form is rather hard, tannic and very sour at times. To fully appreciate the quince, it's best when cooked.

 **SELECTING**
A fully ripened quince will be yellow or golden and should have a fragrant, fruity aroma. Avoid quinces with major bruises, wrinkling, or other signs of damage.

PREPARING
To prepare for cooking, peel the cut in half, then quarters with a sharp knife. Remove the core and seeds, and any damaged areas, and then place the flesh in a bowl of water to prevent browning.

STORING
Quinces bruise easily; any weight placed on them will cause bruising, so store in a single layer. Keep at room temperature for up to a week, or in an unsealed plastic bag in the refrigerator for up to three weeks.

PRESERVING
TWhole fruits do not freeze well, but poached fruit can be frozen. Quinces can also be bottled, or made into quince paste or jam, which both keep well.

 USES
Poach prepared quince with water, sugar, honey and any flavorings you like, such as vanilla bean, star anise, whole cloves or fresh ginger. After 40 to 50 minutes, the quince should have turned pink, tender and fragrant. Use to fill crumbles or pies, or spoon over breakfast oatmeal.

Dulce de membrillo is a popular Spanish quince paste usually served with Manchego cheese. Boil the quince in water with vanilla pod and lemon zest, then strain and puree the quince. Measure the puree and add the same quantity of sugar. Heat purée to dissolve sugar, add lemon juice and cook on low heat until thick and dark pink. Finally, put in low oven to dry. When cool, cut into squares or wedges to serve.

The tanginess of quinces makes them a perfect foil for rich, meaty dishes, too – they often feature in Moroccan tagines and Persian stews.

IN THE GARDEN

Growing quince trees is not difficult as long as you can provide a sunny location. You may need to plant two trees for good pollination, or choose a self-fertile variety.

 CLIMATE
Quince trees are hardy in zones 5 through 9.

 SOIL
Quinces adapt to moist or dry soils, acid or alkaline, but perform best in fertile, well-drained soil.

 PLANTING
Quince trees are happiest in a sunny spot or, in colder northerly areas, plant it against a south-facing or west-facing wall. Small patio quince trees may even be grown in containers.

 GROWING
Quince trees have some drought tolerance, but you should water them during prolonged dry spells - they are hard to over-water.

 HARVESTING
As a rule, quinces do not ripen on the tree but, instead, require cool storage. Begin harvesting quince fruit when it changes from light green-yellow to a golden yellow color in the fall. Pick quinces with care, to avoid bruising.

RASPBERRY

Rubus

Raspberries can vary in color and size, but all deliver an unmistakable sweet, slightly tart flavor. Cultivated varieties are either summer-bearing floricanes, which produce an abundance of fruit within a relatively short period in midsummer, or everbearing primocanes, which bear fruit in the late summer and fall, as well as a summer crop on second-year canes.

VARIETIES

BOYNE This is one of the best raspberries for cold climates. It will consistently produce deep-red, flavorful berries in zones 3-6, where other varieties may experience winter damage.

ROYALTY Royalty is a vigorous purple, primocane raspberry that yields large, sweet berries with great flavor, making it the most popular purple raspberry variety.

ANNE Anne is a fall-bearing primocane variety with sunshine-yellow fruit. These large, sweet, firm berries have a unique flavor with hints of apricot.

JEWEL BLACK Jewel Black is a hardy floricane variety that produces heavy crops of delicious, ebony-colored fruit with an incredible, aromatic flavor.

IN THE GARDEN

Raspberries are among the easiest fruits to grow, and can produce quite a large crop in a relatively small space.

CLIMATE
Raspberries generally grow in zones 4 through 8; however, some varieties tolerate cooler or hotter climates.

SOIL
Raspberries thrive in well-drained soil with a pH between 6 and 7, with ample organic matter.

PLANTING
In spring, plant out potted or bare-root canes 18 inches apart. Cut the newly-planted canes back to nine inches tall to encourage new growth. Raspberry canes grow very tall, so drive in two six foot posts at each end of the row, and stretch galvanized wires between the posts to provide support.

GROWING
Fall-bearing raspberry canes should be cut to the ground in winter. Summer fruiters should be pruned after fruiting.

HARVESTING
To maximize sweetness, pick in the morning. When raspberries are ripe they should pull off the hull easily. Pick only ripe berries because they do not ripen once picked.

IN THE KITCHEN

Fresh raspberries are fragile, difficult to ship, and, therefore, expensive. Once raspberries reach market, they have a shelf life of only a day or two, so growing your own is a cost-effective way to get the freshest fruit..

SELECTING
Raspberries should be plump, dry, firm, well-shaped, and uniformly colored. Don't purchase berries that are withered or crushed.

PREPARING
Raspberries are usually fairly clean and do not need to be washed. If necessary, wash very gently then spread out on a paper towel to dry. Eat or prepare immediately.

STORING
Raspberries are usually fairly clean and do not need to be washed. If necessary, wash very gently then spread out on a paper towel to dry. Eat or prepare immediately.

PRESERVING
Whole raspberries freeze well. Arrange berries in a single layer on a cookie sheet and place in the freezer. Once frozen, transfer to an airtight container and keep for up to a year.

USES
Serve fresh raspberries with ice cream, sorbet, yogurt, or use them in fruit salads, cereals, cakes, and crêpes. Homemade raspberry jam is the perfect way to use a large crop of berries, and the flavor is outstanding.

A simple raspberry coulis is the foundation of many desserts, such as cakes, custards, puddings, ice cream, and sorbets. Puree raspberries, and then push through a sieve to remove seeds. Add sugar to taste, and a little lemon juice to help preserve the color.

Tvinaigrette for a green salad or for grilled chicken, blend raspberries with white balsamic vinegar, oil, honey, rosemary, salt and black pepper to taste.

Or how about a raspberry daiquiri made with fresh, natural ingredients? Muddle 10 raspberries with the juice of a lime and ½ tsp raw sugar. Add 2 ounces of rum and lots of ice and shake well. Pour through a sieve into a martini glass.

NUTRITIONAL VALUE

Serving size 100 g
52 calories
Dietary fiber 6.5 g (26% DV)
Vitamin C 26.2 mg (44% DV)
Vitamin K 7.8 mcg (10% DV)
Manganese 0.670 mg (34% DV)

HEALTH BENEFITS

Antioxidant
Anti-inflammatory
Counter oxidative stress
Help improve coordination, memory, and mood
Reduce risk of diabetes
Helps beneficial gut bacteria

RHUBHARB

Rheum x hybridum

Rhubarb is an herbaceous perennial with thick, angular stems and large, inedible leaves. The edible stems range from red to green, through pink and speckled, and have a strong, tart flavor that can be enjoyed raw or cooked. Although rhubarb is actually a vegetable, its culinary use is mainly as a fruit.

VARIETIES

VICTORIA The large, fat, tender stems are green with a red blush and have a tart, apple-gooseberry flavor. Victoria is considered one of the best rhubarb varieties for cooking. This heirloom variety is easy to grow.

HOLSTEIN BLOODRED Holstein Bloodred is a vigorous grower, with juicy crops of dark, blood-red sticks. purple, and green leaves.

RIVERSIDE GIANT A cold-hardy variety, Riverside Giant is also a vigorous producer, with long, thick green stalks. This enormous plant can grow to 15ft tall by 10ft wide.

TIMPERLEY EARLY Timperley Early is renowned for its superb flavor. It's a very early variety, and good for forcing.

IN THE KITCHEN

The stalks are the only parts of the plant consumed; the leaves are very high in oxalic acid, which can cause severe illnesses if eaten. Rhubarb should be cooked and stored in glass or stainless steel containers (not aluminum, iron, or copper).

 SELECTING Choose firm, crisp stalks with shiny skins. Avoid stalks that are limp, or those with blemishes or split ends.

 PREPARING Trim off the toxic leaves, wash the stalks and pat dry. Use a vegetable peeler to remove any blemishes from the surface of the stalks, but don't cut the stalks until you are ready to use them, or the rhubarb will dry out.

 STORING Remove the leaves from the stalks before you store them. Uncut stalks can be kept in the refrigerator for up to a week, sealed in a plastic bag.

 PRESERVING Cut stalks can be frozen in an airtight bag.

 USES Fresh rhubarb can be very tart, but pairing it with a sweeter fruit reduces the need for extra sugar. Strawberry and rhubarb pie is a classic recipe that combines sweet and tart flavors to great effect.

Rhubarb is an intriguing addition to savory dishes such as Persian lamb with rhubarb. Sweat 2 sliced onions in 2 tbsp butter for four minutes then remove. Dust 2 pounds cubed lamb with flour then brown in the same pan. Add the cooked onion, 1 ½ tbsp ground coriander and 1 quart lamb stock and simmer for 50-60 minutes until tender. Sweat 3 cups chopped rhubarb, 1 cup chopped parsley and 4 tbsp chopped mint in butter for 4 minutes, then add to the stew and season. Serve over rice or pasta, and garnish with toasted pistachios.

Try preserving your rhubarb crop as rhubarb and ginger jam, or rhubarb and date chutney. Or infuse for four weeks with sugar and gin to create vibrant pink rhubarb gin.

IN THE GARDEN

Rhubarb is an easy-to-grow perennial, usually planted as dormant crowns in spring. It is very winter hardy, resistant to drought, and plants remain productive for up to 15 years.

 CLIMATE Rhubarb needs a cool climate, where the average temperature falls below 40F in winter and below 75F in summer.

 SOIL Rhubarb prefers slightly or moderately acid soil, and thrives at a pH of 6.0 to 6.8. Fertilize well.

 PLANTING Plant crowns at least 3 - 4 feet apart after last frost in a semi-shaded plot — rhubarb is one of the few crops that doesn't mind a little shade. Rhubarb can also be 'forced' by covering dormant crowns with clay pots in early spring.

 GROWING Cut off flower stalks as soon as they form to extend cropping. Water during dry weather.

 HARVESTING When harvesting, gently pull the stem from the crown area of the root to remove the base of the stem. Cutting with a knife leaves a stump that may rot and encourage pests.

NUTRITIONAL VALUE

Serving size 100 g, raw
21 calories
Dietary fiber 1.8 g (7% DV)
Vitamin C 8.0 mg (13% DV)
Vitamin K 29.3 mcg (37% DV)
Calcium 86.00 mg (9% DV)
Manganese 0.196 mg (10% DV)
Potassium 288.00 mg (6% DV)

HEALTH BENEFITS

improves digestion
helps prevent Alzheimer's
stimulates bone growth
beneficial for vision and protective to the retina
boosts skin health
optimizes metabolism
improves circulation

SAPODILLA

Manilkara zapota

Sapodilla is a long-lived, evergreen tree native to Central America and the Caribbean. Also known as sapota, chico, naseberry, or nispero, the 2-4 inch, egg-shaped fruit has an exceptionally sweet and malty flavor. Ripe fruit has saggy, brown skin, with soft yellow to brown pulp, sometimes with a reddish tinge, and a grainy texture similar to that of a ripe pear.

VARIETIES

ALANO Rated by many as the finest sapodilla in the world, Alano has medium-sized, oval fruits that are sweet and delicious. It is a slow grower with a compact habit so can be grown in a large pot in cooler climates..

HASYA Hasya is the number one cultivar grown in Mexico. The football-shaped fruit is excellent eating quality and has a reddish hue throughout the pulp. It tends to fruit while quite young.

MAKOK Native to Thailand, Makok is a relatively recent introduction to Florida. The fruit is long and pointed, and is one of the best-tasting in the world.

PROLIFIC As the name suggests, Prolific produces a heavy crop. The flavor is very sweet, like brown sugar, with a slightly gritty texture.

IN THE KITCHEN

Sweet sapodillas go great in fruit salads, flans, ice creams and puddings. Due to their long history of cultivation there, they are also common in many Latin American and Asian recipes.

 SELECTING
Choose sapodillas that are free of soft spots. Lightly scrape the brown skin with your fingernail - mature flesh should have a hint of yellow or red. If the flesh is deep green, the fruit is immature and will not ripen into a sweet fruit.

 PREPARING
Sapodillas are picked when mature, but not fully ripe. Ripen at room temperature for a few days until firm-soft, not mushy. Cut through the fruit, remove the inedible seeds, and spoon out the flesh, or use a sharp knife or peeler to remove the skin.

 STORING
A ripe sapodilla will keep in the refrigerator in a plastic bag or container for about a week.

PRESERVING
Sapodillas can be frozen, but the consistency will change and will be best suited for use in ice creams, breads, pudding, and sauces.

 USES
Sapodillas are commonly eaten raw, or cooked with other fruit, such as apples, pears or quince, or used alone in a pie. For a quick dessert, fold the pulp into whipped crème fraîche to make a fool, or poach the flesh in wine, sugar and lemon juice with cinnamon or vanilla and serve with ice cream.

If you have lots of ripe fruits, try making delicious sapodilla custard with milk, eggs, sugar and cinnamon. Add a caramel sauce and serve upside-down, like a flan.

In Indian kitchens, the sweetness of sapodilla is offset by blending the pulp with yogurt to make a milkshake-like lassi. For a decadent Sapodilla Brandy Smoothie, blend together ½ cup milk, 1 tbsp honey, 1 tsp brandy, ½ cup of sapodilla pulp and 4 cups of ice until smooth.

NUTRITIONAL VALUE

Serving size 100 g
83 calories
Dietary fiber 5.3 g (21% DV)
Vitamin C 14.7 mg (24% DV)
Copper 0.086 mg (4 % DV)
Iron 0.80 mg (4 % DV)

HEALTH BENEFITS

Anti-inflammatory
Antioxidant
Antibacterial
Reduces risk of viral infections
Boosts the immune system
Aids digestive health

IN THE GARDEN

The sapodilla is an attractive tree and, although slow growing, it is wind resistant and long lived. In the tropics it can grow to 100 feet, but grafted examples are much smaller.

 CLIMATE
Thrives in tropical, subtropical and warm temperate climates. Mature trees can withstand 26°-28°F for several hours, but young trees may be killed by 30°F.

 SOIL
Well adapted to many types of soil, including limestone soils, deep loose clay or sandy loam, but good drainage is essential.

PLANTING
Plant seeds in a loose, well-draining potting mix and keep moist - they will take five to eight years to fruit. Sapodilla can be planted close together, 15 – 20 feet, if pruned well. Add fertilizer every 2-3 months during the first year; thereafter, two to three applications per year are sufficient.

 GROWING
Mature trees tolerate dry conditions better than most fruit trees, but irrigate in the dry season to increase productivity.

 HARVESTING
Test if fruit is mature by scratching it with your fingernail (see above). Wash off the sandy scruff before putting aside to ripen.

STRAWBERRY

Fragaria x ananassa

The garden strawberry is well-known for its bright red color, distinctive flavor and juicy texture. Strawberry varieties are grouped by their flowering habit: June-bearing, which produce fruit in the early summer; ever-bearing, which produce more than one crop during the season; and day-neutral, which crop continuously whilst the weather remains good.

VARIETIES

ALLSTAR A vigorous, June-bearing strawberry that produces large, glossy berries with an exceptionally sweet flavor. Their delicate skin makes them ideal for home growers, as they don't ship well.

OZARK BEAUTY The everbearing Ozark Beauty was developed in Arkansas and is well-suited for colder climates as well as higher elevations – with care, it can survive temperatures as low as -30F.

SELVA Selva is a day-neutral type of strawberry that is very widely planted in California and Florida, where it produces large fruit.

WHITE D A white, everbearing strawberry, of a modern, cross-bred type known as pineberries. Although the fruits are relatively small, they are very aromatic with a flavor reminiscent of pineapple.

IN THE KITCHEN

A perfectly ripe strawberry needs no further adornment. But if you do want to cook, there's no shortage of cake, tart and ice cream recipes to make the most of this fragrant, flavorful fruit.

 SELECTING Always choose bright red berries – green or yellow ones won't ripen once picked. Size is not important, but they should be plump and shiny, not dry or shriveled, and have no blemishes or mold.

 PREPARING Strawberries may be rinsed or wiped clean, and gently patted dry. Large fruits should be 'hulled' by cutting out the green cap and stem with a small knife or strawberry huller, then sliced or halved.

 STORING Ripe strawberries do not keep well – no more than a day at room temperature. To store for several days, line a container with a paper towel or clean kitchen towel and place whole, unwashed fruits on top in a single layer. Cover and chill, and wash before eating.

PRESERVING Many cooks prefer frozen strawberries to fresh ones, as they hold their shape better. Simply hull them and put into a plastic bag in the freezer.

Strawberries can also be canned, dehydrated, or made into jam.

 USES Fresh strawberries are popular served simply with cream, ice cream or in a fruit salad. They also make a great filling or topping for cheesecake, tarts, pies and pancakes.

Two unlikely ingredients work especially well with strawberries: black pepper and balsamic vinegar. Macerate berries with a little sugar and a splash of balsamic vinegar, top with a grind of black pepper and serve with vanilla ice cream.

Homemade strawberry ice cream or sorbet is a good way to use a glut of fruit, and keeps well in the freezer. Or try making popsicles: strawberry and yogurt, or strawberry, honey and coconut cream work well.

Strawberries are a great addition to milkshakes, smoothies and other drinks. Enjoy a Strawberry-Basil Refresher by blending lemon juice, sugar, strawberries and basil with a cup of ice cubes, and topping with club soda.

IN THE GARDEN

Although strawberries can be grown from seed, it is more usual to buy young potted plants, or dormant 'bare root' plants. Select a few varieties that fruit at different times to extend the cropping season.

 **CLIMATE** Strawberries tolerate a wide range of conditions, from zones 3 – 10, in full sun or dappled shade.

SOIL Somewhat sandy soil is preferred, with the addition of manure and a balanced fertilizer. They can be grown in compost in pots or special strawberry planters.

PLANTING Plant in rows or on mounded 'hills'. Mulch with shredded pine needles, compost, or straw or place fiber mats under each plant to protect fruits from touching the ground, and to act as a weed barrier.

GROWING Water well during fruit formation and protect from slugs and snails. Remove runners to increase cropping, or allow rooting to propagate new plants.

 HARVESTING Pick individual fruits when uniformly red, plump and shiny.

 NUTRITIONAL VALUE

Serving size 100 g
33 calories
Dietary fiber 2 g (8% DV)
Vitamin C 58.8 mg (71% DV)
Manganese 0.386 mg (18% DV)
Folate (vitamin B9) 24 ☒g (6% DV)

 HEALTH BENEFITS

antioxidant
improves heart health
helps control blood sugar
boosts immune system and skin health
promotes normal tissue growth and cell function
regulates blood pressure

TAMARIND

Tamarindus indica

The tamarind tree originated in the tropical regions of Africa, but is now cultivated worldwide. It produces a pod-like, hard brown fruit containing a fleshy, edible pulp that is often described as sweet-and-sour in flavor. A large, attractive hardwood tree with feathery foliage, tamarind is often planted as an ornamental shade tree in parks and roadsides in the southern United States.

VARIETIES

SWEET TAMARIND "Makham waan" in Thailand, this is a popular fruit snack eaten straight from the pod. It's also used to make desserts and candy, and mixed with sugar and water to make a refreshing drink.

SOUR TAMARIND Pulp from the sour tamarind plays a central role in recipes from Southeast Asia, the Indian subcontinent, the Middle East, south and central America and the Caribbean.

IN THE KITCHEN

Its complex sweet-sour flavor makes tamarind an essential ingredient in many world cuisines. It can be found as unprocessed raw pods, pressed blocks, or concentrate in a jar or can, and lends a tangy note to everything from curries and chutney to cookies and candy.

 SELECTING
Packaged raw pods are generally fully mature with dry, brown shells. Check there are no holes or cracks in the pods, as this could mean bugs or mold have got in. Check packaging to identify either sweet or sour tamarind.

 PREPARING
Open the dried pods, remove the fruit and place in a saucepan with a little water and simmer for 10 - 15 minutes to soften. Cool and gently mash the fruit, then press through a strainer to produce as much pulp as possible while straining out the seeds. The paste is then ready to use.

If starting with a block, soak the tamarind in lukewarm water to soften, then break it up, separating the pulp from the fibers and seeds. Press through a sieve to produce a paste.

 STORING
Raw pods may be kept unrefrigerated for up to a week. Blocks and cans/jars will keep indefinitely unopened, but thereafter should be refrigerated.

 PRESERVING
If made in large quantities, homemade tamarind paste may be bottled or frozen.

USES
Tamarind water - agua de tamarindo - is one of the best-loved aguas frescas in Mexico. The earthy acidity and sweet and sour flavor is most popular on a hot day. It is simple to make; tamarind pulp and sugar are added to hot water. After soaking for 1 ½ hours, the mixture is strained then chilled and served with ice.

Try a mix of tamarind, garlic, chili, sugar and fish sauce to whip up a spicy Vietnamese tamarind dipping sauce to serve with grilled shrimp.

Tamarind also makes a good base for a sweet-sour stir-fry sauce. Mix together 2 tsp tamarind paste, 1/3 cup chicken stock, 2 1/2 tbsp fish sauce, 2 tbsp sugar and 1 or 2 minced fresh red or green chilies. Add to stir-fried chicken, shrimp and/or vegetables and heat through.

IN THE GARDEN

The tamarind is an attractive but fairly large tree, so not be suitable for smaller gardens. Normally evergreen, but leaves may drop in a very hot, dry season. It is wind-resistant and prefers full sun.

CLIMATE
Young trees are cannot take a frost, but mature trees will tolerate brief periods of 28° F.

SOIL
Tamarinds do best in deep, slightly acidic, well drained soils, and can tolerate salt spray but not cold, wet soils.

PLANTING
Plant young trees in a large hole to accommodate the root system; tamarinds are generally too large to be grown in a container.

They can be grown from seed, which germinates within a week. Growth is fairly slow but they begin to produce fruit in 6-8 years.

GROWING
Water young trees until established. Tamarinds withstand drought quite well thereafter and do not require a lot of fertilizer.

HARVESTING
Tamarind matures in late spring to summer, but can be left on the tree for up to six months after maturity to allow the pulp to dry out.

NUTRITIONAL VALUE

Serving size 100 g
239 calories
Dietary fiber 5.1 g (13% DV)
Thiamine (vitamin B1) 0.428 mg (37% DV)
Riboflavin (vitamin B2) 0.152 mg (13% DV)
Niacin (vitamin B3) 1.938 mg (13% DV)

HEALTH BENEFITS

Anti-inflammatory
Antioxidant
Natural laxative
Protects against heart disease
Anti-fungal, antiviral and antibacterial properties
Helps reverse fatty liver disease

UGLI

Citrus reticulata × paradisi

The Ugli, also known as uglifruit, uniq fruit or Jamaican tangelo, is a citrus fruit originally found on the island of Jamaica. It is a naturally occurring hybrid of a Seville orange, grapefruit and tangerine, and is classified as a tangelo. Generally slightly larger than a grapefruit, the rather knobby, misshapen, greenish-yellow rind gives rise to its name – for its 'ugly' appearance.

UGLI The name Ugli is a trademark of the Jamaican company that exclusively grows the fruit. The roundish or teardrop-shaped fruit is easy to peel, with juicy, sweet flesh that tastes more similar to its tangerine parent than its grapefruit heritage.

Ranging in size from 4 inches to 6 inches in diameter, when ripe the thick skin varies in color from green to greenish-yellow, to yellow, and even orange. Inside, the large segments contain few seeds.

IN THE KITCHEN

Ugli fruit adds a subtle citrus tang to both sweet and savory recipes. It can be peeled and eaten like an orange, segment-by-segment, or cut in half and eaten with a spoon, like a grapefruit.

NUTRITIONAL VALUE

serving size ⊠ fruit 122 g
calories 45
dietary fiber 2 g (8% DV)
vitamin C 42 mg (70% DV)
calcium 20 mg (2% DV)

HEALTH BENEFITS

Antioxidant
Anti-inflammatory
Strengthens bones
Boost immune system
Supports skin, muscle, and connective tissue development

SELECTING
Ugli fruit are harvested only once they have fully ripened on the tree, so the fruit found in stores is ready to eat. Jamaican-grown fruit is seasonal from November to May, but is sometimes available in July to September, depending on weather conditions.

PREPARING
No preparation is needed; simply wash, peel and eat.

STORING
Store for up to five days at room temperature, or up to two weeks in the refrigerator.

PRESERVING
To freeze Ugli fruit, divide into sections, removing membranes and seeds. In a saucepan, bring a sugar and water syrup bring to a boil, then cool and pour over Ugli fruit. Freeze in covered airtight containers freezer bags. Keeps for 10-12 months.

USES
Ugli fruit can be used in place of other citrus fruits in recipes.

Draw upon Ugli fruit's roots with a Caribbean pork casserole. Marinate diced pork in sherry for two hours. Gently fry the pork in oil for 3-4 minutes, add shallots and mushrooms and cook for two minutes, then sprinkle on some flour and cook for one minute more. Add chicken broth and seasonings and simmer gently for about 1½ hours until tender. Half way through, cooking add Ugli segments.

Try a twist on *duck a l'orange* by replacing the familiar orange with Ugli fruit to make Ugli duckling, or add Ugli fruit juice and grated rind to egg yolks, oil and mustard to make zingy citrus mayonnaise.

Another twist on a classic is this hot toddy. Place the juice of two Ugli fruit, 2 fl. oz. dark rum and 1 tbsp honey in a small pan and heat gently until honey has melted. Remove from the heat, add a dash of cinnamon and serve.

IN THE GARDEN

The Ugli fruit tree is a tender perennial citrus that grows in Mediterranean or tropical climates. Usually planted as a grafted tree; seeds may not grow true to type.

CLIMATE
Best outdoors in hardiness zones 10 or above, but can be grown in pots and overwintered indoors in colder climates. ?

SOIL
Needs a well-drained, mildly to strongly alkaline soil, pH 7.6 to 9.0. Dig in plenty of compost.

PLANTING
Citrus is best planted in fall in a warm sunny position protected from cold winds. Plant the tree in the ground as deep as it is in the pot/bag. Alternatively, plant in a pot with drainage holes, using a good quality mix, and move around the garden to make the most of the sun during different seasons.

GROWING
Protect young plants from frost. Apply citrus fertilizer in fall and spring.

HARVESTING
Harvest when heavy for their size and slightly yielding – and the uglier the better.

WATERMELON

Citrullus lanatus

The annual, vine-like watermelon originated in West Africa and grows in tropical or sub-tropical conditions. Its sweet, juicy flesh is most commonly red, but varieties may be pink, orange, yellow or white. While the flesh is best enjoyed fresh, the dried seeds are also edible and the rind can be pickled or cooked as a vegetable.

VARIETIES

MILLIONAIRE The Millionaire seedless hybrid delivers all the flavor and succulence of watermelon, but without the seeds. It produces 15-22 lb. fruits with bright red flesh and hard, green-striped rinds.

CRIMSON SWEET A classic 'picnic' watermelon, averaging 25 lb., Crimson Sweet is famed for its high sugar content and great flavor.

SUGAR BABY A smaller 'icebox' melon – sized to fit in your icebox – the dark green Sugar Baby weighs around 8-10 lb. The incredibly sweet flesh contains very few small seeds.

DESERT KING Pale green rind surrounds the yellow-orange flesh of the Desert King watermelon. This heirloom variety produces 20 lb fruits and is drought-tolerant.

IN THE KITCHEN

Containing more than 90 percent water, the low calorie, fat-free watermelon makes a great summer snack. It's a popular addition to fruit salad, or can be juiced for a refreshing drink.

 SELECTING
A ripe watermelon should feel heavy for its size and, when tapped, should produce a deep, hollow sound. It should have a pale yellow patch where it has rested on the ground.

 PREPARING
Watermelon flesh needs very little preparation; simply wipe clean, quarter or slice, and remove the flesh from the thick rind. The large, black seeds can be rinsed and dried before roasting with salt, or with sweet or savory spices.

 STORING
Whole fruits can be stored in a cool, dark place for up to two weeks. Cut slices will keep in the refrigerator for 3-4 days in an airtight container or tightly wrapped in plastic. Cubed watermelon can be frozen – the thawed flesh will be soft, but is still good for smoothies.

 PRESERVING
As well as freezing, watermelon can be dried to make fruit jerky. The rind can be pickled to serve with deli meats and cheeses, or made into sweet watermelon rind jam.

 USES
There are a surprisingly large number of savory watermelon recipes: watermelon BBQ sauces; watermelon salsas; watermelon skewers; and watermelon salads.

Try grilling watermelon with a spicy, Thai-inspired dressing to transform the fruit into a BBQ side dish. Drizzle slices with honey, lime, garlic and chili sauce and grill until caramelized, then serve alongside grilled ribs, chicken or shrimp.

Chilled watermelon soup makes a quick but refreshing dish for a hot summer day. Whizz watermelon flesh with lemon juice, sweet or sparkling white wine and shredded ginger in a blender until smooth. Strain into serving bowls and top with diced watermelon.

IN THE GARDEN

Watermelons are frost-tender and need a long, warm growing season. They tolerate both humid and dry climates, but need full sun to thrive.

 CLIMATE
Can be grown in zones 3-11, but does best in daytime temperatures of 70 - 90 degrees Fahrenheit. Watermelons grown in cool temperatures, below 50 degrees Fahrenheit, will taste bland.

SOIL
Well-drained soil with a light, loamy texture improved with compost, aged manure, or seaweed before planting. Avoid very sandy or clay soils.

 **PLANTING**
In cooler climates, choose a smaller, short-season variety and sow indoors. Watermelon plants need plenty of space - bush varieties can be grown 2 feet apart in rows 4 to 6 feet apart, but vining varieties need 5 to 6 feet between plants and 6 to 8 feet between each row.

 GROWING
Keep soil moist until the fruit reaches tennis ball size, then water only when the top of the soil feels dry.

 HARVESTING
Watermelons don't ripen further once harvested. If it sounds hollow when tapped, the fruit is ripe.

NUTRITIONAL VALUE

Serving size 100 g
30 calories
Dietary fiber 0.4 g (2% DV)
Vitamin C 8.1 mg (14% DV)
Vitamin A 569.00 IU (11% DV)
Potassium 112 mg (3% DV)
Lycopene 4532.00 mcg

HEALTH BENEFITS

Anti-inflammatory
Antioxidant
Lowers risk of heart disease
Reduces hypertension
Improves hydration and digestion
Promotes healthy collagen growth
Lycopene helps reduce cancer risk

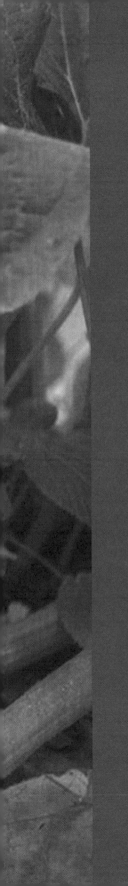

VEGETABLES

In culinary terms, vegetables are any savory plants that we consume at a meal, usually at lunch or dinner. Vegetables include all the edible parts of plants: leaves, stalks, taproots, tubers, bulbs, and flowers. Even savory fruits such as tomatoes and squash are treated as vegetables in many cuisines. Here, we explore gardening and cooking with 60 delicious vegetables.

ACORN SQUASH

Cucurbita pepo

This compact, dark-green squash is shaped like an oversize acorn with thick ridges. The golden-orange flesh boasts a sweet, nutty flavor. Also known as pepper squash, it is native to North and Central America and actually belongs to the summer squash family, though it's considered to be a winter squash.

VARIETIES

EARLY ACORN HYBRID This classic, compact variety is great for container gardening. The 4-pound (1.8 kg) squash has a smooth texture and a sweet, tender flavor. It's ready to harvest in 75 days.

EBONY A lovely green-black hybrid, Ebony has deep-orange flesh with a sweet, dry flavor. The trailing vines spread 10 feet (3 m) and support a dozen 2-pound (0.9 kg) fruits that are ready to pick at 90 days.

HONEY BEAR This super-sweet squash weighs just 1 pound (0.5 kg), perfect for a two-person meal. The vigorous Honey Bear is highly disease resistant and is ready to harvest in 100 days.

TABLE QUEEN The richly flavored heirloom has a ribbed green rind and golden-yellow flesh that turns deeper orange during storage. The fruit of this compact, container-friendly variety is ready in 85 days.

IN THE KITCHEN

The compact acorn squash has a slightly sweet, nutty flavor with a hint of butter. Its fine texture is rarely stringy but is somewhat more fibrous than butternut squash.

SELECTING
Look for smooth, dull skin without any soft spots. The squash should feel hard and heavy for its size. Avoid acorn squash with a bright orange rind—these may be overripe, dry, and stringy. The greener, the better. The stem should be green, not black, and should not be dried out.

PREPARING
Wash the squash, and scrub off any dirt. To make it easier to cut through the hard rind, pierce the skin in a few spots and microwave for three minutes. Allow to cool, then cut in half from stem to end with a large and very sharp knife. Remove the fibers and seeds before cooking.

STORING
Acorn squash can keep for up to two months in a cool, dry location. Once the squash is cut, wrap it and refrigerate it for up to four days. Cooked squash can also be refrigerated for up to four days.

PRESERVING
Baked, cubed, or puréed squash can be frozen for up to 12 months.

USES
Acorn squash is most often baked or roasted, and its bowl shape makes it easy to stuff with hearty fillings.

For a sweet side dish, set cut acorn halves on a baking sheet. Combine melted butter, maple syrup, and brown sugar, and brush on the flesh. To spice it up, sprinkle with cinnamon and nutmeg, or some paprika and cayenne. Roast at 400°F (200°C) for 50 to 60 minutes until a fork easily pierces through the flesh.

If you prefer savory squash, drizzle with olive oil, salt, pepper, and add some cumin, coriander, or smoked paprika.

Try a wintry stuffing: sauté shallots, celery, and thyme; combine with cooked sausage, wild rice, cranberries, and pecans. Stuff and bake until heated.

IN THE GARDEN

To encourage pollination of squash blossoms, plant bee-attracting flowers such as beebalm, mint, or coneflowers nearby. Each acorn squash plant should yield four or five fruits.

CLIMATE
Select a location in full sun, but rotate squash in your garden every couple of years. It grows well in zones 4 and above.

SOIL
Acorn squash needs fertile, well-drained soil with a pH of 6.0 to 6.8. Till the soil down to 8 inches (20 cm).

PLANTING
Sow outdoors after the last frost, or indoors three weeks before the last frost in 3-inch (8 cm) pots. Plant three to five seeds on a mound to protect the roots. Space mounds 36 inches (90 cm) apart. Cover with 1 inch (2.5 cm) of fine soil.

GROWING
Keep the soil evenly moist. Apply a 10-10-10 fertilizer after seedlings emerge and again after blossoms appear.

HARVESTING
Harvest when your fingernail can't pierce the squash's skin. Cut the squash from the vine, leaving about two inches (5 cm) of the stem intact.

NUTRITIONAL VALUE

serving size 100 g (1/2 cup)

calories 56f	iber 4.4 g

vitamin C 16%	potassium 10%
thiamin 15%	iron 8%DV
magnesium 14%	vitamin A 7%

HEALTH BENEFITS

provides antioxidants
boosts immune system
supports healthy vision
nourishes skin
strengthens bones
lowers blood pressure
regulates blood sugar

AMARANTH

Cucurbita pepo

The tall, fast-growing amaranth is a nutrient-rich plant native to the tropics. As a leaf vegetable, amaranth is prized for its mild spinach-like flavor and soft texture. The nutty-tasting seeds are a popular pseudo-grain, much like quinoa. Amaranth often appears as a garden ornamental for its bright, showy flowers.

VARIETIES

RED AMARANTH Also known as blood amaranth, this ancient species traces back to pre-Columbian civilizations. The drought-tolerant amaranth is grown for the grainlike seeds and flavorful leaves.

TRICOLOR This annual is a popular leaf vegetable in the hot climates of Africa and Asia. Also called Chinese spinach or Joseph's coat, tricolor is bushy and compact with attractive red, purple, and green leaves.

LOVE LIES BLEEDING This easy-to-grow annual has sweet, savory leaves and can reach up to 8 feet (2.5 m) in height. It offers a striking display of long, deep-crimson tassel flowers from midsummer to fall.

LIVID AMARANTH A common species in temperate and tropical climates, livid amaranth tolerates a wide range of soil quality and pH. The green leaves and stems are especially tender.

IN THE KITCHEN

The versatile, nutritious amaranth is an excellent addition to any meal. Use the leaves in place of spinach or Swiss chard, or use the nutty, protein-rich seeds in recipes that call for quinoa.

SELECTING
Choose crisp bunches with small leaves and thin, tender stems for the freshest flavor. Avoid those with obvious insect damage or with buds that have flowered. Thick, more mature stems may have a slightly bitter taste.

PREPARING
Rinse leaves well in cold; pat dry. Cut off the roots and tough stalks, but retain the tender stems. You can use the leaves whole, or you can rip or cut them into bite-size pieces.

STORING
Wrap clean leaves in a paper towel and store in a produce bag in the refrigerator. If the roots are intact, store them in a container of water. Use leaves within five days. Refrigerate seeds in an airtight container for up to six months.

PRESERVING
To freeze the leaves, blanch in boiling water for two minutes, plunge in ice water, and dry; store in an airtight container.

USES
Try adding raw, young amaranth leaves to fresh salads or light summer pasta sauces that call for spinach or Swiss chard.

More mature amaranth leaves are slightly astringent, so these are best cooked. The textured leaves hold up well under heat. The simplest way to cook amaranth is boiling the leaves in a pot of lightly salted water for three minutes. Plunge them in cold water and pat dry before adding other ingredients.

For a simple sauté, heat some olive oil over medium-low heat and add minced garlic and, if desired, red chili peppers or mustard seed and cook briefly. Add the amaranth leaves and cook for about 8 minutes. Amaranth also makes a wonderful addition to Asian stir-fries and Indian dals.

The nutty, protein-rich amaranth seeds can be popped, sprouted, or cooked as a porridge. Crushed amaranth seeds make a sweet, gluten-free flour that can be used for baked goods.

NUTRITIONAL VALUE

Serving size 100 g (3/4 cup) boiled leaves
calories 21 protein 2.6 g fiber 2.1 g

vitamin K	75% DV	calcium	21% DV
vitamin C	50% DV	magnesium	15% DV
vitamin A	20% DV	potassium	13% DV
folate	21% DV	zinc	10 % DV

HEALTH BENEFITS

reduces inflammation
provides antioxidants
strengthens bones
lowers cholesterol
boosts heart health
reduces varicose veins
supports healthy vision

IN THE GARDEN

Amaranth is a low-maintenance plant that is tolerant of summer heat and periodic drought. Not only is it a delicious leaf vegetable, but it's also a stunning addition to the garden.

CLIMATE
This tropical plant thrives in warmer climates, but it can also be grown in zones 5 and above, provided it receives direct sunlight.

SOIL
Well-drained loam is best, but amaranth tolerates poor soil as well. The optimal pH range is 5.5 to 7.0.

PLANTING
Sow seeds indoors 6 to 8 weeks before the last frost, or outdoors after the last frost. Sow at a depth of ¼ inch (1 cm) in groups of 3 every 6 inches (15 cm). Space rows 12 to 18 inches (30 to 46 cm) apart.

GROWING
Water amaranth regularly, keeping the top 1 inch (2.5 cm) moist. Feed only poor soil with a general purpose fertilizer.

HARVESTING
Cut or pick young leaves as needed. Snip off the terminal bud to encourage branching of multiple side shoots. Harvest seeds on a dry day just after the first frost.

ARTICHOKE

Cynara cardunculus var. scolymus

The savory artichoke is a perennial thistle of the sunflower family (Asteraceae). Its delectable heart grows at the base of each flower cluster and must be harvested by hand just before the flowers bloom. The broad, arching, silvery-green leaves make a bold statement in any vegetable garden.

VARIETIES

GREEN GLOBE This buttery-tasting artichoke is by far the most common variety in North America. Each prolific plant can produce up to 20 large globes with diameter of up to 5 inches (13 cm).

IMPERIAL STAR This richly flavored variety is often grown as an annual in cooler climates, where perennials can't overwinter. The nearly spineless, glossy-green bulbs grow to about 4 inches (10 cm) wide.

ROMANESCO This Italian heirloom artichoke thrives in the sandy soil of the coastal hills near Rome. The 2-inch (10 cm) thornless bulbs are streaked with bronze and purple, and the nutty-flavored heart is fuzz-free.

VIOLETTO Northern Italy's classic Violetto has an elongated bulb that is about 5 inches (13 cm) long and 3 inches (8 cm) wide. The flavorful, violet-colored fruit matures relatively late in the growing season.

IN THE KITCHEN

Cooking artichokes may seem daunting at first—the large size, spiny tips, and fuzzy chokes can be intimidating. But the exquisite melt-in-your mouth flavor is worth a little extra work.

 SELECTING
Test the weight: Fresh artichokes feel heavy for their size. Look for firm bulbs with tightly packed leaves that squeak when squeezed together. Leaves can be green or purple; avoid those with dry, brown, or splayed tips.

 PREPARING
Use a sharp knife to slice off the top fourth of the bulb and the end of the stem. Cut off the sharp tips of each petal, and peel the fibrous but edible stem. Rinse well and rub with lemon to prevent discoloration.

STORING
Artichokes should remain fresh for about a week in the refrigerator. Sprinkle them with water and store them in a perforated produce bag, or place the stems in a cup of water sweetened with a spoonful of sugar.

 PRESERVING
To freeze cooked artichokes, sprinkle them with lemon juice and place them in airtight containers. Marinated artichokes can be refrigerated for two weeks.

 USES
Whole artichokes can be steamed, boiled, roasted, sautéed, or stuffed. In Europe, the smaller, choke-free bulbs can be eaten raw.

To steam artichokes, set them in a steamer basket or place them directly in a pot filled with two inches of water. Add salt, bay leaf, and lemon juice to the water. Cover, and let the water boil for 25 to 35 minutes. Artichokes are done when you can easily pull a petal from the base.

Enjoy one petal at a time dipped in lemon butter, vinaigrette, or a yogurt and mustard sauce. Trim away the choke and savor the heart. To marinate artichokes, cut the bulbs in half, scoop out the choke, and add to a mixture of oil, lemon juice, salt, pepper, and minced garlic cloves.

IN THE GARDEN

Native to the Mediterranean region, artichokes thrive in warm, dry climates. Along the central coast of California, plants can yield all year long. Artichokes are ready to harvest in 110 to 150 days.

 CLIMATE
Artichokes can grow as perennials in full sun from zones 7 to 11. In zone 4 and below, they perform much better as annuals.

SOIL
Amend your soil with organic compost or humus before planting. Soil should be slightly sandy with a pH between 6.5 and 8.0.

PLANTING
Artichokes flower in their second year, so consider buying container or bare-root plants. Space plants 2 feet (61 cm) apart. Transplant rooted suckers as they appear. Mature perennials live for approximately five years.

 **GROWING**
Artichokes require regular watering and a monthly fertilizer. Protect plants from frost in winter.

 HARVESTING
The peak harvest is in the spring and again mid-autumn. Cut the bulbs leaving up to 2 inches (5 cm) of the stem intact. One plant can produce 20 artichokes a year.

NUTRITIONAL VALUE

Serving size 1 medium bulb (120 g)
calories 64   protein 3.5 g   fiber 6.8 g

folate	27% DV	niacin	10% DV
vitamin K	21% DV	potassium	8% DV
magnesium	16% DV	vitamin B-6	7% DV
vitamin C	11% DV	iron	4% DV

HEALTH BENEFITS

powerful antioxidant
reduces LDL cholesterol
lowers blood pressure
benefits liver function
aids digestion
improves heart health
stabilizes blood sugar

ARUGULA

Eruca sativa

Originally from the Mediterranean, this peppery leaf vegetable is related to kale and Brussels sprouts in the cabbage (Brassicaceae) family. Of the two main types of arugula—regular and wild—the wild type is spicier and more complex than regular arugula and less likely to turn bitter as it matures.

VARIETIES

ASTRO This quick grower has serrated, medium-green leaves that are ready to cut at three weeks. It prefers the cool soil of early spring but is also heat tolerant. The nutty flavor remains mild even as the plant matures.

WILD ITALIAN This delicate, peppery ancient variety retains its flavor all season long. Also known as Sylvetta, it has finely cut leaves that are slow to bolt. The small seeds germinate within eight days.

ROCKET Also known as Roquette, this refreshing, nutty heirloom is a favorite of chefs. Sow in succession for a constant harvest of young tender leaves. Mature leaves have a stronger mustard-like flavor.

IN THE KITCHEN

Arugula spices up mesclum salad blends, lending a robust, peppery flavor to milder greens such as romaine and endive. The leaves and flowers offer a zesty kick to sandwiches, soups, and pizza.

 SELECTING
Look for firm, bright-green leaves that are free of tears and yellow tips. Intact roots help retain freshness. Shorter leaves are generally younger and milder than taller leaves, which can have a stronger peppery, mustard flavor.

 **PREPARING**
Submerge arugula in cold water and swish around to remove debris. Add some vinegar to the water to help remove bacteria. Rinse and drain, then dry the leaves well.

 STORING
Place clean, dry arugula in a produce bag in the refrigerator and use within six days. If the roots are intact, don't wash the bunch; wrap it in a damp cloth and store it in your refrigerator, where it can keep up to 10 days.

 PRESERVING
To freeze arugula, blanch the leaves in boiling water for 30 seconds, then plunge in ice water. Dry completely before storing in an airtight container.

 USES
Arugula is most commonly eaten fresh in salads. Young tender leaves are especially delicious, whereas the stronger, more peppery flavor of mature leaves may be overpowering on their own. These are often combined with milder greens, such as Romaine and endive, in mesclun blends.

You can also add a few fresh arugula leaves to sandwiches for a zesty crunch. Try adding a few leaves to omelets, pastas, and pizzas toward the end of cooking so the leaves don't become too soggy.

Try this classic arugula salad: arugula, blue cheese, pears, and walnuts with a Dijon mustard vinaigrette. A simple lemon vinaigrette with shaved parmesan also complements arugula.

Arugula also pairs well with tomatoes, cucumbers, artichoke hearts, beets, chickpeas, and red onion.

Cooking arugula tends to make the flavor milder, so if your leaves are not quite fresh, try lightly sautéing them in olive oil, minced garlic, and some pancetta.

IN THE GARDEN

Arugula thrives in the cool weather of early spring and fall. It's a great cut-and-come-again lettuce with compact roots that make it ideal for containers. Wild arugula reseeds prolifically.

 CLIMATE
Arugula tolerates frost, so you can sow directly in the garden weeks before the last frost date. Hot summers are not its friend—arugula bolts as temperatures reach about 75°F (24°C).

 SOIL
A neutral soil pH of 6.0 to 6.5 is ideal for arugula. Prepare the seedbed with organic compost.

 PLANTING
As soon as you can work the soil, sow seeds outdoors ¼ inch (6 mm) deep, 1 inch (2.5 cm) apart, and in 10-inch (25 cm) rows. Seeds germinate in five to seven days.

 GROWING
Water arugula regularly, keeping the soil moist. Use a general purpose fertilizer.

 HARVESTING
Harvest leaves at 3 inches (8 cm). Leave 1 inch (2.5 cm) so the plant can regrow. Regular harvesting of smaller leaves helps prevent bolting.

ASPARAGUS

Asparagus officinalis

The tall, fernlike perennial belongs to the Asparagaceae family and dates back to the time of Ancient Egypt. Asparagus is an adaptable, long-lived plant that flourishes in soggy, slightly alkaline soil, where other vegetables would perish. The spears of asparagus have a distinctive, savory umami flavor.

VARIETIES

JERSEY This series includes vigorous cultivars such as Jersey Giant, Jersey Knight, and Jersey Supreme. These hardy, all-male hybrids perform well in colder climates. Supreme produces the earliest spears.

MILLENNIUM The cold-hardy, all-male hybrid boasts a higher yield than some Jersey types and produces for a longer period. The succulent flavor and tight tips are prized by chefs and gardeners alike.

PURPLE PASSION Sweeter and more tender than green varieties, Purple Passion is loaded with antioxidants and adds color to raw salads. The purple fades with cooking, but its luscious flavor lingers.

MARY WASHINGTON This popular heirloom produces long, dark spears with pale-purple tips that grow uniformly. Expect a slightly smaller yield than all-male hybrids and some red berries in autumn.

IN THE KITCHEN

Asparagus has a savory, earthy taste and tends to soak up surrounding flavors. It pairs particularly well with the bold, strong taste of garlic, capers, and Parmesan cheese.

 SELECTING
Choose straight, firm spears that feel crisp, not flexible, when bent. The ends should be moist, not dry or cracked. Thinner spears are more tender, and thicker ones are meatier.

 PREPARING
Rinse spears in cold water and snap off the woody ends. With thicker spears, peel the outer, tougher skin at the ends. Use the spears whole or cut them into bite-size pieces.

 STORING
Immerse the bunch in cold water for a few minutes, then dry. Wrap a damp towel around the ends and store in a bag in the refrigerator for up to a week. To increase its lifespan, trim the ends and place them in a container of water, cover in a bag, and refrigerate.

PRESERVING
For long-term freezer storage, first blanch the spears to preserve their color and stop enzymatic activity. Steam or boil for two to three minutes, then plunge into ice water. Dry thoroughly before sealing in an airtight container.

 USES
The quickest way to prepare asparagus is to add it fresh in a salad with a basic vinaigrette dressing.

To cook asparagus, try steaming it for about five minutes. When done, the spears should be bright green, tender, but slightly crisp. Season with salt and fresh pepper.

Try this mouth-watering lemon-caper sauce with cooked asparagus: Combine mayonnaise or olive oil with Dijon mustard, lemon juice, minced garlic, chopped parsley, and capers. Add salt and pepper and enjoy.

To roast asparagus, spread the spears in one layer on a baking sheet. Coat with olive oil, salt, pepper, and if desired, some garlic powder. Roast at 425°F (220°C) for 15 to 20 minutes. Garnish with Parmesan and lemon slices.

IN THE GARDEN

Asparagus can take two to three years before it produces a full harvest, but once it's established, each crown can produce a half pound (0.25 kg) of spears per season for up to 15 years.

 **CLIMATE**
Asparagus grows well in zones 2 to 8. Choose a site that receives at least eight hours of sunlight daily.

 **SOIL**
The ideal soil pH for asparagus is between 6.5 and 7.5. Work in about 1 inch (2.5 cm) of compost in autumn before planting the following spring.

PLANTING
Transplant year-old crowns in fertile soil. Dig a trench 12 inches (30 cm) wide and 8 inches (20 cm) deep. Space rows 18 inches (46 cm) apart. Drape the roots on mounds and cover the roots with soil. Gradually fill in the trench as the plant grows.

GROWING
Water frequently. Fertilize regularly with compost or manure.

HARVESTING
Harvest spears lightly in the second year for only two weeks; add a week of harvest each successive year. Bend and break off spears, snapping off the most tender part.

NUTRITIONAL VALUE

Serving size 100 g (3/4 cup) raw

calories 20		fiber 2.1 g	
vitamin K	46% DV	iron	12% DV
vitamin A	15% DV	riboflavin	11% DV
folate	13% DV	copper	10% DV
thiamin	12% DV	manganese	10% DV

HEALTH BENEFITS

reduces inflammation
provides antioxidants
aids digestion
boosts cardiovascular system
supports nervous system
lowers blood pressure
aids in collagen formation

BEANS

Phaseolus vulgaris

Also known as haricots verts, string beans, and snap beans, green beans belong to the legume family, though they're often treated as vegetables. Green beans—as opposed to dry beans—are bred to grow quickly but mature slowly, so they're harvested when the pods and seeds are still tender.

VARIETIES

Home gardeners have so many options to choose from when selecting beans for spring planting: compact bush beans that don't require staking, vining pole beans that climb up trellises, yellow "wax" beans, shell beans like edamame, yard-long "asparagus" beans, and large buttery lima beans. Yes, green beans are most often green, but plenty of varieties come in a rainbow of colors, including yellow, red, and purple—though much of the color fades to green with cooking.

SCARLET RUNNER This lovely heirloom (left) is often grown as an edible ornamental. Pick the pods regularly for continuous scarlet blossoms, which attract hummingbirds. The beans mature in 60 days. yellow-green.

JADE The long, slender pods of this tall, upright bush bean grow to about 7 inches (18 cm). This workhorse variety continues to yield even during periods of excessive heat and cold. Jade is ready in 53 days.

CHINESE RED NOODLE (Above) Also known as yard-long beans, these burgundy beauties have pods that grow to 20 inches (51 cm). The vigorous, high-yielding Red Noodle is ready to harvest in 80 days.

PURPLE KING The striking purple pods of this pole bean variety grow on trailing 5-foot (1.5 m) vines all summer long. The juicy, delicious 6-inch (15 cm) pods are ready to pick in about 75 days.

MIDORI GIANT This prolific edamame yields two to three buttery beans per pod on sturdy 24-inch (60 cm) plants. A traditional edamame bush bean, Midori is very adaptable and is ready to harvest in 70 days.

FORDHOOK A popular lima bean that tolerates heat and drought. The bountiful hybrid produces four large beans per 4-inch (10 cm) pod. This is a great variety for warmer climates. The pods mature in 75 days.

GOLD CROP The straight, bright-yellow pods grow to 6 inches (15 cm) and dangle in clusters by the main stem for easy harvesting. This wax bean is a heavy producer and matures in about 50 days.

ROMANO (Above) An heirloom Italian bean, Romano pods are flat, stringless, and grow to about 6 inches (15 cm) long. These broad snap beans boast an outstanding meaty flavor and mature in about 60 days.

DRAGON'S TONGUE
The dramatic cream-and-purple wax bean (above) is sweet and tender with speckled tan seeds. The flat pods of this dual-purpose heirloom reach 6 ½ inches and mature in about 57 days.

TRIOMPHE DE FARCY
A popular French heirloom, this haricort vert bush bean has slender filet pods streaked with pale green. Pick as early as 41 days, when the pods are 3 to 6 inches (8 to 15 cm) long.

BLUE LAKE Developed in the early 1900s, the heirloom Blue Lake boasts a high yield of tender, meaty, deep-green pods on vines that climb up to 7 feet (2.1 m). The 7-inch (18 cm) pods mature in 75 days and grow all season long. They're excellent fresh, frozen, or canned. In the 1960s, a bush hybrid was developed with the same meaty-flavored beans and fine, tender texture. The dark-green, rounded pods reach 6½ inches (17 cm) and are ready to harvest all at once in about 54 days.

IN THE KITCHEN

Freshly picked green beans make a delicious, crunchy snack, and they are easy to add to any meal—in a salad for lunch or as a side dish at dinner. Green beans cook rather quickly, so be careful not to overcook them: Green beans should be tender and crisp, not soggy and bland.

SELECTING
If possible, buy fresh beans loose, not packaged, so you can choose the freshest pods. Select those with the brightest color. Look for firm, crisp pods that snap; pods should not feel limp. Examine the surface: The skin should be tight, moist, and smooth, not wrinkled or lumpy. Avoid beans with brown spots or bruises.

PREPARING
Rinse beans just before cooking. Trim off the tips but don't chop the pods into smaller pieces before cooking: Cutting green beans before cooking causes most of the nutrients to leach out. Pull out the strings if there are any.

STORING
Place unwashed fresh beans in an airtight container or produce bag, and refrigerate them in the produce drawer for up to seven days.

PRESERVING
To freeze fresh beans, blanch them in boiling water for three minutes. Plunge into ice water, and dry. Store them in an airtight container for up to nine months.

To pressure-can your beans, boil them for four minutes, pack them into sterilized jars, and fill with water, leaving an inch of headspace. Add a spoon of salt. Place in a pressure canner and follow the manufacturer's instructions.

USES
You can eat green beans raw, provided you wash them first. Raw beans, however, contain a small amount of toxins—but the younger the pods, the lower the toxin content.

The best method of cooking beans is steaming, which retains the most nutrients. Add 2 inches (5 cm) of water to a large pot, and bring to a boil. Rinse the pods, place them in the steamer basket, and cover. Steam for five minutes. (Remember to cook green beans whole whenever possible to preserve the nutrients.)

Try this popular side dish: green beans almondine. Sauté a shallot in some butter, and add slivered almonds, lemon zest or lemon juice, salt, and pepper. Drizzle on steamed or boiled green beans.

Steamed green beans figure prominently in the classic French salad niçoise. Arrange the following ingredients separately around a wide salad bowl: grilled tuna steak, a diced hard-boiled egg, tomato wedges, cubed potatoes, and olives. Dress with a lemon-mustard vinaigrette.

To roast green beans, place them in a layer on a baking sheet and toss with olive oil, garlic, salt, and pepper. Add any of the following: bacon bits, mushrooms, onions, cherry tomatoes, or sliced carrots. Roast at 425°F (220°C) for 10 minutes or until tender.

IN THE GARDEN

Green beans are easy to grow in most climates and in a variety of soils. With so many varieties to choose from, you can experiment with different green beans each year. Remember that beans fix the soil with nitrogen, so rotate beans in your garden every few years.

 CLIMATE
Green beans do well in hardiness zones 3 through 10. Choose a spacious site in the garden that receives full sunlight every day.

SOIL
Green beans prefer well-draining soil that is slightly acidic with a pH between 6.0 and 6.8, but beans are highly adaptable. Turn the soil several times before sowing seeds to loosen the dirt and prevent weeds from germinating.

PLANTING
If using a trellis or pole supports, be sure to set them in place before sowing the seeds. Sow seeds outdoors after the last frost date—seedlings are sensitive to frost. Sow seeds at a depth of 1 inch (2.5 cm). Space bush beans 3 inches (8 cm) apart, and pole beans 8 inches (20 cm) apart. Space rows every 3 feet (1 m).

GROWING
Water green beans regularly, preferably using a drip irrigation system to protect the leaves from too much moisture. If that isn't feasible, water green beans in the morning to allow moisture on the leaves to evaporate. Avoid nitrogen fertilizers, which promote lush leaves but skimpy pods.

 FUN FACT

Once known as "string beans," modern green beans have been bred without those pesky strings—the tough, inedible fiber on the side of the bean.

 **HARVESTING**
Pick beans when the leaves are dry but the seeds are not yet bulging. Harvest regularly to encourage new growth.

 **COMPANION PLANTS**
Because green beans release nitrogen into the surrounding soil, you can do double-duty by planting heavy-feeding vegetables and berries near green beans. Some excellent companion plants are beets, broccoli, carrots, celery, corn, cucumbers, eggplant, nasturtium, peas, potatoes, strawberries, and tomatoes. Avoid planting onions or peppers nearby—they inhibit the growth of green beans.

BEET

Beta vulgaris

Beets are the edible taproot of the herbaceous biennial beet plant of the Amaranthaceae family. For millennia, the sweet beetroot has been grown as a food, a medicine, and a dye. Ancient Romans believed it was an aphrodisiac; indeed, beets contain the mineral boron, which enhances sex hormones.

VARIETIES

DETROIT BEET Dark red with very sweet flesh. These perfectly round 3" beets have striking deep red flesh. Baby beets make excellent eating, and harvesting them helps promote the growth of the remaining beets.

DETROIT BEET Dark red with very sweet flesh. These perfectly round 3" beets have striking deep red flesh. Baby beets make excellent eating, and harvesting them helps promote the growth of the remaining beets.

FORMANOVA Also known as Cylindra, this Danish heirloom has a rich buttery flavor. The cylinder shape offers more uniform slices than round beets. It matures in 55 days and is great for canning.

GOLDEN This heirloom 2-inch (5 cm) golden-orange beet taste mellower, sweeter, and less earthy than red beets, but it is just as nutritious. Plant Golden heavily because the germination rate is low.

IN THE KITCHEN

Beets are packed with nutrients and so versatile in the kitchen. The sweet, earthy taste of beets pairs well with bright, fresh flavors. Be mindful that the red pigment betalain can stain.

 SELECTING
Look for beets with fresh green leaves still intact, or at least part of the stem remaining. Beets should be firm with no bruising or soft spots.

 PREPARING
Cut off the tips and leaves within an inch of the beet. Rinse off debris with a vegetable scrubber; pat dry.

 STORING
Store beets in a produce bag in the refrigerator for up to 10 days. Loosely wrap greens in a paper towel and store in a bag in the refrigerator for up to three days.

 PRESERVING
Freeze cooked cubed or halved beets for up to a year.

 USES
Beets are crunchy and delicious when eaten raw, but roasting beets sweetens their flavor and intensifies their color. Beets can also be sautéed, boiled, steamed, or pickled. Peel away the skin after cooking, then slice, chop, or mash.

To roast beets, cut them in half, and toss with olive oil, salt, pepper, a dash of thyme. Roast at 400°F (200°C) for 30 to 40 minutes, turning a couple of times. Let cool, and pull away the skin. Slice or cut into cubes.

To make borscht, grate beets and combine with kefir or buttermilk, diced cucumber, scallion, dill, salt, and pepper. Sprinkle with chopped boiled egg.

For a refreshing citrusy salad, combine roasted beets or chopped beet greens with orange segments, a soft goat cheese, and hazelnuts. Drizzle with olive oil, balsamic, salt, and pepper.

Sweet beets also go well with sharp greens such as spinach and arugula.

To make pickled beets, first boil for 30 minutes. Next, boil vinegar, sugar, cloves, allspice, and salt for five minutes. Pour over the beets, and refrigerate for at least an hour.

IN THE GARDEN

The cool-season beet is a favorite garden vegetable in northern climates: Beets are easy to grow and tolerate frost well. To mark rows, combine radish seeds along with beet seeds.

 CLIMATE
Beets thrive in zones 2 to 10. Choose a site in your garden with full or part sun.

 SOIL
Beets do well in a light, fertile soil with a pH between 6.5 and 7.5. Turn over the soil with compost or manure before planting because the taproots like to grow deep.

 PLANTING
Sow seeds outdoors three weeks before the last frost date, or indoors five weeks before the last frost. Sow at a depth of ½ inch (1.3 cm). Space seeds 2 inches (5 cm) apart.

 GROWING
Water well and mulch when established. Choose a fertilizer that's high in phosphorus and low in nitrogen.

 HARVESTING
Beets mature in 50 to 70 days. If you wait too long to harvest, the beets will become tough and woody. To harvest greens, cut them when they reach 6 inches (15 cm).

NUTRITIONAL VALUE

Serving size 100 g (3/4 cup)
calories 44   protein 1.7 g   fiber 2.8 g

vitamin B-6	52% DV	phosphorus	6% DV
folate, mcg	27% DV	magnesium	5% DV
potassium	7% DV	iron	4% DV
vitamin C	6% DV	zinc	3% DV

HEALTH BENEFITS

lowers blood pressure
improves athletic performance
reduces inflammation
aids digestion
boost brain function
reduces risk of cancer

BOK CHOY

Brassica rapa subsp. chinensis

This ancient Chinese cabbage, also known as pak choi, is a popular cruciferous vegetable in Southeast Asia and China. The leaf blades grow on a bulb, much like celery, and the hearts at the center of the stalks are viewed as a delicacy in some cuisines. Bok choy is the main ingredient in kimchi.

VARIETIES

BLACK SUMMER This attractive hybrid boasts deep-green oval leaves with light-green stalks. Reaching 12 inches, Black Summer is very slow to bolt and is great for winter harvest. It's ready to eat in 45 days.

PURPLE PACCHOI. Purple leaf tops contrast with green veins and stems. Harvest them within three weeks as 4–6" baby-leaf greens, their best spring use. For fall crops you may allow them to grow 8–10".

MEI QING CHOI This dwarf Shanghai hybrid is vase-shaped with light-green stalks and dark spoon-like leaves. It grows to 8 inches (2.5 cm) tall and resists heat and cold. Enjoy Mei Qing Choi in 35 days.

PURPLE PACCHOI. Purple leaf tops contrast with green veins and stems. Harvest them within three weeks as 4–6" baby-leaf greens, their best spring use. For fall crops you may allow them to grow 8–10".

IN THE KITCHEN

The crunchy bok choy stalks have a mild, sweet flavor with just a hint of mustard. Bok choy is delicious raw in salads or added to Asian stir-fries. Use it in any recipes as a substitute for celery.

SELECTING
Bok choy bulbs should have a rich, vibrant green color. Avoid bulbs with dried-out or rubbery leaves. For soups, choose varieties with larger leaves; for stir-fries, select the varieties with longer and narrower stalks.

PREPARING
Just before using bok choy, cut off the root end of the bulb, as with celery, and rinse individual stalks thoroughly under cold water to remove trapped dirt and debris.

STORING
Store unwashed bok choy in a perforated produce bag in the refrigerator for up to five days. Or you can wash the stalks, dry them, roll them in paper towels, and store in a produce bag in the fridge.

PRESERVING
To freeze bok choy, first blanch it in boiling water for two minutes, plunge into ice water, and dry. Place in an airtight container, and store in the freezer for up to 10 months.

USES
Bok choy is as delicious raw as it cooked. Toss some fresh bok choy into your salads or slaws. This classic Asian vegetable also tastes great in soups, sautées, and stir-fries.

When you cook bok choy, chop it into bite-size pieces, and cook the white stalks first for a few minutes, then add the greens.

For a quick stir-fry, heat olive oil and minced garlic. Add chopped bok choy, snow peas, and mushrooms, and cook for a few minutes. For extra protein, add some cubed tofu or shredded chicken. Drizzle with sesame oil and soy sauce.

Try making the traditional Korean dish kimchi by fermenting bok choy. Cut the bok choy into strips, and place it into a bowl. Add salt and water, and set a plate on top of the bok choy to weigh it down. Let it sit for at least three hours. Strain; combine sugar, pepper flakes, and two cups of water, and add to the bok choy. Add daikon, ginger, garlic, and scallions. Place in a jar, and let sit for 24 hours. Store in the refrigerator.

IN THE GARDEN

Bok choy prefers cooler seasons and tends to go to seed in hot summer climates. It tolerates below freezing temperatures—a light frost sweetens the flavor and adds a bit of crispness.

CLIMATE
Bok choy does well in zones 4 to 7. Choose a site that will have some shade—bok choi needs only about six hours of sunlight per day.

SOIL
Amend your soil with organic matter and be sure it drains well. The ideal pH is between 6.0 and 7.0.

PLANTING

Sow seeds outdoors one or two weeks before your last frost date, or indoors four weeks before the last frost. Sow seeds ¼ inch (0.6 cm) deep, 1 inch (2.5 cm) apart, and in rows about 18 inches (46 cm) apart. Seeds germinate within four to eight days.

GROWING

Water constantly; drought can lead to bolting. Use fertilizer sparingly.

HARVESTING

Harvest before flowering, in about 45 days. Cut the plant about 1 inch (2.5 cm) above the ground and fertilize to encourage a second harvest.

BROCCOLI

Brassica oleracea

An Ancient Roman creation from wild cabbage, broccoli has a smooth, dark-green crown of florets that resembles a bouquet of miniature trees. The word *broccoli* means "the flowering top of a cabbage head." This cruciferous vegetable is a powerhouse of vitamins, minerals, and phytonutrients.

VARIETIES

CALABRESE An Italian heirloom, Calabrese produces the classic medium-size crowns and readily sprouts side shoots after the first harvest. It matures in zones 3 to 10 in about 65 days.

EARLY PURPLE The Early Purple Broccoli Plant produces extremely flavorful heads of broccoli that are bright purple. Once the main head is removed this variety will continuously produce many offshoots.

PURPLE SPROUTING This cold-hardy English heirloom has lovely purple florets. In milder climates, this long-season variety can overwinter. All parts are edible: florets, leaves, and stems. It's ready in 120 days.

EARLY PURPLE The Early Purple Broccoli Plant produces extremely flavorful heads of broccoli that are bright purple. Once the main head is removed this variety will continuously produce many offshoots.

IN THE KITCHEN

The peppery taste of broccoli pairs well with sharp cheeses such as Parmesan and cheddar and strong flavors like garlic and anchovies. Add broccoli to salads or serve it as a side dish.

 SELECTING
Select compact crowns with a dark-green color, firm stalks and stems, and compact bud clusters. Avoid heads with blooming yellow flowers—these are past their prime.

 PREPARING
Place the broccoli head in a colander and rinse under cold water; shake dry. Cut the florets from the main stalk, moving in a circle from the outside toward the middle. Peel away the woody part of the stem and julienne the tender part.

 STORING
Wrap dry and unwashed broccoli loosely in produce bags, but don't seal them. Use broccoli within three days for the freshest flavor, but it should keep for up to 10 days in the refrigerator.

 PRESERVING
Freezing raw broccoli imparts a bitter flavor, so you should always blanch florets and stems before freezing: Boil for three to five minutes, plunge in cold water, and dry thoroughly. Freeze for up to one year.

 USES
Fresh raw broccoli florets are a quick and delicious snack that goes great with dip, but a quick blanching brightens florets and softens the tough texture and bitter taste.

Boiling broccoli greatly reduces its nutrient content, so it's best to steam, roast, or microwave.

Roasting broccoli strips it of the bitterness and adds a warm, nutty flavor. To roast, place broccoli florets in a single layer on a baking sheet, and drizzle with olive oil, sliced garlic, salt, and pepper at 425°F (220°C) for 20 minutes.

Broccoli is a colorful addition to stir-fries: Heat olive oil, garlic, and ginger in a wok; add broccoli, soy sauce, vegetable broth, sesame oil, and your favorite vegetables. Sprinkle with sesame seeds.

IN THE GARDEN

Broccoli is a cool-season vegetable that should be harvested in late fall or early winter. Established broccoli plants can tolerate a light frost and temperatures down to 26°F (–3°C).

 CLIMATE
Broccoli prefers full sun in zones 3 to 10. In zones 7 and warmer, broccoli can overwinter for an early spring harvest.

 SOIL
Broccoli needs well-drained, rich soil with a pH between 6.0 and 7.0. Amend soil with organic matter before planting.

 PLANTING
Sow seeds indoors 6 to 8 weeks before the last frost, and outdoors in early summer for a fall crop. Sow 1/2 inch (1.3 cm) deep and 16 inches (40 cm) apart in a staggered pattern. Space rows 36 inches (1 m) apart.

 GROWING
Keep the soil consistently moist, and fertilize regularly. Mulch soil to reduce water evaporation.

 HARVESTING
As soon as the crown is firm and tight, and before the buds flower, cut the stem about 6 inches (15 cm) below the base of the crown. Side shoots will form with smaller heads.

NUTRITIONAL VALUE

Serving size 100 g (1-1/4 cup)
calories 34   protein 3g   fiber 2.6g

vitamin C 120% DV	riboflavin 9% DV
vitamin K 85% DV	phosphorus 9% DV
folate 16% DV	potassium 7% DV
vitamin B-6 13% DV	iron 5% DV

HEALTH BENEFITS

powerful antioxidant
strengthens bones
strong anti-inflammatory
protects against cancer
regulates blood sugar
supports heart health
aids digestion
boosts brain function

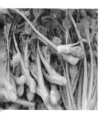

BROCCOLI RABE

Brassica ruvo

A favorite green of Southern Italy, broccoli rabe may resemble broccoli, but it's actually more closely related to turnip greens. Also known as rapini, its small florets, deep-green leaves, and thin stalks have a pungent, zesty flavor. The edible, yellow flowers add a bright touch to salads and pastas.

VARIETIES

SESSANTINA In Italian, Sessantina refers to 60—the days until harvest. There's also Quarantina (40) and Novantina (90). The fewer the days, the shorter the plant. Sessantina grows to 18 inches (46 cm) tall.

EARLY FALL RAPINI
The tender shoots of this vigorous heirloom have a lively, mustard flavor. Plant it in early fall for a winter harvest, in about 50 days. It tolerates a light frost and grows to 16 inches (40 cm). 18 inches (46 cm) tall.

SORRENTO This Italian variety (above) has blue-green leaves and florets that are relatively large. This is the quickest broccoli raab to mature— just 40 days. Sorrento has some of the largest, most uniform dark green florets in the early category, averaging 3-4 inches across. It grows upright to 30 inches. A choice pick for the early gardener. Harvest the tender leaves, stems, and unopened flower buds; they have a hearty yet mild broccoli flavor.

IN THE KITCHEN

The nutty, slightly bitter broccoli rabe has a chewy texture that doesn't always appeal to everyone. But when it's cooked right, broccoli rabe makes a rich, flavorful side dish of greens.

NUTRITIONAL VALUE

Serving size 100 g (1-1/4 cup), cooked
calories 25   protein 3.8   fiber 2.8 g

vitamin K 210% DV	vitamin B-6 17% DV
vitamin C 41% DV	vitamin E 17% DV
vitamin A 25% DV	iron 13% DV
folate 18% DV	calcium 12% DV

HEALTH BENEFITS

powerful antioxidant
supports healthy vision
nourishes skin
strengthens bones
regulates blood sugar
reduces risk of cancer
boosts cardiovascular system
improves nerve function

SELECTING
Look for firm, dark-green stems and tight florets. Avoid bunches with wilted, yellow leaves and heads that have flowered.

PREPARING
Trim away tips that are discolored, and peel the skin of thicker, woody stems. Rinse in cold water until the water runs clear.

STORING
Refrigerate unwashed broccoli rabe in a produce bag for up to a week, though it will be freshest if used within a couple of days.

PRESERVING
To freeze broccoli rabe, first wash well and remove tough stems. Blanch for two minutes in salted boiling water, and plunge into ice water. Drain, dry, then store in the freezer for up to three months.

USES
The earthy, robust flavor of broccoli rabe is a bit overpowering to eat these greens raw. Heating broccoli rabe mellows some of the acrid flavor by breaking down the enzyme that is responsible for the pungent bite. Keep in mind that chopping the leaves tends to release more of the bitter enzyme, so use your leaves whole instead.

Always blanch broccoli rabe before using it in a recipe. Sweet balsamic vinegar also tames the harsh bite of broccoli rabe. Sauté some garlic and anchovies, add the greens, then drizzle with balsamic vinegar that has been reduced. Season with salt and red pepper flakes. This tastes great alone or as a pasta sauce.

Rich, cool sauces complement these pungent greens, too. Try crumbling a rich cheese like gorgonzola over sautéed or roasted broccoli rabe, or melt a creamy cheese such as fontina for a hearty sauce.

Other pairings that work well with broccoli rabe are lemon dressings or yogurt sauces, which balance out the bitterness and bring out the earthy nuttiness. Combine plain Greek-style yogurt with cumin, garlic, and a dash of cayenne.

IN THE GARDEN

This quick grower is a cut-and-come-again vegetable that you can enjoy for a long season. About four weeks after sowing, pinch the terminal bud to trigger the growth of side shoots.

CLIMATE
Broccoli rabe is easy to grow in zones 3 to 9. Choose a site in full sun. In milder climates, plant in late summer or fall for a late fall or early spring harvest.

SOIL
Broccoli rabe prefers fertile, well-draining soil with a pH between 6.0 and 7.5. Rake in a layer of 8-8-8 fertilizer to the planting bed.

PLANTING
Sow outdoors in early spring, as soon as you can work the soil.

Sow ¼-inch (1.3 cm) deep, 2 inches (5 cm) apart, and in rows 18 inches (46 cm) apart. Seeds germinate in about five days.

GROWING
Keep the soil evenly moist, and fertilize regularly. Control weeds.

HARVESTING
Cut leaves and flowering stalks when they reach 7 inches (18 cm) and the buds are still closed. Water the plants well after harvesting, and fertilize to coax out a second harvest.

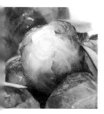

BRUSSELS SPROUTS

Brassica oleracea, Gemmifera group

Brussels sprouts are cabbage-like buds that grow along a thick stalk. This cruciferous vegetable is part of the mustard family (Brassicaceae), and was first cultivated in its namesake city in Belgium during the 13th century. Brussels sprouts are packed with anti-inflammatory phytonutrients.

VARIETIES

HESTIA The apple-green 1-inch (2.5 cm) sprouts grow uniformly on 30-inch (76 cm) plants. Hestia tolerates both warm and cold temperatures, and is ready to harvest in about 100 days.

JADE CROSS This dwarf hybrid produces an abundant yield of 1 ¼ inch (8.5 cm) deep-green oval sprouts on 28-inch (71 cm) plants. It matures in 85 days, and is ideal for cool regions with short growing seasons.

ROSELLA PURPLE This is a specialist sprout variety from Europe, it offers smaller yields of dark red sprouts, but has a milder, delicate, nuttier flavor than standard green types. Rosella Purple keeps its color when cooked.

IN THE KITCHEN

The bitterness of Brussels sprouts shouldn't deter you from eating this nutrient-rich vegetable. Cooking sprouts correctly brings out the nutty, savory flavor and crunchy texture.

 SELECTING
Look for firm, brightly colored sprouts. Avoid those with loose, yellow leaves. Smaller sprouts are often more flavorful. Buy sprouts on the stalk if you can, and store them with the stalk intact.

 PREPARING
Trim the dry ends, and peel off yellow or damaged leaves. Before cooking, either cut the sprouts in half lengthwise, or use a sharp knife to score each base with an X for more even cooking.

 STORING
Store fresh, unwashed, untrimmed sprouts in a produce bag in the crisper drawer of the refrigerator for up to a week, but sprouts taste freshest when they're used within four days.

 PRESERVING
To freeze Brussels sprouts, first remove them from the stalk, trim off damaged leaves, then soak them in warm water for about 10 minutes. Rinse well, and dry each sprout individually. Store sprouts in an airtight container in the freezer for up to a year.

 USES
You can boil or steam Brussels sprouts, but those methods don't really enhance their flavor or texture. Overboiling can easeily leave them tasting bitter and mushy.

The best method for preparing Brussels sprouts is either roasting or sautéing, which enhances the savory flavor, minimizes the bitterness, and retains the delightful crunch.

First, cut the sprouts in half and toss them with olive oil, garlic, salt, pepper, and lemon juice, then sauté or roast. To sauté, heat some oil in a pan over medium heat and sauté for about six minutes per side. To roast, place the sprouts in a single layer on a baking sheet and roast for 400°F (200°C) for 15 to 17 minutes, until the sprouts are tender and crispy brown.

IN THE GARDEN

The slow-growing Brussels sprouts require the cool weather of early spring or fall to mature. They are best when planted for an early winter harvest, after a light frost has sweetened them up.

 CLIMATE
Brussels sprouts prefer a site in full sunlight but tolerate light shade in zones 2 to 9.

SOIL
Work in 6 inches (15 cm) of compost or manure before planting, and till the top 12 inches (30 cm) of soil. Aim for a heavy, neutral soil with a pH between 6.0 to 6.8.

 PLANTING
Planting time will depend on your region. Start seeds outdoors in areas with mild winters, and indoors in cooler regions. Sow seeds ¼ inch (6 mm) deep. Space seedlings 18 inches (46 cm) apart in wide rows.

GROWING
The shallow roots require even moisture and thick mulch. Feed every three weeks with a nitrogen-rich fertilizer.

HARVESTING
Harvest firm buds at about 1-inch (2.5 cm) wide, beginning from the bottom. Snap off the leaf stem just below the bud.

 NUTRITIONAL VALUE

Serving size 100 g (5 sprouts), cooked
calories 36   protein 2.7   fiber 2.8 g

vitamin C 109% DV	thiamin 9% DV
vitamin K 35% DV	phosphorus 8% DV
folate 15% DV	potassium 7% DV
vitamin B-6 14% DV	riboflavin 6% DV

 HEALTH BENEFITS

powerful antioxidant
strong anti-inflammatory
reduces cancer risk
regulates blood sugar
benefits cardiovascular system
reduces blood triglycerides

BUTTERNUT SQUASH

Cucurbita moschata

An offshoot of crookneck, butternut squash was bred for a straighter neck and a more compact size. The bell-shaped winter squash has a fine tan skin and a dense, moist, dark-orange flesh. All parts of this squash are edible: the fine rind, the sweet flesh, the cream-colored seeds, and the orange blossoms.

VARIETIES

EARLY BUTTERNUT
An excellent medium-size squash with sweet flesh. The vines of this semi-bush variety grow to 60 inches (1.5 m). The fruits weigh about 4 pounds (1.8 kg) and mature in 85 days.

VIOLINA DI RUGOSA
The Italian heirloom produces violin-shaped squash with wrinkly tan skin and dry, dark-orange flesh. The sweet fruits grow to 5 pounds (2.3 kg) and mature in about 100 days. aking brings out its honey-sweet flavor.

HONEYNUT This mini squash grows on a semi-vining plant and produces fruits with a sweet, complex flavor. The rind matures from dark green to burnt orange in about 110 days. The 5" long fruit weigh from 1 to 1-1/2 lbs. and have a sweet and rich flavored deep orange flesh. The rind starts off a dark green, turns tan and then a rich burnt orange color at full maturity. Intermediate resistance to powdery mildew. Plant as early as possible due to long maturity.

IN THE KITCHEN

A classic addition to an autumn meal, butternut squash has a nutty, earthy flavor and can be prepared as a sweet side dish, puréed into a rich soup, or added to nutritious muffins and cakes.

 SELECTING
The squash should feel heavy and hard, with no soft spots. The skin should be smooth and matte; if it's shiny, it was likely picked early and waxed. Look for an intact stem.

 PREPARING
Wash the skin. Cut the squash in half lengthwise if roasting. To cube, trim off the ends, cut in half crosswise, scoop out the seeds, and if desired, peel. Cut each section in half lengthwise, slice, then cube.

 **STORING**
Do not refrigerate whole butternut squash. Peeled and cut squash, however, should be refrigerated and used within five days.

PRESERVING
Allow the squash to cure, or dry, for two weeks on a rack in a warm, dry area with good air circulation. Then store the squash in a cool, dark area for up to two or three months. Keep it out of the sunlight, which can cause the squash to over-ripen.

 USES
The possibilities are limitless with butternut squash. It's best when roasted, but it can be steamed, sautéed, baked, or grilled.

Choose either a sweet or a savory flavor: Highlight butternut squash's sweetness with cinnamon, nutmeg, and brown sugar, and serve with pears and cream, or add it to your favorite muffin mix. Try savory recipes to balance out the sweetness and add an earthy flavor with shallots, sage, thyme, and bay leaf.

It's especially delicious in raviolis, dumplings, and pies. You can roast the seeds, too.

To roast butternut squash, cut it in half and place on a baking sheet, cut side up. Drizzle with a butter, brown sugar, salt, and pepper. Roast at 400°F (200°C) for 50 minutes, or until the flesh feels tender when pierced with a fork.

To roast cubed squash, toss with olive oil, salt, and pepper. Spread in one layer on a baking sheet and roast at 400°F (200°C) for 25 to 30 minutes, turning once.

IN THE GARDEN

For each member in the household, grow one to two squash plants. Each will yield about four or five squashes in 85 to 110 days. Provide plenty of growing space for each squash plant.

 CLIMATE
Squash thrives in full sun in just about any zone, once temperatures have reached 65°F (18°C). Seedlings are very tender and sensitive to frost.

 SOIL
Prepare a bed with fertile and slightly acidic soil with a pH of 5.5 to 6.8.

 PLANTING
Sow seeds directly after the last frost date, at a depth of 1 inch (2.5 cm) and about four seeds per 18-inch (46 cm) hill. Each hill should have about 25 square feet (2.3 square meters) of space.

 GROWING
Water regularly, but do not overwater. Apply a 5-10-10 fertilizer regularly for these heavy feeders. Mulch around the plants.

 HARVESTING
Fruits can tolerate a light frost but not temperatures below 28°F (-2°C). Cut the stems 1 inch (2.5 cm) from the fruit when the skin is hard and the stems are dry.

CABBAGE

Brassica oleracea capitata

Originally from Southern Europe, cabbage derives its name from the French word *caboche*, or "head," and grows from a bud at the top of a short stem. The broad, overlapping leaves are either smooth or crinkly savoy. Green cabbage has a grassy, cruciferous flavor, whereas red cabbage is bold and peppery.

VARIETIES

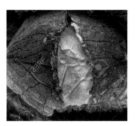

JANUARY KING This curly-leaf cross has stunning leaves of deep purple, dark green, and cool blue. The winter-hardy heads weigh 4 pounds (1.8 kg) and are known for their outstanding flavor. Harvest in 160 days.

LATE FLAT DUTCH This beautiful blue-green heirloom produces a solid cabbage head that doesn't split. The impressive heads reach 10 to 15 pounds (4.5 to 6.8 kg) and are ready to pick in 100 days.in 160 days.

RUBY PERFECTION The rich burgundy heads are a dense 3½ pounds (1.6 kg). The striking leaves are perfect to use as wraps or in slaws. Ready in 85 days, this is an excellent midseason cabbage.

SAVOY PERFECTION This heirloom savoy has attractive, dark-green crinkly leaves that sweeten after a light frost. The tender heads reach up to 7 pounds (3.2 kg), and are ready midseason in 90 days.

IN THE KITCHEN

This humble cabbage is truly versatile in the kitchen: Its crisp, sturdy leaves are essential ingredients in coleslaw, sauerkraut, and stir-fries. It's also great as a filling in wraps and dumplings.

 SELECTING
Choose a crisp, tight head that feels heavy for its size. Stems should be firm, and few leaves should be loose. Avoid discolored or damaged heads.

 PREPARING
Discard withered outer leaves. Rinse the leaves individually in cold water, and dry completely.

 STORING
Refrigerate cabbage heads for up to two weeks in the produce drawer. To preserve nutrients, do not cut the cabbage until you're ready to use it.

 PRESERVING
A popular method of preserving cabbage is curing it in brine as sauerkraut. To freeze cabbage, blanch shredded cabbage in boiling water for two minutes, plunge in ice water, and dry; freeze in an airtight container for up to six months.

 USES
When raw, cabbage can have a rubbery texture, but it softens and sweetens with cooking.
To make your own sauerkraut, finely chop and crush cabbage, submerge in salted water, cover, and let sit for several days.

Here's an easy Asian lettuce wrap recipe: sauté cubed chicken in oil, add garlic, onion, shredded cabbage, and carrots. Blend soy sauce, grated ginger, peanut butter, chili paste, and cilantro. Combine with chicken and spoon onto Bibb lettuce leaves.

To make a healthy coleslaw, combine plain yogurt with mayonnaise. Add minced onion, vinegar, mustard, sugar, salt, celery seed, and pepper. Toss with shredded cabbage, carrots, and celery.

Try stuffed cabbage leaves: Combine cooked meat, rice, onions, crushed tomatoes, brown sugar, and thyme. Remove the hard middle rib of each cabbage leaf, stuff with filling, and roll up the leaf. Bake at 350°F (175°C) for one hour.

IN THE GARDEN

Cabbage is easy an easy cool-weather crop to grow in the garden or in containers. The hardy biennial can withstand a light frost and temperatures down to 20°F (–7°C).

 **CLIMATE**
Cabbage grows well in zones 3 through 9 in direct sunlight. Partial shade may lead to loose heads.

 SOIL
The ideal soil for cabbage is rich in organic matter and has a pH of 6.5 to 7.0. Amend the soil with nitrogen-rich blood meal in the fall before planting.

 PLANTING
Start seeds indoors four to six weeks before the last frost, or sow directly as soon as the soil can be worked. Sow seeds ½ inch (13 mm) deep; thin plants to 18 inches (46 cm) apart in rows 3 feet (1 m) apart.

GROWING
Water cabbage regularly—the roots need to remain evenly moist. Feed cabbage midseason with a nitrogen-rich fertilizer.

HARVESTING
Cabbage is the sweetest when harvested in cool weather. Cut cabbage heads when they are firm to the touch and the base reaches at least 4 inches (10 cm) across.

NUTRITIONAL VALUE

Serving size 100 (1-1/4 cup), raw

calories 25	fiber 2.5 g

vitamin K 63% DV	thiamin 5% DV
vitamin C 50% DV	iron 5% DV
folate 11% DV	magnesium 5% DV
vitamin B-6 10% DV	calcium 4% DV

HEALTH BENEFITS

lowers blood pressure
benefits cardiovascular system
reduces risk of cancer
aids digestion
lowers cholesterol
reduces inflammation
boost immune system

CARROT

Daucus carota subsp. sativus

A familiar root vegetable in cuisines worldwide, carrots were first grown more than 3,000 years ago in the vicinity of Afghanistan. This herbaceous, biennial belongs to the parsley family (Apiaceae) and has a crunchy taproot that is usually bright orange, though cultivars can be yellow, red, purple, or pink.

VARIETIES

Of the five main varieties, Nantes is particularly sweet, with a cylindrical shape and a blunt rounded tip. Chantenay carrots are shorter and stubbier with broad shoulders and a tapered tip. Imperator are the longest with thin roots and are produced on a large scale in North America. The conical Danvers carrots are not quite as long as Imperator types but tolerate heavy soil quite well. The fifth type is the popular mini carrot or baby carrot.

ATLAS A petite Parisian market–type carrot, Atlas grows to just 2 inches (5 cm) and is perfect for shallow soils or container gardening. This sweet, round baby carrot has a yellow core and is ready in 75 days.

DANVERS HALF LONG A common heirloom carrot in North America, Danvers is a dependable deep-orange root that grows up to 8 inches (20 cm) long. It thrives in a variety of soils, is ready to harvest in 75 days.

MALBEC This elegant, bordeaux beauty produces long, uniform roots up to 10 inches (25 cm). The Imperator-type Malbec has a small core and great texture. This hybrid is ready to harvest in 70 days.

MOKUM The Nantes-type pencil carrots are perfect for early bunches. Sweet and crisp, it retains its flavor in hot weather and sweetens with a light frost. Harvest baby carrots at 36 days, and full-size carrots in 58 days.

NAPOLI An early Nantes cultivar, Napoli is delicious as a baby or a full-size carrot. The cylindrical 7-inch (18 cm) root is smooth with strong tops and matures in 58 days. It performs well even in heavy clay soil.

PURPLE HAZE An Imperator-type root, Purple Haze has a bright, complex flavor. The deep-purple skin surrounds a crisp, bright-orange interior. It grows to 7 inches (18 cm) and matures in 73 days.

GOLD NUGGET The flavorful golden-yellow taproot of this Nantes-type carrot grows to about 8 inches (20 cm). It boasts a strong top, a thin core, and strong bolt-resistance. It matures in about 57 days.

HERCULES The cone-shaped Chantenay-type carrot grows to 7 inches (18 cm) and is delicious even when harvested in summer. Shallow or rocky soil is not a problem for Hercules. It's ready to enjoy in 65 days.

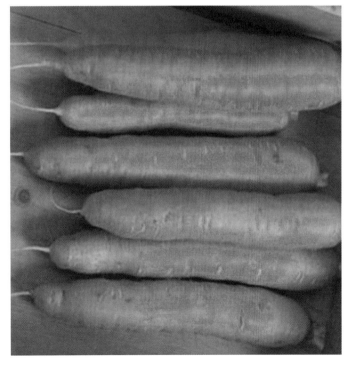

WHITE SATIN The crisp, creamy-white roots of this hybrid are cylindrical and grow to 9 inches (23 cm). White Satin is highly adaptable, though it tends to get green shoulders. It matures in 68 days.

YELLOWSTONE This lemon-yellow Imperator hybrid has consistent color down to the core, and it pairs well with Purple Haze and White Satin. The thick green tops crowd out weeds. It's ready in 73 days.

BOLERO

This classic Nantes-type cultivar produces a thick taproot that tapers to a blunt tip and grows up to about 7 inches (15 cm) in length. Bolero boasts a rich, sweet flavor and a crisp, juicy texture. This high-yielding variety is also very resistant to disease. Its tall, strong tops make harvesting a snap. Bolero matures in about 75 days and is appropriate for both fall and winter harvests. It's excellent either fresh or stored.

IN THE KITCHEN

Raw, crunchy carrots are a quick, healthy snack, and they are just as nutritious when cooked. Although vitamins are often depleted with cooking, the beta-carotene in carrots is very heat-stable—in fact, steaming carrots enhances the body's ability to absorb beta-carotene and then convert it to vitamin A.

SELECTING

Choose carrots that have smooth skin and are firm and crisp, not rubbery. The brighter the orange color, the greater the beta-carotene content. Smaller carrots are generally a bit more tender.

PREPARING

Cut off the leaves. Rinse the carrots and gently scrub them with a vegetable brush. No need to peel organic carrots, only conventional ones to remove pesticides. Cut away any green parts of the stem, which have a bitter taste.

STORING

Cut off all but an inch of the greens, which draw moisture from the carrot and cause them to wilt prematurely. To keep carrots crisp and well hydrated, place them in a container of water and refrigerate for up to a month, replacing cloudy water as necessary.

PRESERVING

To freeze carrots, keep small carrots whole, and slice larger carrots. Blanch them in boiling water for three minutes. Plunge into ice water, dry well, and store in airtight containers. For the best flavor, freeze the youngest, most tender carrots of the bunch. Alternatively, you can pickle carrots: Heat a cup of rice wine vinegar with brown sugar, salt, and pepper until the sugar dissolves. Cool the mixture, then pour over carrots, seal, and marinate for two hours. Store in the refrigerator for up to two weeks.

USES

Carrots can be eaten raw or shredded, sliced, diced, or julienned.

Nosh on raw carrots as a snack or crudité; toss them in salads and slaws; cook them as a side dish; or add them to soups, stews, and stir-fries. Carrots also lend a sweet, earthy flavor to juices and baked goods such as carrot cake or muffins.

Carrots pair well with celery and onion, and this trio of vegetables is essential for vegetable broths and pot roasts.

As a side dish, try easy glazed carrots: Place sliced carrots in a pot with a some chicken broth and simmer until tender; add butter, brown sugar, maple syrup, salt, and white pepper. If desired, spice it up with cinnamon, nutmeg, and cayenne pepper.

Roast a medley of winter root vegetables. Cut any of these vegetables in even sizes: carrots, potatoes, sweet potatoes, parsnips, beets, or butternut squash, and toss with olive oil, rosemary, salt, and pepper. Arrange in one layer on a baking sheet, and roast at 400°F (200°C) for 25 to 40 minutes, turning once. For more flavor, add onions, garlic, and thyme, or sprinkle with fresh parsley before serving.

IN THE GARDEN

Carrots are fun and easy to grow in most climates. Just remember to time the harvest for cooler weather—carrots sweeten when touched by frost. For a dramatic display in your kitchen, try planting carrots in an array of colors—from cream and gold to scarlet and crimson.

CLIMATE
Plant carrots in full sun in cooler climates, and in part shade in warmer climates. Scorching heat makes carrots taste bitter.

SOIL
Carrots require rich, deep soil that's loose and fluffy so the taproots can grow unobstructed. Remove stones from the soil and till down to 18 inches (46 cm). Amend heavy soils with compost. A pH range between 6.0 and 6.8 is ideal for carrots.

PLANTING
Sow seeds three weeks before the last frost date, and then every two to three weeks through midsummer for a continuous harvest. Sow seeds ¼-inch (6 mm) deep, and at least 2 inches (5 cm) apart. Space rows 10 inches (25 cm) apart.

GROWING
Keep the soil evenly moist, watering from above, if possible, rather than by drip irrigation. Do not fertilize or plant near heavy feeders. Too much nitrogen leads to forked carrots and heavy green leaves. Cover shoulders that pop up with dirt to prevent them from greening and turning bitter.

HARVESTING
Begin harvesting baby carrots when the green tops reach about 5 inches (13 cm) and carrots are about 4 inches (10 cm) long. This also serves to thin the row and encourage neighboring carrots to develop more fully. Carrots sweeten with a bit of frost, but if you leave carrots in too long, they get woody.

OMPANION PLANTS
Plant carrots near tomatoes, which provide shade and natural insecticides. Carrots also aerate the soil, which benefits tomatoes. Other good companions for carrots are leeks, rosemary, sage, and chive, which all repel carrot flies. Avoid planting carrots near dill, coriander, and parsnips.

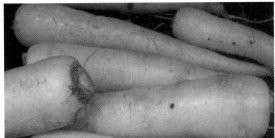

FUN FACT
The wild carrot, known as Queen Anne's Lace, is actually purple and it was first used in ancient times as a medicine, not as an edible vegetable.

CASSAVA

Manihot esculenta

The tall, graceful cassava plant is a perennial shrub of the spurge family (Euphorbiaceae) and is native to western Brazil. Also known as manioc and yuca, cassava is harvested for its starchy, chewy tubers. These nutty, nutrient-dense roots are also the source of tapioca and garri starch.

VARIETIES

SWEET CASSAVA
Once this cassava gets established, propagate with stems cuttings every two to three years. In warmer climates, cassava roots are ready to harvest as early as eight months after planting. Cassava is the third-largest source of food carbohydrates in the tropics, after rice and maize. It is a major staple food in the developing world, providing a basic diet for over half a billion people. It is one of the most drought-tolerant crops, capable of growing on marginal soils. Cassava can be cooked in many ways. The root of the sweet variety has a delicate flavor and can replace potatoes. It can be made into a flour that is used in breads, cakes and cookies.

VERTICAL PLANTING
In this method, plant the cuttings vertically with two thirds of the stem buried in the soil. Shoots will develop from the exposed nodes, and roots will grow from those below.

HORIZONTAL PLANTING
In an sunny, open location in the garden, dig a trench about 3 inches (8 cm) deep and lay the stem cutting inside. Cover with fine soil, and keep evenly moist.

DIAGONAL PLANTING
Place the cassava stem cutting into the soil at an angle, with two thirds of the stem underground, and one third above the ground. Press the soil around the stem to secure it in place.

IN THE KITCHEN

Cassava contains twice the starch of potatoes—and twice the calories! Be sure to cook cassava before eating: It contains the toxic chemical cyanide, which is neutralized by cooking.

SELECTING
Smell the roots: Fresh cassava tubers have a fresh, bright scent. Look for pure white centers that are firm and blemish-free. Discard tubers with black spots or any discoloration.

PREPARING
Use a sharp knife to cut the root into 3-inch (8 cm) segments. Stand the segments vertically on a cutting board and slice the hard, waxy skin, then peel away the rest of the skin. Cut the pieces lengthwise in quarters, then cut away the woody core.

STORING
Ideally you should store whole cassava unpeeled in a cool, dark place for up to a week. Place peeled cassava in a container of water, then refrigerate for up to a month, provided you change the water every two or three days.

PRESERVING
To freeze cassava, peel it, and cut it into chunks. Freeze in an airtight container for six months.

USES
A simple way to prepare cassava root is to boil it in lightly salted water until tender, about 15 to 30 minutes. Remove the tough core. Add cooked cassava to any recipes that call for potatoes. Use the water to thicken soups and stews.

Cassava is delicious fried: Cut the root into small pieces, and deep fry as you would french fries. Or try making cassava chips by deep-frying slices of cassava.

Try these Dominican-style cassava fritters: Grate a ½ pound (0.23 kg) of cassava, add a spoon of sugar and aniseed, salt, and combine with an egg. Heat 1 inch (2.5 cm) of oil in a pan, form patties with 2 T. (30 ml) of the mixture, and fry on both sides.

For some Caribbean comfort food, try the classic creamed, mashed cassava. Boil cassava chunks until very soft, for about an hour. Drain, reserving the liquid, and mash the yucca with some milk, some of the cooking liquid, and butter. Add a dash of cinnamon and nutmeg.

IN THE GARDEN

The towering subtropical cassava grows up to 12 feet (4 m) tall with elegant, tropical-looking palmate leaves, but it can take as long as 18 months before it's ready for the first harvest.

CLIMATE
Cassava needs eight months of warm weather and full sun. In cooler zones, grow cassava as an annual outdoors or grow it indoors in a large pot in a sunny area.

SOIL
Cassava tolerates drought but prefers moist, well-drained soil with a bit of sand. Loosen the soil about 12 inches (30 cm) deep.

PLANTING
Start plants from propagules, 3-inch (8 cm) stem cuttings with several nodes. Place the cuttings directly on soil in a pot in a sunny area indoors. Mist regularly. Transplant outdoors when it's warm and when sprouts are about 2 inches (5 cm) long. Plant 3 inches (8 cm) deep.

GROWING
Fertilize cassava in the spring. Propagate often: Roots tend to get woody after a few years.

HARVESTING
Lift cassava out by the roots. Cut the roots from the base of the plant.

CAULIFLOWER

Brassica oleracea var. Botrytis

An offshoot of wild Cypriot cabbage in the 15th century, cauliflower has since adapted to various climates around the world. Creamy-white heads are the most common type, but cauliflower cultivars now come in a rainbow of colors—from deep purple to coral orange to spikes of green.

VARIETIES

CHEDDAR This hybrid has smooth and uniform heads with a dense, rich texture. The cheerful bright-orange color even brightens with cooking. The heads grow to 6 inches (15 cm) across in 68 days.

GRAFFITI These striking purple heads grow to about 7 inches (18 cm) wide. Graffiti has a mild, sweet flavor and is nutritious too— this purple beauty is packed with antioxidants. It's ready to harvest in 75 days.

GREEN MACERATA The attractive apple-green heads have a sweet, delicate flavor and grow to about 2 pounds (1 kg). This self-blanching Italian heirloom is vigorous and hardy, and matures in 70 days.

SNOWBALL This self-blanching European heirloom develops bright-white heads up to 8 inches across. The leaves protect the head from the sun as it matures. The mild-flavored heads are ready in 65 days.

IN THE KITCHEN

Cauliflower's delicate flavor makes it the perfect canvas to try out any number of culinary creations. Try savory ingredients like capers and anchovies or simply drizzle with melted butter.

 ### SELECTING
Choose firm, compact heads; avoid cauliflower that has soft spots, which indicate spoilage. Examine heads for brown spots or dark flecks on the curds. Cauliflower should have a uniform color and be blemish-free.

PREPARING
Peel away the outer leaves of the head, and trim off the stem. Use a peeler to skim off discolored spots. Cut the florets from the stem in even pieces, and rinse under cold water.

STORING
Place whole, unwashed heads in a produce bag, and refrigerate for up to two weeks. Store heads with the florets facing up to prevent moisture build-up on the buds. Use precut florets within a day or two.

 ### PRESERVING
To freeze florets and prevent them from sticking together, pre-freeze them: Arrange florets in a single layer on a baking sheet, place them in the freezer for a few minutes, then store them in an airtight container.

 ### USES
Cauliflower can't really shine when it's boiled—and overcooked cauliflower is downright mushy and bland. Its mild flavor and texture benefit from roasting with strong flavors such as garlic and cayenne pepper, or sharp cheeses such as Parmesan. The delicate cauliflower is delicious in creamy soups and casseroles.

Try this simple recipe for cauliflower au gratin: Sauté minced garlic and cubed ham in a cast-iron skillet; add cauliflower florets, and cook until tender. Blend a spoonful of flour with some heavy cream, and add to the skillet. Season with salt, pepper, and cayenne. Sprinkle with Gruyère or other melting cheese, and broil until lightly brown, about 5 minutes. Serve with fresh chopped parsley.

IN THE GARDEN

Cauliflower can be a challenging vegetable to cultivate. It's a sensitive plant that requires even temperatures, consistent moisture, good drainage, and proper air circulation.

CLIMATE
Cauliflower does well in zones 2 through 11. It needs at least six hours of sunlight per day.

SOIL
Provide well-draining soil amended with rich organic matter. Aim for a pH of 6.0 to 7.5. Prepare the soil by tilling down about 12 inches (30 cm).

PLANTING
Sow seeds directly three weeks before the last frost date, or indoors up to six weeks before the last frost. Do not disturb the roots. Sow seeds ½-inch (13 mm) deep and 10 inches (25 cm) apart. Space rows every 3 feet (1 m).

GROWING
Water cauliflower regularly for even moisture; the heads become stressed when growing conditions fluctuate. Fertilize every three weeks.

 ### HARVESTING
Harvest heads when they are firm but before flowering. Keep one set of leaves intact to protect the head.

NUTRITIONAL VALUE

Serving size 100 g (3/4 cup)
calories 23   fiber 2.3 g

vitamin C 59% DV	choline 8% DV
vitamin K 14% DV	phosphorus 5% DV
vitamin B6 13% DV	thiamin 4% DV
folate 11% DV	riboflavin 4% DV

HEALTH BENEFITS

strengthen bones
boosts cardiovascular system
protects against cancer
aids digestion
reduces inflammation
regulates blood sugar

CELERY

Apium graveolens

Celery was first cultivated in the salty marshlands of the Mediterranean and the Middle East. Ancient Greeks and Romans used wild celery as a flavoring, and ancient Chinese used it as a medicine. Over time, the strings were bred out of the petioles of most varieties, leading to more succulent stalks.

VARIETIES

BRILLIANT CELERIAC
The knubbly, nutty-flavored relative to celery has large round roots with buff skin. The inside is pure white and flavorful. Brilliant is ready to harvest in 100 days. Try it in soups and stews.

GIANT RED The largest of the red-stalk varieties, this heirloom has purple-red stalks and yellowish-pink hearts with a fresh, crunchy flavor. It's cold hardy and disease resistant. Harvest Giant Red in 85 days.

PEPPERMINT STICK
This red-and-white-striped heirloom has tender stalks and flavorful leaves, too. It reaches 24 inches (60 cm) and is slow to bolt. Peppermint Stick is ready to enjoy in 85 days.

TALL UTAH
The thick, dark-green stalks of this heirloom grow to 12 inches (30 cm) tall. This longtime favorite celery has compact hearts and is very cold hardy. Tall Utah matures in 100 days.

IN THE KITCHEN

The crispy, crunchy celery is a staple ingredient that lends texture to soups, stews, and pot roasts. Celery is also a delicious, low-calorie snack that you can munch on plain or dipped in hummus.

 **SELECTING**
Choose bright-green stalks that are in a tight bunch. The stalks should be crisp, not droopy. The leaves should look fresh and light green with no yellow or brown spots.

PREPARING
Cut off the bottom and tips of the celery. Rinse each stalk under cold water, rubbing away dirt near the base. Cut and peel away any stringy fibers.

STORING
Store celery in a produce bag and refrigerate for up to two weeks. If you'd like to use one stalk at a time, trim off the ends of the stalks, rinse in cool water, and dry. Wrap them in a paper towel, and store in a produce bag in the refrigerator.

PRESERVING
To freeze celery, cut the stalks into 3-inch (8 cm) strips, and blanch them in boiling water for three minutes. Plunge into ice water, dry, and store in airtight containers in the freezer for up to six months.

USES
One of the most popular and convenient ways to eat celery is to munch on it raw. If you don't like it plain, try dipping it into a healthy spread like hummus or tzatziki.

Celery is often used as a base for soups and stews, especially in combination with onions, carrots, and bell peppers. It lends a firm texture while absorbing other flavors well. Celery is often added to stuffings and salads for a zesty flavor. Try pairing celery with fennel, zucchini, or green beans.

For a simple side dish, try braising celery: Cut stalks into bite-size strips on the bias. Heat some butter, and sauté celery with salt and pepper for five minutes. Add some broth, and cook for several minutes until celery is tender and the sauce is reduced. Serve with chopped celery leaves.

To make celery soup: Heat olive oil in a large pot, and sauté onion and garlic. Add chopped celery, diced potato, chicken stock, and parsley. Simmer for 30 minutes until tender. Purée in a blender and serve hot.

NUTRITIONAL VALUE

Serving size 100 g (1 cup) raw
calories 14   fiber 1.6 g

vitamin K 39% DV	vitamin C 4% DV
folate 9% DV	riboflavin 4% DV
vitamin B-6 6% DV	calcium 4% DV
potassium 6% DV	magnesium 3% DV

HEALTH BENEFITS

powerful antioxidant
reduces inflammation
aids digestion
alkalizes the body
lowers cholesterol
regulates blood pressure
supports liver health

IN THE GARDEN

Celery is a long-season vegetable that doesn't care for heat. It can be a bit fussy to grow, but once you've eaten celery fresh from the garden, you won't want to go back to store-bought.

 CLIMATE
Celery grows well in zones 2 to 10 in full or part sun. It prefers the cooler days of spring and fall.

 SOIL
The ideal pH for celery is between 5.8 and 6.8. Amend the soil with compost before planting.

 PLANTING
Soak seeds overnight before planting. Start seeds indoors 8 to 10 weeks before the last frost. Press seeds onto the starter soil, but don't cover them. Transplant outdoors two weeks before the last frost date. Space plants 10 inches (25 cm) apart.

 GROWING
Celery is a thirsty plant. Water regularly for large, juicy stalks. Mulch to preserve moisture. Side dress celery's shallow roots with a 5-10-10 fertilizer.

 HARVESTING
Pick stalks as needed after they reach 8 inches (20 cm). Harvest stalks beginning with the outside of the plant.

COLLARD GREENS

Brassica oleracea var. viridis

Collard greens are herbaceous annual or biennial plants of the mustard family (Brassicaceae). The dark-green leaves are deeply lobed and grow on thick stems. Although botanically similar to kale, collards have broader leaves and no frills. Collards are a rich source of minerals and vitamins A and C.

VARIETIES

GEORGIA SOUTHERN
This 1800s heirloom is a longtime favorite. It has a rich sweet flavor, with not much bitterness, and it tolerates heat and frost well. The plant grows to 3 feet (1 m) in about 50 days.

JERNIGAN YELLOW
This hybrid has a sweet, buttery flavor that's milder than other collards. The yellow-tinted leaves are very uniform and grow to 23 inches (58 cm) tall and mature in about 75 days.

OLE TIMEY BLUE
The large blue-green leaves have striking purple veins. They're upright and easy to harvest for their delicious kale flavor. Old Timey grows to 24 inches (60 cm) in about 60 days.

TIGER HYBRID
This upright plant features thick, savoyed leaves in deep blue-green. Pick leaves as needed, and encourage new growth for a repeat harvest. It matures in 69 days.

IN THE KITCHEN

Collards have a mild, earthy, and smoky flavor but readily soak up surrounding flavors. They pair well with lighter dishes such as chicken, fish, and beans, and taste great with citrus foods.

 SELECTING Choose crisp, small leaves for the freshest flavor. Avoid greens that are wilted—those are past their prime and will taste bitter. Examine leaves for blemishes or insect damage. Thicker, larger, and more mature leaves will have a stronger, slightly bitter taste.

 PREPARING Soak collards in cold water with vinegar to remove dirt and bacteria. Rinse until the water runs clear, and dry thoroughly. Remove the tough stems and central ribs. Use the smaller, more tender leaves for salads, and the more mature leaves as a side dish.

 STORING Place collards in a produce bag and push out any excess air before sealing the bag. Refrigerate collards in the produce drawer for up to a week.

 PRESERVING To freeze collards, clean them well, and tear larger leaves into smaller pieces. Blanch the greens in boiling water for three minutes, plunge into ice water, and dry. Seal in airtight containers.

 USES Steam or boil collards in a small amount of salted water to preserve nutrients.

Try this simple sauté: Heat olive oil over medium heat, and sauté onions and minced garlic. Add chopped collard greens, salt, lime juice, and red pepper flakes. Stir in some broth and simmer until the greens are tender, about 10 minutes. Serve with white beans.

The Brazilian recipe couve à mineira is a meatier dish of sautéed greens: Cook diced bacon until crispy; add minced onion and garlic, and sauté. Roll up the collard leaves, slice thinly, and add to the skillet along with a spoonful of cider vinegar and sliced smoked sausage. Sprinkle with crushed red pepper or smoked paprika. Cook for five minutes or until tender.

IN THE GARDEN

Although collards are popular in the Southern U.S., they are actually a cold-season crop. Plant collards with a fall harvest in mind. A touch of frost will sweeten the rich, dark-green leaves.

 **CLIMATE** Choose a sunny location with filtered shade during the hottest part of the day. The frost-tolerant plant grow in all hardiness zones.

 SOIL The soil should be rich, loamy, and fast-draining. Aim for a pH range between 6.5 to 6.8, though collard greens are adaptable to a variety of soils.

 **PLANTING** Sow seeds directly after danger of a heavy frost has past, or start indoors four to six weeks before the last frost. Sow at a depth of ¼ inch (6 mm), and thin seedlings to 18 inches (46 cm) apart.

 GROWING Water plants regularly for an even supply of moisture. Feed with a 15-0-0 fertilizer, and mulch.

 HARVESTING Cut or pick young leaves as needed when the leaves are 6 to 8 inches (15 to 20 cm) tall, about 75 days. Harvest leaves from the outside in, to encourage new shoots.

NUTRITIONAL VALUE

Serving size 100 (1/2 cup)

calories 33		fiber 4g
vitamin K 400%		calcium 14%
vitamin A 42%		iron 11%
vitamin C 24%		vitamin B-6 10%
choline 17% DV		riboflavin 8%

HEALTH BENEFITS

strengthens bones
reduces cancer risk
regulates blood sugar
powerful antioxidant
nourishes skin and hair
improves mood and sleep

CORN

Zea mays

Also known as maize, corn is a cereal plant that belongs to the grass family (Poaceae). Although corn is actually a grain, it is treated as a vegetable in cuisines worldwide. First domesticated in Mexico 10,000 years ago, corn comes in a rainbow of kernel colors—yellow, white, red, blue, and black.

VARIETIES

AMERICAN DREAM
This excellent bicolor hybrid has a rich, sweet flavor. It grows to 7 feet (2.1 m) tall and is adaptable to a variety of conditions. American Dream is ready to harvest in about 77 days.

GOLDEN BANTAM An heirloom from 1902, Golden Bantam quickly became the standard for sweet yellow corn. Each 5-foot (1.5 m) stalk often bears two 6-inch (15 cm)ears. It matures in 80 days.

SILVER QUEEN This classic hybrid yields sweet, tender corn on towering 8-foot (2.4 m) stalks. The large ears grow to 9 inches (23 cm) long with 15 rows of pearly white kernels. It's ready to enjoy in 92 days.

SWEETNESS This hybrid lives up to its name. The delectable bicolor kernels grow on well-wrapped 8-inch (20 cm) ears and sturdy 6-foot (1.8 m) stalks. This robust variety matures within 68 days.

IN THE KITCHEN

Fresh corn on the cob tastes so sweet that you can enjoy it plain or with just a touch of butter and salt. But corn is so versatile—try adding it to salads or chowders, or bake a loaf of cornbread.

SELECTING
Choose fresh ears of corn without peeling the husks: The silky tassels at the top should be brown and sticky, not black and dry. The husk should be tight, green, and a bit moist. If you see little holes in the husk, those could be worm holes. Feel along the husk for plump kernels; avoid ears with soft spots.

PREPARING
To shuck corn, pull back the outer leaves, one at a time, and hold onto them as you snap off the stem. Grab the tassels at the top and pull those away. Trim off the ends of the ears, and rinse the ears in cold water.

STORING
Wrap unhusked corn a damp paper towel and place in a produce bag. Refrigerate for two days.

PRESERVING
To freeze corn, blanch in boiling water for five minutes, plunge into ice water, and dry on a towel. Store in an airtight container for up to six months.

USES
To make corn on the cob, boil corn in salted water, and cook for five to seven minutes. To freshen up more mature corn, add some milk, sugar, or lemon to the water. Drizzle with butter and salt.

Enjoy roasted corn on the cob: Place unhusked corn on a baking sheet, and roast at 400°F (200°C) for 20 minutes. Or wrap in aluminum foil and grill.

Try this easy recipe for puréed corn: Cut off the kernels from roasted corn, and combine with butter, lemon juice, salt, and pepper. Blend to desired thickness. If desired, sprinkle with smoked paprika or cayenne. Serve warm.

Melt butter in a large pot, add scallions, celery, bell pepper, and cook for five minutes. Add 1 cup corn kernels, diced potatoes, broth, salt, and pepper. Simmer for 15 to 20 minutes, until vegetables are tender. In a blender, combine 2 cups corn kernels with cream and purée. Add to pot, simmer for 10 minutes. Serve with chopped scallions and some crème fraîche.

IN THE GARDEN

Corn requires a lot of space to grow and to pollinate properly. Because corn is wind pollinated, be sure to allocate at least four rows and at least 100 square feet (9.3 m2) per variety.

CLIMATE
Corn performs well in hardiness zones 2 though 9 in full sunlight.

SOIL
Well-draining, fertile soil is best, but corn is adaptable. The optimal pH range is between 6.0 and 7.0.

PLANTING
Sow seeds outdoors after the last frost date. Sow 2 inches (5 cm) deep and 6 inches (15 cm) apart. Thin seedlings to every 12 inches (30 cm). Plant in rows 30 inches (76 cm) apart. To avoid cross-pollination, space different varieties 400 feet (122 m) apart.

GROWING
Corn is a thirsty plant and requires about 2 inches (5 cm) of water per week. Feed corn with a high-nitrogen fertilizer every few weeks. Mulch to protect roots,

HARVESTING
Harvest about 20 days after the silks appear. The corn kernels should be full, milky, but firm.

CROOKNECK SQUASH

Cucurbirta pepo

The classic summer squash, crookneck is also known as yellow squash. Crookneck, which gets its name from the graceful curve in its neck, has a delicate, buttery flavor similar to zucchini but sweeter and slightly nutty. The fine, bright-yellow skin can be smooth or covered in bumpy warts.

VARIETIES

DELTA This prolific bush hybrid produces 8-inch (20 cm) fruit with a smooth, bright-yellow skin and a dense, buttery flesh. Delta squash is highly disease resistant and is ready to harvest in about 55 days.

EARLY SUMMER These compact fruits grow to 6 inches (15 cm) long and have bumpy yellow skin. The tender flesh has a delicious flavor and delicate texture. Early Summer matures in about 53 days.

SUMMERPAC This reliable bush hybrid sets bright 6-inch (15 cm) fruits all summer long. The fruits have a smooth, wart-free skin and flavorful flesh. A prolific and heat-resistant variety, it's ready in 47 days.

SUNNY SUPERSETT An early-bearing crookneck, this hybrid boasts high yields of glossy, thin-skinned fruits that mature to 7 inches (cm) within 38 days. The fruits have a sweet and nutty flavor.

IN THE KITCHEN

Summer squash is a remarkably versatile vegetable. Its flesh is juicy with a mild, earthy flavor, and it tastes just as delicious in savory dishes as it does in sweet muffins and quick breads.

 SELECTING Choose crooknecks with firm, shiny, bright-yellow skin that is blemish-free; avoid those with bruising. Look for squash with a fresh, green stem that's not dried out. Hold the squash: It should feel heavy for its size.

 PREPARING Handle the squash gently—its thin skin is fragile and easily damaged. Some squash have small prickles on the skin—gently rinse these off under cold water. No need to peel the rind unless it's rather thick. Trim off the ends.

STORING Wrap the squash in a produce bag in the refrigerator, where it will keep for up to two weeks. If you have squash blossoms, use those right away.

 PRESERVING To freeze crookneck squash, wash and slice it first. Then steam it or blanch it in boiling water for three minutes. Plunge the squash slices into ice water, then dry thoroughly. Place them into an airtight container and freeze for up to 12 months.

 USES For a fresh, easy summer sauté, heat some olive oil in a skillet and add chopped onion and garlic. Add thinly sliced crookneck squash, salt, pepper, and fresh marjoram, dill, or cumin seed. Sauté for five minutes or until tender.

Use julienned squash as a crudité or add it to salads, slaws, soups, stir-fries, and pasta sauces. Crookneck is equally scrumptious in sweet baked goods such as muffins and quick breads. Try adding some sweet spices like cinnamon, nutmeg, cloves, or ginger.

To roast squash, cut it into 1-inch (2.5 cm) pieces and place on a baking sheet; toss with olive oil, lemon juice, salt, garlic powder, smoked paprika, and cayenne pepper. Bake at 400°F (200°C) for 45 to 60 minutes or until tender. Serve warm.

IN THE GARDEN

Harvest crookneck when it's still young for its delightfully tender flesh and mild, nutty flavor. This compact, bush-type squash is ideal for smaller beds and container gardening.

 CLIMATE Crookneck squash prefers a location in full sunlight. It grows well in almost any climate, from zone 3 through 11.

SOIL Crookneck prefers rich, well-draining soil. Amend the top 3 inches (8 cm) with compost. The ideal pH is from 6.0 to 6.8.

 **PLANTING** Sow seeds directly after the last frost date. Plant four seeds per hill at a depth of 2 inches (5 cm).

Space rows 36 inches (1 m) apart. Thin to one or two seedlings per hill.

 GROWING Water crookneck at least once a week, and more often during dry spells and hot weather. Use low-nitrogen 5-10-10 fertilizer at planting time and every four weeks. Plant bee-friendly flowers nearby for better pollination.

 HARVESTING Cut the stem just above the young squash about eight days after the plant flowers.

HEALTH BENEFITS

boosts immune function
reduces inflammation
regulates blood sugar
benefits nervous system
supports heart health
strengthens bones
supports healthy vision

CUCUMBER

Cucumis sativus

The crisp, cool cucumber is actually a fruit that's commonly treated as a vegetable in cuisines worldwide. Cucumbers belong to the gourd family (Cucurbitaceae) and grow on trailing vines much like squash. Low in calories but high in nutrients, cucumbers are refreshing and healthy summer food.

VARIETIES

Originally from India, cucumbers have been cultivated for the past 3,000 years and have adapted to various climates around the globe. The fruits generally fall into three groups: slicing, pickling, and seedless. Slicing varieties are long with fine skin and are most often eaten fresh. The chunkier, shorter pickling varieties are intended for preserving as pickles. The seedless types, also known as burpless, have been bred without seeds. All types are delicious to eat raw.

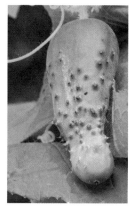

BOSTON PICKLING
An heirloom that produces continuous yields of small, straight cucumbers with thin skin and a green color. Harvest from long vines when cucumbers are 3 to 7 inches—in about 55 days.

DIVA
An award-winning slicing cucumber, Diva yields sweet fruits with no bitter taste and a superbly crisp texture. The smooth, thin-skinned hybrid is a seedless Beit Alpha–type cucumber that produces only female flowers and sets fruit without pollination. Enjoy high yields of disease-resistant cucumbers that reach 6 to 8 inches (13 to 20 cm). Diva is ready to harvest in about 58 days and is best when picked young.

HEALTH BENEFITS

benefits cardiovascular system
supports healthy vision
nourishes skin
promotes healthy vision
provides antioxidants
protects against cancer

NUTRITIONAL VALUE

Serving size 100g (1 cup)
calories 16   protein 0.6 g   fiber 0.7 g

vitamin K 7% DV	copper 4% DV
vitamin C 4% DV	phosphorus 4% DV
vitamin B-6 4% DV	biotin 3% DV
folate 4% DV	thiamin 3% DV

PAINTED SERPENT

Also known as Armenian Cucumber, this coiling cuke is one of the oldest heirlooms. Its excellent flavor brightens any salad. Harvest at 8 to 18 inches (20 to 46 cm) within 72 days.

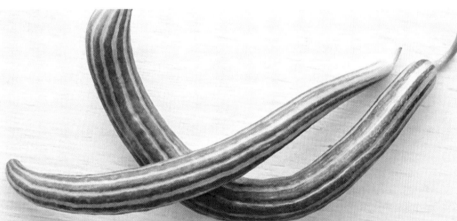

LEMON A unique round and yellow heirloom from the 1800s, Lemon cukes grow to the size of a tennis ball. They mature from a deep orange to a brilliant yellow in about 65 days. Delicious fresh or pickled.

PARISIAN PICKLING

This French heirloom has a dark-green skin and firm flesh with few seeds. It's perfect for pickling or eating fresh. These tiny cornichons are ready to harvest at 3 inches (8 cm) in 60 days.

IN THE KITCHEN

Cucumbers are a delightfully refreshing summer vegetable. Fresh cucumbers pair well with tomatoes and red onions tossed with a cool, creamy dressing or a tangy lemon vinaigrette. Cucumbers add a crispy, mouth-watering flavor to green salads, creamy sauces, cold soups, and meaty sandwiches.

SELECTING

Select firm cucumbers with dark-green skin (unless it's a different variety) without any yellowing areas. Gently feel for soft spots, which would indicate that the cucumber has started to rot. Smell the cucumber: It should have a fresh, clean scent; an older fruit will have an off odor.

PREPARING

Wash cucumbers under cold water and use a scrubber to clean off any dirt or spines. Slicing cucumbers will generally have smoother skin, which does not have to be peeled. You may want to peel conventional cucumbers to remove chemical residues and any waxy film.

STORING

To retain the fresh flavor and the cool crunch, place dry, unwashed cucumbers in a produce bag, and store them in the vegetable drawer of your refrigerator. Be sure it's not too cold, which could damage the fruits. They should remain fresh for about a week.

PRESERVING

To pickle your cukes, cut them into quarters or slices, and place them in a sterilized jar. Combine fresh dill, garlic cloves, white vinegar, salt, and peppercorns; place in the jar. Fill with distilled water, and secure the lid. Shake the contents, and set aside for 24 hours. Enjoy!

USES

Cucumbers are a wonderful snack on their own. Add a touch of salt and drizzle a bit of honey on them for a sweet and nutritious snack.

Cut cucumbers into quarters and use them in a platter of crudités with some creamy yogurt sauce or cheese dips.

Better yet, make a dipping sauce out of the cucumbers—try this classic Greek tzaziki sauce: Peel cucumbers, and remove the seeds. Finely dice the cucumbers and strain, pressing out the liquid. Combine plain Greek yogurt, lemon juice, crushed garlic cloves, freshly chopped dill, salt, and white pepper. Refrigerate for at least an hour or overnight to allow the flavors to blend.

Marinated cucumbers are a tangy and easy dish to make: Cut the cucumbers lengthwise, remove the seeds, and slice them. Place them in a salad bowl along with sliced red onion and cherry tomatoes. Combine olive oil, white wine vinegar, lemon juice, salt, and white pepper. Toss with vegetables and chill for at least an hour.

Cucumbers are also delicious in soup. Try this cold gazpacho recipe: In a blender, combine equal parts tomatoes and cucumbers. Add a slice of bread, garlic, wine vinegar, olive oil, and purée until smooth. Strain, then chill for at least an hour.

214

IN THE GARDEN

A must for every home gardener, cucumbers are easy to grow—once the danger of frost has past. As vining or bush plants, cucumbers do require a fair amount of water and fertilizer, but these prolific plants will reward you with a delicious and bountiful harvest.

CLIMATE
Cucumbers are a warm-season crop and are highly sensitive to frost. Plant in zones 4 through 11 in a sunny location once the danger of frost has past.

SOIL
The soil should be well-draining and very fertile for these heavy feeders. Work plenty of organic compost or manure into the soil before planting. Till about 8 inches (20 cm) down. The soil temperature should reach 70°F (21°C) for best results. Cucumber seeds will not germinate when the soil temperature is below 50°F (10°C). The ideal soil pH is between 6.0 and 6.8, although cucumbers will tolerate a pH up to 7.0.

PLANTING
Install trellises for vining cucumbers before planting, so as not to disturb roots later. Ideally you should sow seeds outdoors two weeks after the last frost date. If you want a head-start, sow seeds indoors in individual pots three weeks before you plan to transplant them. Sow three seeds 1 inch (2.5 cm) deep, and about 12 inches (30 inches) apart for vining types, and 24 inches (60 cm) apart for bush types.

GROWING
Water cucumbers regularly—they thrive in evenly moist soil. Try to water plants in the morning and avoid wetting the leaves. Mulch to conserve moisture. Feed with a low-nitrogen fertilizer at planting and again every three weeks. Spray the vines with sugar water to attract bees and encourage pollination.

HARVESTING
During peak harvest, pick cucumbers every other day to encourage new growth. Harvest fruits before their skin gets too tough and the fruits become bitter. Start picking slicing cucumbers at 6 to 8 inches (15 to 20 cm), pickling cukes at 2 to 3 inches (5 to 8 cm), and burpless ones up to 10 inches (25 cm).

 FUN FACT

Cucumbers aren't just for eating! For a soothing at-home spa treatment, place cucumber slices on your eyes or blend a purée as a refreshing facial.

DANDELION GREENS

Cichorium intybus

Dandelion greens are not actually true dandelions but part of the chicory family. Dandelion greens, a longtime favorite bitter in Italy, have bright-green leaves with a nutty, earthy flavor. The youngest leaves are the most tender and the least bitter, and they're are a rich source of vitamins and antioxidants.

VARIETIES

CICORIA ITALIAN
These true Italian dandelion greens are delicious in mesclun salads or cooked as a spinach substitute. This variety matures in 65 days, but harvest earlier for the most tender leaves.

CLIO Very upright and uniform, Clio is easy to harvest as a cut-and-come-again green. Its leaves are remarkably tender and resist bolting. Harvest baby leaves in 35 days, and mature leaves at 45 days.

ITALIKO RED The garnet ribs and contrasting deep-green leaves add a dramatic flair to salad mixes. The tangy Italiko Red is ready to harvest in 35 days for baby leaves, or in 56 days for full-size greens.

CATALOGNA SPECIAL
Use these bright-green leaves in fresh salad mixes. Harvest the tender, spoon-shaped baby leaves at 28 days, or the full-size, jagged leaves at 48 days. It's slow to bolt and stands upright.

IN THE KITCHEN

One of the first tender greens available in spring, dandelion leaves are a delightful addition to salad mixes. Use dandelion greens as you would arugula, beet greens, or mustard greens.

 **SELECTING**
Choose crisp bunches with small leaves and thin, tender stems for the freshest flavor. Avoid yellow or wilted leaves or those with insect damage. Larger, mature leaves will have more of a bitter taste.

PREPARING
Rinse the greens in cold water two to three times; pat dry. Trim away the tough stems, and discard any discolored or damaged leaves.

STORING
Wrap clean leaves in a paper towel and store in a plastic bag in the refrigerator. Greens will remain fresh for three to five days. Be careful not to store them in freezing temperatures, which will cause them to wilt.

PRESERVING
To freeze dandelion greens, first blanch them in boiling water for two minutes. Plunge them into ice water, and dry thoroughly. Store the greens in airtight containers for up to six months.

USES
Add tender young dandelion greens to any mesclun-style salad mix. Or add dandelion greens to light summer pasta sauces that call for arugula or beet greens.

Mature dandelion greens have a more pronounced bitter flavor, so these are best cooked. The simplest method is to steam the leaves for two minutes and drizzle with a balsamic vinaigrette.

For a simple sauté, heat olive oil in a skillet and add onion, garlic, and if desired, red pepper flakes. Add dandelion greens and cook for about five minutes.

Try an Indian variation of dandelion green sauté: Heat olive oil and mustard oil in a skillet, and sauté onion, garlic, garam masala, and red chillies for three minutes. Slice the dandelion greens into strip and sauté for five minutes. Serve over rice with chickpeas.

For pesto sauce with dandelion greens, combine the following in a blender: dandelion greens, olive oil, garlic, pine nuts, salt, lemon zest, and Parmesan.

NUTRITIONAL VALUE

serving size 1 cup (55 g)
calories 25   protein 1.5 g   fiber 1.9 g

vitamin K 550% DV	thiamin 10%
vitamin A 112%	iron 10%
vitamin C 33% DV	calcium 8% DV
riboflavin 13%	potassium 5%

HEALTH BENEFITS

powerful antioxidant
reduces inflammation
regulates blood sugar
lowers cholesterol
improves blood pressure
helps control weight

IN THE GARDEN

Dandelion greens are a cool-season plant that prefers an early spring or late fall harvest. Temperatures of 75°F (24°C) and higher will cause most varieties of these greens to bolt.

 CLIMATE
Dandelion greens grow best in zones 4 to 9 in full to part sun. The ideal temperature is about 60°F to 65°F (15.5°C to 18°C).

 SOIL
Well-draining, fertile soil is best, but dandelion greens are adaptable. The ideal pH range is between 5.5 and 7.0.

 PLANTING
Start seeds indoors eight weeks before the last frost, or sow outdoors after the last frost date.

Sow at a depth of ⅛ inch (3 mm), 6 inches (15 cm) apart. Space rows 12 to 18 inches (30 to 46 cm) apart. For baby greens, sow in a 4-inch (10 cm) band.

 GROWING
Water dandelion greens twice a week, keeping the soil evenly moist. Feed with a general purpose fertilizer.

 HARVESTING
Cut or pick young leaves as needed. The youngest greens will be the most tender.

EGGPLANT

Solanum melongena

The subtropical eggplant is a perennial plant that originated in South Asia. Also known as aubergine or brinjal, eggplant is related to tomatoes and peppers of the nightshade family (Solanaceae). Most commonly a rich purple, eggplant cultivars also come in pure white, pale lavender, and glossy black.

VARIETIES

ARETUSSA A striking white eggplant that yields plenty of mild-tasting fruits early in the season. The 8-inch (20 cm) fruits are a uniform cylindrical shape and have a spineless green calyx. It's ready in 50 days.

CALLIOPE This lovely, white-and-purple Indian hybrid can be picked for baby fruits at 2 inches (5 cm) long, or full-size at 4 inches (10 cm). Calliope has a spineless calyx and matures in 64 days.

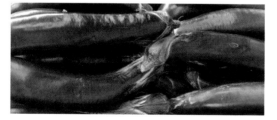

ORIENT CHARM The skin of this beauty ranges from lavender to rich purple, tapering to a touch of white near the green calyx. Fruits grow to 10 inches (25 cm) long on vigorous plants, and mature in about 65 days.

JAYLO This stunning eggplant has a shiny black skin and superb flavor. The vigorous and high-yielding Jaylo develops firm skins early and can be harvested at a half pound (0.2 kg). It matures in 65 days.

IN THE KITCHEN

A delicious, hearty vegetable that's packed with nutrients. It's so versatile in the kitchen—eggplant can be puréed into a dip, grilled as a side dish, or served as a nutritious main course.

 SELECTING
Choose a small or medium eggplant that feels heavy for its size. The skin should be glossy, smooth , and firm. The stem should be green, not dry or brown.

PREPARING
Cut the stem from the eggplant. Use a paring knife to peel the skin of more mature eggplants; no need to peel tender young fruits. Slice into ½-inch (13 mm) pieces, place in a colander. Sprinkle with salt, and place a heavy pot on the slices as a weight to squeeze out the liquid. Dry the slices before using.

STORING
Store eggplant at room temperature—not the refrigerator. It does not like temperatures below 50°F (10°C). Store it uncovered on a counter out of sunlight and away from melons, bananas, and onions. Use within three days.

 PRESERVING
To freeze eggplant slices, blanch for three minutes in boiling water, plunge into ice water, and dry well. Place in airtight containers and freeze for up to nine months.

 USES
Try the classic Italian classic eggplant Parmesan: Sauté garlic, tomatoes, salt, pepper, and basil. Combine breadcrumbs with Parmesan in a bowl. Dredge eggplant slices in flour, then egg, followed by breadcrumb mix. Place on a baking sheet, and bake at 425°F (220°C) for 20 minutes, flipping once during baking.

Here's an easy recipe for baba ghanoush, a Greek dip: Cut the eggplant in half lengthwise, sprinkle with olive oil and salt, and roast at 425°F (220°C), cut side up, for one hour; allow to cool. Scoop out the flesh, strain, and purée in a blender with olive oil, lemon juice, tahini, garlic, salt, and pepper. Refrigerate for an hour to let the flavors meld. Serve with pita bread.

For a simple sauté, heat some olive oil in a skillet and add minced garlic and, if desired, red chili peppers or mustard seed and cook briefly.

IN THE GARDEN

This tropical vegetable needs high temperatures to thrive. The warmer soil of raised beds and containers are excellent choices for eggplant. Plan in advance for a late-summer harvest.

 **CLIMATE**
Eggplant grows best in zones 4 through 10 in full sunlight.

SOIL
Eggplant needs well-draining loamy or sandy soil with a neutral to slightly acidic pH from 5.8 to 6.5.

PLANTING
Install a trellis before planting. Consider purchasing young plants from a nursery. To start from seed, begin eight to 10 weeks before the last frost. Seeds require temperatures above 70°F (21°C) to germinate. Sow seeds ½ inch (13 mm) deep, and 12 inches (30 cm) apart, in 24-inch (60 cm) apart.

GROWING
Keep eggplants evenly moist. Use a 5-10-10 fertilizer, and mulch around the plants. Pinch terminal buds for more branching.

HARVESTING
For baby eggplant, pick fruits that are about ½ pound (225 g); for minis, ¼ pound (110 g). Fruits mature in 50 to 75 days from transplanting.

NUTRITIONAL VALUE

Serving size 100 g (1 cup)
calories 24   protein 1g   fiber 3.4 g

Vitamin B-6 7% DV	Folate 4% DV
Copper 7% DV	Niacin 4% DV
Thiamin 6% DV	Magnesium 3% DV
Manganese 5% DV	Iron 3% DV
Manganese 5%	Magnesium 3% DV

HEALTH BENEFITS

benefits cardiovascular system
aids digestion
protects against cancer
strengthens bones
supports brain function
regulates blood pressure

ENDIVE

Cichorium endivia

The pale, yellow-green endive is a bitter leaf vegetable that belongs to the chicory family and is related to radicchio and escarole. The lacy-leaved variety of is also known as frisée or chicory, and the tight smooth spears are known as Belgian endive. Endive has a sweet, full flavor and a crisp, refreshing bite.

VARIETIES

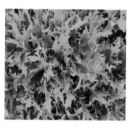

DE LOUVIERS This French heirloom has finely curled, lacy leaves and a yellow heart with an excellent, tangy flavor. It's a fast grower, heavy producer, and a delight in the garden. Enjoy it in 75 days.

RHODOS Also known as a frisée, Rhodos is a small, mild endive with frilly, toothed, pale-green leaves. The most tender leaves of these full-size heads are near the heart. Rhodos is ready to enjoy in 42 days.

FRISEE Frisee (Pronounced "free-ZAY") is a curly variety of endive with pale-green, yellowish, finely cut leaves. Though it can have a slightly bitter flavor, Frisee is much milder than other varieties.

WITLOOF CHICORY This dual-purpose endive is best known as the standard for forcing Belgian endive spears, but it's lacy greens can be harvested too. Greens are ready in 60 days, and spears in 160 days.

IN THE KITCHEN

The pale, creamy white leaves of endive make it an elegant addition to raw salads and crudités. When endive is cooked, the mildly bitter flavor mellows into a sweeter, softer taste.

SELECTING
Choose crisp bunches with smooth, unblemished leaves and tight heads. Belgian endive should be creamy white or pale yellow; it the spear is green, it's been exposed to too much light.

PREPARING
Rinse lacy leaves in cold water; pat dry. To prepare the Belgian endive spears, remove the outer leaves, trim off the base, and cut out about 1 inch (2.5 cm) of the bitter core. Cut the head in half, quarters, or slices.

STORING
Wrap spears or heads in a paper towel and store in a plastic bag in the refrigerator. Leaves remain fresh for about five days. Store seeds in an airtight jar in the refrigerator for up to six months.

PRESERVING
To freeze endive, blanch the leaves for two minutes in boiling water, plunge into ice water, and dry. Store in airtight bags for up to six months.

USES
Belgian endive spears are delicious braised. Try this easy recipe: Cut endive spears lengthwise, and slice into the core for even cooking. Place endive onto a baking sheet, and drizzle with olive oil, salt, and pepper. Roast at 425°F (220°C) for 50 minutes.

Stuff individual Belgian endive leaves with smoked salmon and goat cheese, or use the leaves in a platter of crudités for scooping dips.

Combine both endive spears and lacy frisée in salads with cruciferous vegetables. Try this recipe: Roast Brussels sprouts, and combine with sliced Belgian endive, chopped frisée, and walnuts. Drizzle with a mustard vinaigrette.

Belgian endive pairs well with salmon. To prepare an endive cream sauce, sauté chopped onion in butter in a large skillet. Add sliced Belgian endive, and sauté until tender. Add crème fraîche or heavy cream, Dijon mustard, salt, and pepper. Simmer until thickened. Serve over poached salmon with parsley sprigs.

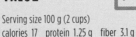

IN THE GARDEN

Belgian endive is the lettuce that you need to grow twice before you can eat it! Plant it, dig up the root, and put it in cold storage. Plant it again—in the dark—and the creamy heads emerge.

CLIMATE
This cool-weather leaf vegetable grows best in zones 3 to 9. Plant in full sunlight; in warmer regions, plant in part shade.

SOIL
Well-drained loam is best for endive. Amend the soil with compost before plant. The optimal pH range is between 5.5 and 7.0.

PLANTING
Sow seeds indoors 6 to 8 weeks before the last frost, or outdoors after the last frost. Sow at a depth of ¼ inch (1 cm), 10 inches (25 cm) apart. Space rows 12 inches (30 cm) apart.

GROWING
Keep endive consistently moist. Apply a general-purpose fertilizer at planting. Provide light shade when temperatures exceed 75°F (24°C).

HARVESTING
Cut the plant just above soil level when it reaches 6 inches (15 cm). For Belgian endive, cool the roots, then plant in the dark to force the white spears.

ESCAROLE

Cichorium endivia var. latifolia

Escarole is a leaf vegetable belonging to the genus Cichorium, which includes several similar, bitter, leafed vegetables. There are two main varieties: curly endive, which has narrow, green, curly outer leaves and is sometimes called chicory, and escarole, or broad-leaved endive, whichhas broad, pale green leaves and is less bitter than the other varieties.

VARIETIES

BIONDA CUORE PIENO The most popular escarole in Italy, Bionda has a delicate flavor and light-green heads that turn blond, especially when blanched. It's drought tolerant and matures in about 65 days.

CORNETTO BORDEAUX This large, upright heirloom boasts exceptional flavor and bright-green leaves with full white ribs. It's cold resistant, and is best enjoyed for a fall harvest. It's ready in 75 days.

EROS A compact, early escarole variety, Eros has dense, full heads of slightly bitter, wavy leaves that resemble leaf lettuce. Enjoy it in mixed salads or lemony sautés. Eros is ready to harvest within 45 days.

NATACHA A beautiful escarole, Natacha produces large, heavy heads of lush, medium-green leaves. It's highly resistant to disease, bolting, and tipburn, even in warmer weather. Harvest these greens in 50 days.

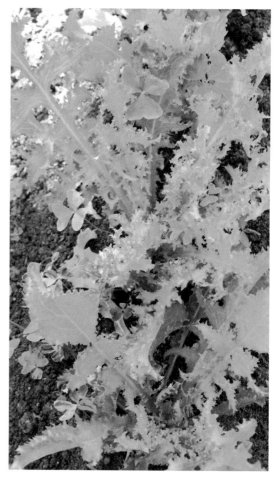

IN THE KITCHEN

Not everyone appreciates the mildly bitter flavor of escarole. To balance out its sharpness, pair escarole with citrus flavors such as lemon and orange, or drizzle with a balsamic vinegar.

 SELECTING
Choose crisp bunches of escarole with vibrantly colored leaves. Avoid those with bruised or yellowing leaves.

 PREPARING
Cut off the stem and separate the leaves. Rinse individual leaves under cold water to remove trapped dirt. Dry escarole only if you're using it in a fresh salad. Chop or tear the leaves to your desired size.

STORING
Wrap clean leaves in a paper towel and store in a produce bag in the refrigerator. Escarole should remain fresh for up to two weeks if properly stored.

 PRESERVING
To freeze escarole, blanch the leaves for two minutes, then plunge into ice water. Dry well before placing the leaves into an airtight containers. Freeze for up to six months.

 USES
When using raw escarole in salads, choose the inner, paler leaves, which have a milder flavor. The outer, darker green leaves are a bit chewier and more bitter. Use all the leaves when cooking because heat reduces the bitterness and imparts a sweeter flavor.

Escarole is delicious either sautéed, braised, or grilled. Sprinkle chopped escarole on pizza or add it to your marinara sauce.

Escarole's strong flavor pairs well with a variety of foods: citrus and vinegar, garlic, onion, anchovy, strong cheeses such as Gorgonzola, and fruits.

Try this classic Italian escarole and white bean soup: Cook bacon in a large saucepan, remove, and chop. Sauté garlic, chopped escarole, red pepper, and salt for two minutes. Purée a cup of cooked cannellini beans with chicken stock; add to the skillet with a cup of whole beans, bacon, and a cup of water. Simmer for 15 minutes; sprinkle with Parmesan cheese.

IN THE GARDEN

Escarole is often blanched in the garden to reduce its chlorophyll content—and, thus, its bitterness. Protect escarole from the sun by tying the outer leaves together three weeks before harvest.

 **CLIMATE**
Cool-weather escarole grows best in zones 4 to 8 in full sunlight.

SOIL
Escarole prefers well-worked, well-draining soil. Amend with aged compost before planting. The optimal pH range is between 5.0 and 6.8.

PLANTING
For spring planting, start seeds directly four to six weeks before the last frost. Sow at a depth of ¼ inch (1 cm), and space seedlings 10 inches (25 cm). Space rows 18 inches (46 cm) apart. Sow every two weeks in midsummer for a continuous fall harvest.

GROWING
Keep plants evenly moist to prevent bitterness. Side dress with compost during the growing season.

HARVESTING
Escarole is rather heat tolerant, but plan to harvest before the weather exceeds 85°F (29°C). Cut plants when they are at least 5 inches (13 cm) tall.

NUTRITIONAL VALUE

Serving size 100 g (3/4 cup)

calories 15	fiber 2.8 g

Vitamin K 212% DV	Zinc 6% DV
Folate 20% DV	Calcium 4.6% DV
Vitamin A 10% DV	Thiamin 5% DV
Iron 7% DV	Potassium 5% DV

HEALTH BENEFITS

boosts immune function
benefits cardiovascular system
protects against cancer
provides antioxidants
boosts metabolism
regulates blood pressure
strengthens bones

FENNEL

Foeniculum vulgare

Originally from the Mediterranean region, the cool-season fennel plant grows to about 2 feet (60 cm) tall and has feathery foliage resembling dill. The leaf stalks overlap at the base, forming a tight white bulb that tastes like anise. All parts of fennel are edible, including the bulb, stalk, leaves, and seeds.

VARIETIES

ANTARES An excellent hybrid with a strong licorice flavor, Antares has dark foliage and a sweet 5-inch (13 cm) bulb. This fragrant fennel is highly bolt resistant and attracts beneficial insects. It's ready in 58 days.

ORAZIO The large, rounded bulbs of Orazio are very uniform and have a fresh anise flavor. It grows quickly to 5 inches (13 cm) wide and is ready to harvest in 50 days for baby size, and 80 days for full size.

PRELUDIO This prolific hybrid yields large, heavy bulbs that are uniform in size. Preludio can be planted for an early fall harvest in most climates. It's ready in 50 days for baby size, and 80 days for full size.

SOLARIS The heavy bulbs have a delicate anise flavor and a juicy texture. Solaris grows well in all seasons. Its bulbs are especially delicious at baby size—about 3-inches (8 cm) across—at about 50 days.

IN THE KITCHEN

Fresh fennel has a pleasant anise flavor and celery-like crunch, but cooking it brings out a mellow, savory taste. Fennel pairs especially well with chicken, lamb, fish, and pork sausage.

 **SELECTING**
Choose fennel that has a smooth, unblemished outer layer so you don't have to discard too much of the bulb later. Look for a firm, young bulb; older bulbs can taste leathery and tough when roasted.

PREPARING
Cut off the stalk above the bulb and save the fronds to garnish your meal. Trim the bottom and remove any damaged areas. Cut the bulb into quarters, and slice off the core for more even cooking.

STORING
Trim the stalks about two inches above the bulb. Wrap all parts of the fennel loosely in a produce bag, and refrigerate for up to 10 days.

PRESERVING
To freeze fennel, quarter the bulb, remove the core, and blanch for three minutes in boiling water, plunge into ice water, and dry. Store in airtight containers for up to six months. Its flavor will keep, just not its crispness.

USES
Try adding thinly sliced raw fennel to any of your fresh salads for a bright, licorice flavor and a great crunch. It pairs well with fresh orange slices and tangy lemon dressings.

To roast fennel, toss quartered fennels bulbs with olive oil, thyme, salt, and white pepper, and roast at 425°F (220°C) for 40 minutes. Sprinkle with Parmesan cheese and fennel fronds.

Roast fennel along with other vegetables such as carrots, parsnips, potatoes, or cherry tomatoes.

Try this refreshing fennel and pomegranate side dish: Sauté minced garlic and shallot in olive oil; add sliced fennel and celery, broth, parley, salt, and pepper; simmer for eight minutes. Sprinkle with pomegranate seeds, hazelnuts, lime juice, and fennel fronds. For a salad, combine the above ingredients, except for the broth and garlic; drizzle with a lime vinaigrette.

Add fennel to marinara and sausage pasta sauces, to coleslaws, white bean salads.

IN THE GARDEN

Fennel is a multipurpose vegetable: Its anise-flavor bulb is delicious as are the fern-like leaves. But fennel will also attract pollinators, especially swallowtail butterflies, to your garden.

CLIMATE
Fennel performs best in zones 3 to 10 in full sunlight. In warmer climates, it grows as a perennial. Fennel is at its best when planted for a fall harvest.

SOIL
Well-drained loam is best, but fennel is not finicky when it come to soil pH—between 6.0 to 7.5 is fine.

 PLANTING
Sow outdoors after the last frost date. Sow 10 seeds per foot (30 cm) at a depth of ¼ inch (1 cm).

Thin seedlings to 6 inches (15 cm) apart. Space rows 18 inches (46 cm) apart.

 GROWING
Keep plants evenly moist. Feed fennel with nitrogen-rich fertilizer. Mulch around plants to preserve moisture and protect the roots.

 HARVESTING
You can harvest fennel at either baby-size or full-size bulbs. Mature fennel should be harvested right away because it tends to bolt quickly.

FIDDLEHEADS

Matteuccia struthiopteris

Ferns are nonflowering, vascular plants with graceful arching fronds. Ferns grow freely in meadows and marshy environments on almost every continent. Their fiddleheads—the tender, tightly coiled scrolls of newly emerging leaves—are a delicacy and one of the first springtime edibles.

VARIETIES

BRACKEN FERN
Also known as Fiddlehead Fern, Bracken has large, divided, dark-green leaves with red and yellow streaks at its base. This adaptable fern grows quickly to about 4 feet (120 cm) in height.

EUROPEAN OSTRICH
This large, elegant fern has arching, light-green fronds that grow quickly to about 5 feet (1.5 m) tall. A herbaceous perennial, European Ostrich tolerates full shade.

LADY FERN The finely cut, lacy leaves of Lady Fern are emerald green and grow to 3 feet (1 m) tall on erect stalks that may be green, red, or purple. Lady fern tolerates full sun if the roots are kept moist.

KING OSTRICH The graceful arching fronds of this lustrous deep-green fern resemble the plumage of an ostrich. Growing to 4 feet (1.2 m), King Ostrich is the most popular fern for harvesting fiddleheads.

IN THE KITCHEN

Fiddlehead fronds are a springtime delicacy. The graceful spiral shoots can be prepared much like any other vegetable. Their delicate savory flavor is similar to asparagus and spinach.

 SELECTING
If foraging for fiddleheads in the wild, pick bright-green fronds that are tightly coiled. Be sure to properly identify the species you're harvesting—some ferns are toxic. If purchasing fiddleheads, look for tight coils with at least an inch (2.5 cm) of stem intact. Young fiddleheads should have papery scales that brown, not white.

 PREPARING
Trim away dry stems. Swish the fronds in a bowl of cold water to remove any trapped dirt and peel off brown paper covering.

 STORING
Store clean, dry fronds in a produce bag in the refrigerator, but don't trim the stems yet. Or store them in a bowl of water, refreshing the water daily. Fronds will remain fresh for up to three weeks.

 PRESERVING
To freeze, blanch them for three minutes in boiling water, plunge into ice water, and dry before placing them in an airtight containers. Fronds will keep for up to eight months.

 USES
Some fiddleheads are toxic raw and must be cooked before eating. Boil them in salted water for about seven minutes before using them in sautés, pasta sauces, or salads.

For a simple sauté, heat butter in a skillet and sauté minced shallots. Add whole fiddleheads and portobello mushrooms, and sauté for five minutes. Stir in crème fraîche or sour cream and drizzle with lemon juice.

Try roasting fiddleheads: Toss fronds with olive oil, garlic, lemon juice, mustard, capers, thyme, chili pepper, salt, and pepper. Arrange in a single layer on a baking sheet. Roast at 450°F (220°C) for 10 minutes.

For a fern salad, try this recipe: Combine fronds with a goat cheese, pecans, and cranberries. Dress with a lemon balsamic vinaigrette.

IN THE GARDEN

Unlike most annual vegetables, perennial ferns are shade-loving plants that need consistently moist soil. Find a location in your garden that has morning sun but afternoon shade.

 **CLIMATE**
Fiddleheads ferns thrive in moist woodlands and marshland in zones 3 through 8 in partial shade.

 SOIL
Well-drained loam is best. Amend the soil with compost, but do not fertilize when planting. Ferns prefer a neutral to acidic soil with a pH between 4.0 and 7.0.

 **PLANTING**
Because ferns must be established before harvesting the fiddleheads, consider purchasing plants from a nursery to get a head-start. Ferns will then spread in clumps through their rhizomes.

 GROWING
Keep ferns even moist; water them frequently during dry spells. Mulch to protect the plants. Feed only lightly if at all—ferns are sensitive to fertilizer.

 HARVESTING
Allow newly planted ferns to become established before you harvest them. In the third year, harvest up to half of the fiddleheads.

NUTRITIONAL VALUE

Serving size 100 g (1 cup)
calories 34   protein 4.5 g   fiber 0.4 g

Vitamin C 36% DV	Iron 13% DV
Niacin 33% DV	Magnesium 8% DV
Vitamin A 20% DV	Potassium 8% DV
Riboflavin 15% DV	Zinc 8% DV

HEALTH BENEFITS

reduces blood pressure
regulates blood sugar
provides antioxidants
benefits cardiovascular system
boosts immune function
supports healthy vision
promotes weight loss

GARLIC

Allium sativum

Native to Central Asia, garlic is one of the most commonly used seasonings throughout human history. Hundreds of varieties of the bulb are now available, but they all fall into two main categories: the slow-growing hardneck varieties with a central stalk, and the larger softneck types with "braiding" leaves.

VARIETIES

CONTI FAMILY A 100-year-old Italian heirloom, the hardneck Conti has large buff coves with purple streaks. The white and purple bulbs contain six to nine mild-flavored cloves.

EARLY PURPLE ITALIAN This popular, extra-large softneck is mildly spicy and makes excellent braids. It also performs well in the heat. Each 2-inch (5 cm) bulb yields eight to 12 cloves.

ELEPHANT Elephant garlic lives up to its name. The huge 4-inch (10 cm) bulbs can weigh up to a pound (0.5 kg). Each bulb contains four to six large cloves with an intense green-onion flavor.

GERMAN RED This robust garlic has the heat of a chili pepper. A vigorous hardneck, German Red yields about eight to 10 cloves per 2-inch (5 cm) head. Its thin dark-purple skin is easy to peel.

IN THE KITCHEN

The aromatic garlic is a foundational ingredient in cuisines worldwide. Raw garlic has a robust, pungent flavor that mellows to a nutty and slightly sweet flavor when cooked.

SELECTING
Choose solid, compact bulbs with smooth, unbroken skin. Feel around for soft or damp spots, which indicate that the garlic is rotting.

PREPARING
Separate the cloves from the bulb by setting a pan on the bulb and applying some pressure to break them apart. To remove the skin from a clove, press down on the clove with the flat side of a large kitchen knife.

STORING
Moisture is not garlic's friend. Store garlic at room temperature in a dark, dry place with good air circulation. A mesh bag in the pantry is ideal. Braid a few bulbs of softneck varieties together and hang them in your pantry.

PRESERVING
To freeze garlic, purée it with a little bit of water and spoon it into ice cube trays. Once frozen, store them in airtight containers up to a year.

USES
Garlic can be eaten fresh, roasted, or sautéed. Infuse oil and vinegar salad dressings with whole or crushed garlic cloves.

Roast or sauté garlic cloves with any other vegetables: asparagus, potatoes, turnips, parsnips, carrots, beets, Brussels sprouts, or squash.

Roast garlic on its own, so you can store it for later. To roast, combine garlic cloves with the skin on, olive oil, and salt; place on a baking pan in one layer. Roast at 350°F (175°C) for 45 minutes. Allow to cool, snip off the tips, and squeeze out the soft pulp. Refrigerate for a week, or freeze for up to a year.

Try this classic French recipe—chicken with 40 garlic cloves. Cook chicken thighs in a covered cast-iron pot for 20 minutes. Remove and drain. Sauté 40 garlic cloves, onion, and herbes de Provence. Add white wine and reduce by half. Add chicken thighs, chicken stock, thyme, tarragon, parsley, salt, and pepper. Cover and cook for 90 minutes. Drizzle with butter.

IN THE GARDEN

Garlic is a cold-weather crop that's easy to grow and requires very little space in your garden. Plant garlic cloves in the middle of the fall and enjoy fresh garlic cloves by late fall or early spring.

CLIMATE
For the first two months of growth, garlic needs a temperature of 32° to 50°F (0° and 10°C). Zones 1 to 7 are ideal.

SOIL
Choose an area that was not recently used for onions. Clear the bed of rocks from the first 6 inches (15 cm) of soil. Amend with compost or manure and a general purpose fertilizer.

PLANTING
Plant garlic cloves 2 inches deep with the pointy side up. Space the cloves 6 inches (15 cm) apart, in rows 12 inches (30 cm) apart. Mulch with 4 inches (10 cm) of straw or chopped leaves to protect the roots from heaving.

GROWING
Fertilize when the leaves emerge. In spring, cut off the flower stalks to encourage bulb growth.

HARVESTING
When the leaves have turned brown, you can harvest the bulbs, usually in July or August.

GINGER ROOT

Zingiber officionale

Ginger root is an aromatic perennial herb that grows in tropical and subtropical climates. Native to Southeast Asia, ginger has been used medicinally for thousands of years. The primary bioactive compound in ginger root is gingerol, which is a powerful anti-inflammatory and antioxidant.

VARIETIES

GINGER The blossoms of this tropical plant grow in clusters of bright yellow, vivid pink, and deep scarlet above glossy, lance-shaped leaves. This elegant reed-like plant grows to about 3 feet (1 m) tall.

PROPAGATION Choose a fresh rhizome that has several well-developed "eyes," or buds. Break the rhizome into sections, each with several buds, or plant the entire piece. Be sure the buds are facing up.

GROWTH Ginger root grows slowly, expanding its rhizomes underground in dense clusters. It needs temperatures between 70° and 80°F (21° and 27°C) to thrive. The soil should be moist but never soggy.

IN THE KITCHEN

Spicy ginger root adds a zesty warmth to Asian and Indian cuisines—from stir-fries to curries. Ginger also adds a refreshing flavor to herbal teas, baked goods, and fruit salads.

SELECTING
Look for ginger roots with smooth, tan skin and a fresh fragrance. The rhizomes should feel heavy for their size. Larger ginger is more mature and spicier, though more fibrous. Avoid dried, wrinkled flesh that's past its prime.

PREPARING
Just before using, peel off the tan skin with a paring knife or a vegetable peeler. Trim away any dried-out ends. Cut ginger into thin slices or julienne strips, or finely grate as needed.

STORING
Store ginger root on the kitchen counter for up to a week. Or wrap ginger tightly in a produce bag, and store it in the crisper drawer of the refrigerator. Ginger should stay fresh for up to three weeks.

PRESERVING
Peel and slice ginger root, sprinkle with sea salt, and let it sit for an hour. Boil rice wine vinegar with sugar, and reduce. Pour the liquid over the ginger slices, soak for three minutes, then strain the liquid. The pickled ginger slices will turn pink.

USES
Ginger root is a versatile food that tastes great with a variety of meats, vegetables, grains, and fruits. Ginger pairs especially well with garlic; in Indian cuisine, a garlic-ginger paste is a basic necessity and the foundation of so many traditional recipes.

Ginger is excellent in beverages as well. Try making a batch of lemon-ginger tea: Simply boil some water, add slices of lemon and ginger; allow to simmer for 10 minutes. Serve hot or cold, and sweeten with honey if desired.

Try this elegant dessert of poached figs in a lemon-ginger sauce. Boil water with sugar, and add julienned ginger root and lemon zest. Boil until thickened. Add figs and simmer for 5 minutes.

IN THE GARDEN

Ginger root has a warm, zesty flavor that is often used as a spice, though it's actually a rhizome vegetable. Ginger is also grown as an ornamental plant for its exotic flowers and graceful leaves.

CLIMATE
Find a protected area with filtered light. Ginger does not tolerate frost, wind, or direct sunlight.

SOIL
Ginger root needs rich, well-draining soil. Amend with compost, and remove rocks from the top 6 inches (15 cm). Add a slow-release fertilizer at planting.

PLANTING
Purchase ginger rhizomes from a nursery or from your grocery store. If the latter, soak the ginger in water overnight to remove any growth retardants. Plant in the soil about 3 inches (8 cm) deep.

GROWING
Water plants regularly, but don't allow the roots to get soggy. Feed with a liquid fertilizer such as seaweed extract every few weeks. Mulch around the plants.

HARVESTING
In about eight to 10 months, when the leaves die back, ginger is ready to harvest. Dig up all or part of the rhizome.

NUTRITIONAL VALUE

Serving size 5 slices (11 g)

Calories 9	Fiber 0.2 g

Vitamin C 1% DV	Iron 1% DV
Vitamin B-6 1% DV	Magnesium 1% DV
Niacin 1% DV	Phosphorus 1% DV
Calcium 1% DV	Potassium 1% DV

HEALTH BENEFITS

powerful antioxidant
benefits cardiovascular system
improves asthma symptoms
aids digestion
boosts immune function
reduce nausea and morning sickness
improves breath

JICAMA

Pachyrhizus erosus

Native to Mexico and Central America, jicama is a round starchy root vegetable with a tan, papery skin. It has a juicy and crunchy flesh with a sweet, nutty flavor that tastes like a cross between potato and savory apple. Jicama is also known as yam bean, Mexican potato, and Mexican turnip.

VARIETIES

JICAMA The two varieties of jicama (pronounced HEE-ka-ma) are *jicama de agua* and *jicama de leche,* which refer to the viscosity of their juices. The tubers of the *leche* form are generally longer and have a thick, milky juice, whereas the tubers of the *aqua* type are rounder with a juice that runs clear. The texture and consistency of the *aqua* type is preferred and is more commonly cultivated.

DESCRIPTION Jicama is a subtropical perennial vine in the legume family and is a towering presence in the garden. With proper support, jicama can reach 16 feet (5 m) in height. Jicama produces green beans similar to lima beans, but these are toxic, as are all other parts of jicama—except for the enormous taproot. Typically, jicama is grown as an annual because harvesting the roots kills the plant.

IN THE GARDEN

The subtropical jicama plant needs nine months of frost-free weather to establish its roots. In climates with only five warm months, jicama can still be grown, but its tubers will be a smaller size.

 CLIMATE
Jicama thrives in hot, humid climates with a moderate amount of rainfall. Plant jicama in zones 7 to 10 in full sunlight.

SOIL
Jicama prefers moist, well-draining, sandy loam with a pH range between 6.5 to 8.0, but it tolerates more acidic soil.

PLANTING
In cooler climates, start seeds indoors eight to 10 weeks before the last frost date, using bottom heat. Space seedlings 12 inches (30 cm) apart. Alternatively, plant tuber sections, which will allow for a quicker harvest.

 GROWING
Water plants when the top inch of soil is dry. Do not overwater jicama. Snip off flowers to encourage better root development.

 HARVESTING
Dig up the plant before the first fall frost or when the vine begins to die. Carefully use a trowel to dig around the tubers.

IN THE KITCHEN

The mild, sweet flavor of fresh jicama pairs well with just a squeeze of lime juice and some chili powder, as it's often served in Mexico, but jicama is also delicious cooked.

 SELECTING
Choose jicama roots that are firm with a smooth skin. Avoid tubers with dry, cracked, or bruised skin. There should be no soft or wet spots. The smaller, younger tubers are generally sweeter.

 PREPARING
Jicama can be eaten raw, but first remove the toxic bark-like skin. To peel, first slice off the top section with a sharp knife, and place that flat on the work surface. Use a paring knife, not a vegetable peeler, to cut away the skin.

 STORING
Store whole jicama in a cool, dry place for up to three weeks; jicama gets moldy when wet. When storing peeled and cut jicama, however, wrap it in a produce bag and refrigerate for up to two weeks.

 PRESERVING
Jicama can remain fresh for up to six months when stored in the freezer. Wrap dry, whole jicama in aluminum foil and freeze. For precut jicama, first dry each section thoroughly, then place it into an airtight container.

 USES
Slice fresh, raw jicama into strips and serve along with creamy dip or a tangy vinaigrette.

Jicama makes a great base for salsa: Finely dice jicama and combine with diced tomato, red onion, jalapeño, cilantro, black beans, and lime juice. Serve with tacos or tortilla chips.

Try this jicama slaw: Combine lime juice, white wine vinegar, olive oil, sugar, red pepper flakes, and salt. In a large bowl, combine julienned jicama, carrots, cucumber, and red bell pepper; shredded cabbage and carrots; and chopped red onion and cilantro. Toss with the dressing and enjoy.

Bake a batch of jicama fries: Toss boiled jicama sticks with olive oil, paprika, onion and garlic powder, and salt. Bake at 425°F (220°C) for 30 minutes.

 NUTRITIONAL VALUE

serving size 100 g (3/4 cup)

Calories 38	Fiber 4.9 g

Vitamin C 27% DV	Vitamin E 3% DV
Iron 6% DV	Magnesium 3% DV
Vitamin B-6 3% DV	Phosphorus 3% DV
Folate 3% DV	Potassium 3% DV

 HEALTH BENEFITS

provides antioxidants
benefits cardiovascular system
aids digestion
boosts gut biome
protects against cancer
helps regulate weight

KALE

Brassica oleracea var. acephala

A close relative to wild cabbage, kale is a green or purple leaf cabbage whose central leaves do not form a head like other cabbages. Originally cultivated in 2000 BC in the Eastern Mediterranean, the superfood kale now consists of dozens of cultivars that have adapted to regions around the world.

VARIETIES

RED WINTER The dark-green leaves of Red Winter have lovely red-purple veins. The dense, fluffy texture is softer than curly types, and it's also a bit sweeter. Red Winter grows to 24 inches (60 cm) in about 50 days.

PORTUGUESE A sweet, tender kale, this heat-tolerant plant boasts large, flat leaves with white stems and veins. Portuguese grows to 36 inches (90 cm) and is ready to harvest in about 60 days.

LACINATO Also known as dinosaur kale and Tuscan kale, Lacinato is an heirloom variety that goes back to the 1700s. The mild, sweet blue-green leaves are especially delicious after the first frost. It reaches 36 inches (90 cm) in 65 days.

IN THE KITCHEN

The blue-green leaves of kale are one of the most nutrient-dense foods in the world—no wonder it's become such a popular food. Add these healthy cabbage leaves to salads, soups, and smoothies.

SELECTING
For salad greens, look for smaller leaves, which are more tender and mild. Larger leaves can be tough and course. Be sure leaves are moist, crisp, and blemish-free. Avoid those with yellow or brown spots.

PREPARING
When using flat-leaf kale, fold each leaf in half lengthwise and cut away the tough central rib (discard the rib or save it for stock), and chop the leaves to the desired size. For curly-leaf kale, pull the leaves from the central stem, and tear into bite-size pieces. Wash well.

STORING
Wrap dry, unwashed kale leaves in paper towels and store them in a produce bag. Refrigerate for up to a week.

PRESERVING
To freeze kale, first cut away the stems, then blanch the leaves in boiling water for two minutes, plunge into ice water, and dry well. Store in airtight containers for up to a year.

USES
Toss young, tender kale leaves into any salad. The strong, earthy taste of kale pairs well with savory umami salad dressings such as creamy garlic, lime-chili, or peanut-sesame.

Caldo verde soup is a classic Portuguese comfort food. Try this rustic recipe: In a large soup pot, sauté chopped onion in olive oil for two minutes. Add thinly sliced potatoes and water; over and simmer for 20 minutes. In a skillet, cook thinly sliced chorizo sausage; drain. In the soup pot, mash tender potatoes and add sausage and thinly sliced kale. Simmer for five minutes. Serve hot.

Kale smoothies are packed with nutrients. Try this refreshing recipe: In a blender, combine chopped kale, unsweetened milk, plain yogurt, banana, pineapple, creamy peanut butter, and honey. Blend to desired consistency.

For a savory side dish, sauté minced onion and garlic in olive oil in a large pot. Add chopped kale, red pepper flakes, and salt. Cook for five minutes.

NUTRITIONAL VALUE

serving size 100 cup (1 1/2 cups)

Calories 28	Fiber 2 g

Vitamin K 335% DV	Riboflavin 9% DV
Vitamin C 53% DV	Iron 10% DV
Vitamin A 23% DV	Vitamin B-6 7% DV
Calcium 14% DV	Potassium 7% DV

HEALTH BENEFITS

powerful antioxidants
promotes healthy gut biome
benefits cardiovascular system
protects against cancer
boosts immune function
supports healthy vision
nourishes skin
helps dissolve kidney stones and gallstones

IN THE GARDEN

Hardy, cool-weather kale benefits from a light frost before harvesting to sweeten its tender leaves. Kale will continue to grow until the temperatures drop to about 20°F (–7°C).

CLIMATE
This leafy green grows well in either full sun or part shade. Plant it anytime in zones 3 to 10.

SOIL
Kale prefers well-draining, loamy soil with a neutral to sightly acidic pH between 5.5 and 6.8. Amend the soil with compost and 10-10-10 fertilizer at planting.

PLANTING
Sow seeds directly in early spring at a depth of ¼ inch (1 cm), and 3 inches (8 cm) apart. Space rows 18 inches (46 cm) apart. Thin seedlings 12 inches (30 cm) apart.

GROWING
Keep plants evenly moist but do not overwater. Mulch to retain moisture. Apply a general purpose fertilizer after you begin harvesting the first leaves to encourage new growth.

HARVESTING
Pick leaves as needed, beginning with the outer ones. Harvest the whole plant after a frost has sweetened the leaves.

KOHLRABI

Brassica oleracea var. gongylodes

The biennial kohlrabi plant is a type of cabbage in the mustard family (Brassicaceae) that is harvested for its bulbous stem. This unusual vegetable tastes a bit like a turnip, but it's sweeter and a bit milder. Kohlrabi cultivars come in a range in colors—from pure white to pale green and deep purple.

VARIETIES

KOLIBRI A gorgeous purple variety, Kolibri boasts uniform 3-inch (8 cm) bulbs with gleaming amethyst skin and white, almost fiber-less flesh. This succulent hybrid is ready to harvest in about 50 days.

SWEET VIENNA This super-early variety can be planted outdoors before the last frost. The 3-inch (8 cm) bulbs have a mild, sweet flavor and a crisp, juicy texture. It reaches 15 inches (38 cm) in 45 days.

KOSSAK An enormous kohlrabi, Kossak keeps its sweet flavor even as it grows to a whopping 8 inches (20 cm) across. Harvest before it starts to elongate for the best flavor. Kossak matures in 80 days.

EARLY WHITE VIENNA This early variety has smooth, pale-green skin and a mild white flesh that tastes like sweet turnips. The bulbs are best at 3 inches (8 cm) wide, in about 55 days.

IN THE KITCHEN

Kohlrabi is a popular vegetable in Indian cuisine, and it pairs well with traditional Indian spices such as ginger, turmeric, and coriander. The leaves are also edible and taste great in salads.

 SELECTING
Look for firm, smaller bulbs no more than 3 inches (8 cm) across that feel heavy for their size. These are generally the most tender. Choose bulbs with intact leaves that are crisp and bright green.

 PREPARING
Remove the leaves and stalks. Scrub the bulb, rinse, and dry. Peel the tough outermost layer with a vegetable peeler. Cut the bulb in half, from the top down, and then into quarters. Remove the core, and slice or chop as needed.

 STORING
After the stalks and leaves have been removed, wrap the clean bulb loosely a damp kitchen towel. Place it in a produce bag, and refrigerate for up to two weeks. Use the leaves right away or refrigerate for up to two days. Precut kohlrabi will keep for just a few days.

 PRESERVING
To freeze kohlrabi, cut it into chunks or slices. Blanch in boiling water for three minutes, plunge into ice water, and dry. Place in an airtight container and freeze for up to 10 months.

 USES
This Indian curry brings out the sweet flavor of kohlrabi: Toss cubed kohlrabi with olive oil, minced garlic, and salt. Arrange in a single layer on a baking sheet. Bake at 450°F (230°C) for 20 minutes. In a saucepan, sauté chopped onion, and mustard and cumin seeds. Add diced tomato, kohlrabi, lemon juice, curry powder, chili powder, and salt. Add water for consistency, and cook for 10 minutes. Serve warm over basmati rice.

Here is a sweet and simple kohlrabi soup: Sauté chopped onion, celery, and carrots in butter for 15 minutes. Add sliced kohlrabi, chicken stock, thyme, bay leaf, salt, and white pepper; simmer until kohlrabi is tender. Remove the bay leaf, and purée. Sprinkle with chopped kohlrabi greens.

IN THE GARDEN

The peculiar-looking kohlrabi is not the most popular vegetable, but it's delicious, easy to grow, and quick to mature. In German, the aptly named *kohlrabi* means "cabbage turnip."

 CLIMATE
Kohlrabi grows well in zones 6 to 11 in full sunlight. As a cool-weather vegetable, kohlrabi prefers temperatures between 40° and 75°F (4° and 24°C).

 **SOIL**
Plant kohlrabi in rich, well-draining soil that is not too loose. The ideal pH range is 5.5 to 6.8, but it tolerates more alkaline soil up to 7.5.

PLANTING
Sow seeds outdoors three weeks before the last frost, or in midsummer. Sow ½ inch (13 mm) deep, and 1 inch (2.5 cm) apart. Space rows 18 inches (46 cm) apart. Thin seedlings to every 4 inches (10 cm).

 GROWING
Keep kohlrabi evenly moist. It's a heavy feeder: pply a 10-10-10 fertilizer at planting and every few weeks.

 HARVESTING
For the sweetest flavor and best texture, harvest most varieties of kohlrabi before they reach 3 inches (8 cm) across.

NUTRITIONAL VALUE

Serving size 100 g (2/3 cup)

Calories 29	Fiber 1.1 g

Vitamin C 72% DV	Magnesium 5% DV
Vitamin B-6 12% DV	Iron 4% DV
Potassium 7% DV	Thiamin 3% DV
Phosphorus 6% DV	Calcium 3% DV

HEALTH BENEFITS

aids digestion
provides antioxidants
regulates blood pressure
benefits cardiovascular system
strengthens bones
boosts immune function
supports healthy vision

LEEKS

Allium ampeloprasum

The leek is a hardy perennial of the onion family and has been cultivated for millennia for the mild-flavored white stalk. Leeks fall into two main types: The more common is the summer leek, which is harvested later in summer; winter leeks grow slowly all winter long and emerge in springtime.

VARIETIES

LANCELOT The long, white shafts of this heavy-yielding leek grow to 14 inches (36 cm). Lancelot's uniform shafts have a fine, delicate flavor. This variety is very disease resistant and is ready in 80 days. .

BLUE SOLAISE This blue-green French heirloom is very hardy and can overwinter even in cooler climates. The tall stalks turn bluer in cool weather. This mild and sweet leek matures in 105 days.

HANNIBAL The mild-flavored leek is a stout, reliable fall variety. The dark-green leaves cascade from long, thick white stalks. A heavy producer, Hannibal matures in 105 days, but can be harvested at baby size.

GIANT MUSSELBURGH This smooth, mild Scottish heirloom has been gracing Scottish soups since the 1830s. Its thick, white stalks reach up to 3 inches (8 cm) across and are ready to harvest in 100 days.

IN THE KITCHEN

Leeks have a mild, onion-like taste. The edible portions of the leek are the white base (above the roots and stem base), the light green parts, and the lower parts the dark green leaves.

SELECTING
Choose leeks that have the most white and pale green—these are the edible portion of the leek. Stalks should be firm and crisp. Avoid leeks with withered of yellow tops. Thinner leeks are generally more tender.

PREPARING
To clean these notoriously dirty plants, first trim off the stem. Cut the leeks about 1½ inches (4 cm) above the white section. Discard the tough, dark-green tops. Cut the white section in half lengthwise, and separate all the leaves. Soak, then rinse.

STORING
Wrap unwashed leeks in a produce bag in the vegetable drawer of your refrigerator for up to two weeks. Cooked leeks should be eaten within one or two days.

PRESERVING
Leeks do not freeze well. Instead, dry them: Place sliced leeks on a baking sheet, and bake at 145°F (63°C) until crisp.

USES
Leeks are delicious braised. Try this recipe for braised leeks with Parmesan: Heat olive oil in a cast-iron skillet, add clean quartered leeks, and sauté for three minutes. Add dry white wine, and cook for 20 to 25 minutes. Sprinkle with Parmesan, and broil until the cheese melts.

Leek and potato soup is a classic: In a large pot, sauté chopped onion, celery, and leeks until soft. Add minced garlic and cook, then add broth, cubed red potatoes, thyme, parsley, salt, and pepper. Cover and simmer for 20 minutes, or until the potatoes are tender. Cool slightly, then purée in a blender until smooth. Add broth for desired consistency. Sprinkle with chopped cooked maple-glazed bacon and parsley.

Leek and bacon quiche: Sauté sliced leeks with thyme, salt, and white pepper. Remove from heat, and add chopped cooked bacon, eggs, cream, and Gruyère cheese. Pour into prebaked pastry shells, and bake at 375°F (190°C) for 30 minutes.

NUTRITIONAL VALUE
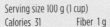

Serving size 100 g (1 cup)

Calories 31	Fiber 1 g

Vitamin K 25% DV	Vitamin A 5% DV
Iron 11% DV	Vitamin E 3% DV
Vitamin B-6 9% DV	Calcium 3% DV
Vitamin C 6% DV	Magnesium 3% DV

HEALTH BENEFITS

reduces inflammation
benefits cardiovascular system
protects against cancer
aids digestion
regulates blood sugar
boosts brain function

IN THE GARDEN

Leeks are trouble-free in the garden and very cold hardy. Try growing several varieties—early summer types and slow-growing winter types—for a year-round supply of leeks.

CLIMATE
Leeks are cool-season vegetables with a long growing season. Select either a summer or winter type of leek for your particular climate.

SOIL
Plant leeks in well-draining, fertile, slightly acidic soil. The ideal pH range from 6.0 to 6.8, although leeks will tolerate a slightly more alkaline soil.

 PLANTING
Leeks are most often transplanted in the garden as seedlings. To maximize the white part of the leek, dig a 6-inch (15 cm) furrow, and plant the seedlings at the bottom, fairly close together. As they grow, gradually fill in the furrow.

GROWING
Water plants regularly. Fertilize leeks only once midseason.

HARVESTING
Dig up leeks as soon as they reach the desired size. Gently lever them out with a fork.

LETTUCE (LEAF)

Lactuca sativa

Loose leaf lettuce is one of the easiest, most popular types of salad greens to grow. Loose leaf lettuce is a fast-growing annual and forms very loose heads in shades of burgundy red or brilliant green. The tops of the ruffled leaves are tender and mild-flavored, and the stems have a fresh, crispy bite.

VARIETIES

MERLOT The darkest of all red-leaf lettuce varieties, Merlot is packed with antioxidants. The crisp, wavy-edged leaves are excellent for cut-and-come-again harvest. Merlot is ready to enjoy in 55 days.

BLACK SEEDED SIMPSON Developed in the 1870s, this sweet and tender heirloom is still very popular. The frilly, light-green leaves can be harvested early. Mature leaves are ready in 60 days.

RED SALAD BOWL This maroon-red lettuce is heat tolerant and slow to bolt. It also does not turn bitter as it matures. The tender baby leaves are especially sweet and delicious at 28 days.

SALAD BOWL This heirloom lettuce has green large-lobed leaves that are crisp and tender. The award-winning Salad Bowl is heat tolerant and slow to bolt. It reaches 15 inches (38 cm) in about 45 days.

IN THE KITCHEN

Loose leaf lettuce goes well in any type of salad. The mild taste and crisp texture of loose leaf are the perfect backdrop for citrus flavors, pungent cheeses, and crunchy roasted nuts.

 SELECTING
Choose fresh, crisp bunches with moist, firm green stems. Avoid bunches with damaged, dried-out, or yellowing leaves. Whenever possible, purchase lettuce at a farmer's market, especially if you can find bunches with the roots still intact.

 PREPARING
Rinse leaves in cold water to remove dirt trapped between curls. Remove the tough stems. Tear the leaves into bite-size pieces—chopping lettuce with a knife bruises the fragile leaves.

 STORING
Wrap the lettuce in a paper towel, and store it in a produce bag in the refrigerator for up to five days. Avoid the coldest part of the refrigerator, because freezing temperatures cause lettuce to wilt.

PRESERVING
Lettuce does not freeze well. The cell walls break down when frozen, causing the leaves to become mushy. To keep lettuce crisp, it should be stored above freezing temperatures.

 USES
The mellow taste of loose leaf lettuce pairs well with bright citrus and creamy cheeses. Try this refreshing mandarin and red leaf lettuce salad: In a small bowl, whisk together olive oil, cider vinegar, Dijon mustard, honey, salt, and pepper; add minced red onion. In a salad bowl, combine red leaf lettuce, mandarin pieces, and chopped red and yellow bell peppers. Crumble feta cheese over the salad, and toss with vinaigrette.

Try this pear, walnut, and goat cheese salad: Lightly roast walnuts, and chop into halves. Whisk together olive oil, lemon juice, Dijon mustard, salt, and pepper. In a salad bowl, combine lettuce and pear slices. Toss the salad with the dressing, and crumble goat cheese and nuts on top.

IN THE GARDEN

Grow a fresh supply or loose leaf lettuce from spring to fall. Lettuce is easy to plant in strategic nooks in your garden: Plant with radishes and carrots or under the shade of tomatoes.

 CLIMATE
Lettuce prefers cool weather and tends to bolt in the heat of summer. Plant in full sunlight in cool weather and provide shade as the weather warms up.

SOIL
Prepare a well-draining fertile bed with loose soil. The optimal pH for loose leaf lettuce is between 5.8 and 6.5 .

PLANTING
Start seeds indoors six weeks before the last frost date, or outdoors when the soil is workable. Sow seeds ¼ inch (1 cm) deep. Space rows 12 inches (30 cm) apart.

GROWING
Keep the soil moist; mulch to preserve moisture and discourage weeds. Sprinkle the leaves on hot days to cool the leaves. Apply a nitrogen-rich fertilizer at planting and every few weeks.

 **HARVESTING**
Pick tender leaves every two or three days in the mornings. Harvest mature leaves promptly.

NUTRITIONAL VALUE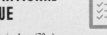

serving size 1cup (30 g)

Calories 4	Fiber 0.3 g

Vitamin K 39% DV	Thiamin 2% DV
Vitamin A 12% DV	Riboflavin 2% DV
Folate 3% DV	Vitamin C 1% DV
Iron 3% DV	Niacin 1% DV

HEALTH BENEFITS

reduces inflammation
boosts nerve function
lowers cholesterol
promotes restful sleep
provides antioxidants
protects against cancer
boosts heart health

LETTUCE (HEAD)

Lactuca sativa

You have three great choices in head lettuce, each with its own unique benefits: Iceberg lettuce is typically defined by its mild flavor and crisp texture; Butterhead lettuce (eg Boston and Bibb lettuce) form heads, but they are more loose than iceberg; Romaine can also be considered a head lettuce, but its head is long and oval—it is rich in vitamins C, K and A..

VARIETIES

ICEBERG Also known as crisphead lettuce, Iceberg has a very juicy crunch. The tight, glossy-green head resembles cabbage, but the flavor of Iceberg is very mild. This lettuce is ready to harvest in 85 days.

BUTTERHEAD The bright-green leaves of this variety have a succulent, buttery flavor and a delicate texture. Also called Boston lettuce, the widely adaptable Butterhead matures in about 52 days.

MUIR The heads of this Batavian lettuce are light green and very flavorful. Muir is heat tolerant and very slow to bolt. The heads form early and can be harvested as minis before they mature at 50 days.

DEER TONGUE A compact heirloom Bibb variety, Deer Tongue has unique olive-green leaves that grow in a pinwheel shape. Harvest baby-size leaves at 28 days, and mature ones at 50 days.

IN THE KITCHEN

Head-type lettuces have a delicate flavor and are excellent in fresh salads with other vegetables. Combine them with sharper lettuce varieties such as radicchio or endive to balance out the flavors.

SELECTING

Choose fresh, crisp bunches with moist, firm green stems. Avoid bunches with damaged, dried-out, or yellowing leaves. Whenever possible, purchase lettuce at a farmer's market, especially if you can find bunches with the roots still intact.

PREPARING

Rinse individual leaves in cold water to remove trapped dirt. Remove the tough stems. Tear the leaves into bite-size pieces—chopping lettuce with a knife bruises the fragile leaves.

STORING

Wrap the whole head of lettuce in a paper towel, and store it in a produce bag in the refrigerator for up to seven days. Avoid storing lettuce in the coldest part of the refrigerator.

PRESERVING

Lettuce does not freeze well. The cell walls break down when frozen, causing the leaves to lose their crispness and wilt.

USES

Try making this classic wedge salad with iceberg lettuce and a blue cheese dressing: For the dressing, combine sour cream, minced garlic, crumbled blue cheese, lemon juice, salt, and pepper in a small bowl. Cut iceberg lettuce into wedges; arrange on individual plates, and drizzles with dressing and chopped bacon.

Pair the buttery flavor of Bibb lettuce with rich avocado and a tangy lime vinaigrette: Slice avocado into thin wedges. In a small bowl, whisk together olive oil, lime juice, mustard, salt, sugar, and white pepper. In a salad bowl, arrange the lettuce, avocado, sliced scallions, and chopped cilantro. Toss with dressing.

Use the cup-like leaves of butterhead lettuce for Asian chicken wraps: Sauté minced onion and garlic, and add diced chicken; cook until chicken is no longer pink. Stir in tamari sauce and teriyaki sauce, and season with pepper. Spoon onto lettuce leaves, sprinkle with sesame seeds, and serve warm.

IN THE GARDEN

Head-type lettuce takes a bit longer to mature than loose leaf varieties. Inter-plant the two types of lettuce for a continuous harvest of salad greens, but give head lettuce room to grow.

CLIMATE

Lettuce prefers cool weather and tends to bolt in the heat of summer. Plant in full sunlight in cool weather and provide shade as the weather warms up.

SOIL

Prepare a well-draining fertile bed with loose soil. The optimal pH for loose leaf lettuce is between 5.8 and 6.5 .

PLANTING

Start seeds indoors six weeks before the last frost date, or outdoors when the soil is workable. Sow seeds ¼ inch (1 cm) deep. Space rows 12 inches (30 cm) apart.

GROWING

Keep the soil moist; mulch to preserve moisture. Sprinkle the leaves on hot days to cool the leaves. Apply a nitrogen-rich fertilizer at planting and every few weeks.

HARVESTING

Pick tender leaves every two or three days in the mornings. Harvest mature leaves promptly.

MUSHROOM

Agaricus bisporus

Although the mushroom is commonly classified as a vegetable, it is of course neither a vegetable nor a plant but rather the savory fruit of a fungus. The ground-hugging mushroom is also a superfood that's loaded with nutrients, and it's the only food in the produce aisle that contains vitamin D.

VARIETIES

Mushrooms are in a food kingdom all to themselves. At least 10,000 species of mushrooms grow worldwide—and many more are likely still undiscovered—but only a small fraction of them are edible. The mushrooms we see in the grocery store are the umbrella-shaped fungi with the basic structure of the standard "button" mushroom, consisting of a stem, a cap, and gills on the underside. Mushrooms are most often cultivated but adept foragers can gather them in the wild. Only twenty species are commercially cultivated.

WHITE BUTTON Also known as the common or table mushroom, this is the most cultivated mushroom in the world. A favorite among chefs, it's versatile and has a mild flavor, which intensifies with cooking.

PORTOBELLO The large, meaty portobello is really an oversize Cremini. Portobello's cap is flat and buff, and the fibrous white stem is dense and chewy. When cooked, it acquires a smoky, earthy umami flavor.

CREMINI The brown flesh and stem of Cremini are dense and meaty. It's similar to White Button, but Cremini is more mature and has a richer, nuttier flavor. It's the standard mushroom in Italy and France.

PINK OYSTER This blushing beauty grows swiftly in vibrant pink bouquets, then bleaches to white as it matures. The tropical Pink Oyster is rather delicate, though, and has a relatively short shelf-life.

ENOKI The elegant, snow-white Enoki grows on tall, slender stems in tightly packed clusters. It can reach up to 4 inches (10 cm) when mature. Enoki has a mild, fruity flavor and a slight crunch.

CHANTERELLE The dense, wavy caps of Chanterelle are a gorgeous golden-orange. Its chewy, white meat has a peachy scent and a peppery, earthy flavor. Chanterelle can reach up to 2 pounds (0.9 kg).

NUTRITIONAL VALUE

Serving size 100 g (1 cup)
Calories 22   Protein 3 g   Fiber 1 g

Selenium 45% DV	Phosphorus 12% DV
Riboflavin 31% DV	Vitamin B-6 8% DV
Niacin 24% DV	Thiamin 7% DV
Vitamin K 17% DV	Potassium 7% DV

HEALTH BENEFITS

Provides antioxidants
Benefits heart health
Lowers cholesterol
Regulates blood sugar
Strengthens bones
Lowers blood pressure

WHITE OYSTER This carnivorous, flat-topped mushroom has a smooth, velvety texture and a delicate flavor. The broad white or tan caps span up to 10 inches (25 cm) across in shelf-like arrangements.

SHITAKE A rich, meaty mushroom, Shitake has a tawny cap and a white stem. Cooking brings out a smoky flavor. Dating back 100 million years, Shitake is the second most cultivated mushroom in the world.

PORCINI Prized in many cuisines for its rich, nutty flavor, Porcini is a chef's delight. The chestnut-colored mushroom imparts an earthy umami flavor to soups, risottos, and pasta sauces.

MOREL The unique honeycomb cap of the earthy-tasting Morel is attached to a hollow white stem. Morel is strictly a foraging mushroom; its fragile growing conditions cannot be replicated.

TRUFFLE The darling of all mushrooms, the Truffle has a musky scent and a savory, earthy flavor. This finicky delicacy grows underground and is especially difficult to harvest—thus its hefty price tag.

PADDY STRAW Worldwide, straw mushrooms rank third in consumption. They are cultivated throughout East and Southeast Asia and used extensively in Asian cuisines.

IN THE KITCHEN

The savory umami flavor and meaty texture of mushrooms add substance to any meal. Mushrooms are delicious either sautéed on the stove top, roasted in the oven, or grilled outdoors. They pair especially well with onions, garlic, thyme, and soy sauce.

SELECTING

Look for the largest, firmest mushrooms that are nice and plump. They should be dry but not dried out; avoid mushrooms that look wet or slimy. The caps should be smooth and blemish-free without any dark soft spots.

Examine the gills under the cap: Mushrooms with exposed gills have a stronger flavor, whereas those with a closed veil are generally milder.

PREPARING

Lightly brush away dirt from mushrooms—you don't have to wash them. If your mushrooms are very dirty, however, rinse them quickly under cold water to gently remove debris. Dry them right away so that they don't absorb too much water, which will then be released during cooking.

Trim away only dried-out ends of the stems. The stems of most mushrooms are edible, except for Shitake, which has a tough woody stem that should be removed. You can, however, add it to flavor soups.

STORING

Keep mushrooms in their original packaging and store them in the refrigerator for up to a week, though some varieties are more prone to spoilage. If you purchased mushrooms loose, place them in a paper bag, and store them in the main part of your refrigerator.

PRESERVING

Not all types of mushrooms freeze well. Try flash-freezing mushrooms individually first, then store them together in an airtight container for up to six months. Cooked mushrooms will keep in the freezer for up to a month.

Mushrooms such as Porcini and Shitake can be dried for long-term storage. First, brush away any dirt, and thoroughly dry the mushrooms. Next, slice them into ⅛-inch (3 cm) pieces; this will reduce the amount of drying time in the oven. Place the mushrooms slices in a single layer on a baking sheet, and dry them at 150°F (65°C) for one hour. Store them in an airtight container.

USES

Mushrooms are highly versatile. Milder varieties such as White Button are delicious raw: Just slice them and add to salads. Meatier types like Portobello are excellent for grilling or stuffing.

One of the simplest method to cook mushrooms is to sauté them in butter with garlic and onions, and season them with thyme, salt, and pepper.

Try this marinated mushroom recipe: Sauté salted mushrooms in olive oil, until they release about half their liquid; cool. Combine olive oil, red wine vinegar, garlic, basil, thyme, oregano, salt, and pepper; toss with mushrooms. Sprinkle with parsley.

IN THE GARDEN

Growing mushrooms is not quite the same as tending to a vegetable garden. To cultivate mushrooms, first choose a simple variety of mushroom to grow and collect or purchase some spores. Next you can either purchase a complete growing kit or assemble one yourself.

CLIMATE
Choose an area that is cool, dark, and free from pests or pets that might disturb the mushrooms. Basements are excellent locations to start cultivating mushrooms.

SOIL
Prepare a bed of fertile soil about 2 inches (5 cm) deep in a flat pan or other container. Determine the appropriate type of substrate for your mushroom variety; it could be either straw, sawdust, or wood chips. Sterilize the substrate by soaking in boiled water or heating in a pressure cooker to kill off bacteria. Apply the substrate over the soil.

PLANTING
Purchase spores from a dealer or collect your own spores from store-bought mushrooms. To collect your own, first remove the stem of a mushroom, and place the cap gill-side down on a sheet of colored paper (so you can see the spores). Cover the cap with a mug to protect the mushroom from contaminants. In about 24 hours, remove the mug and mushroom cap; you'll see a "spore print" on the paper made of millions of spores.

GROWING
Inoculate or implant the mushroom spores over the substrate. This is the mycelium, which will spread across the substrate, providing a surface for its "fruits," or mushrooms, to grow. Adjust the growing conditions, such as temperature and humidity, for your particular mushroom species. Use a humidity tent if needed.

In about three weeks, look for "pinning" on the surface, which indicates that the spores are sprouting.

HARVESTING
To harvest the mushrooms, simply pull or twist them away from the substrate. Begin harvesting smaller mushrooms in as little as four weeks. Reapply spores for new growth.

FUN FACT
The largest living organism in the world is a honey fungus that's 2.4 miles (3.8 km) wide and resides in the Blue Mountains of Oregon.

MUSTARD GREENS

Brassica juncea

Perhaps the sharpest-tasting of all the bitter greens, mustard has a strong, peppery flavor reminiscent of horseradish—even after cooking. Originally from the Himalayas, the cruciferous mustard plant has been cultivated for thousands of years. It's also known as Chinese mustard and Indian mustard.

VARIETIES

SCARLET FRILLS A colorful additions to fresh salads, Scarlet Frills has ruffled burgundy leaves with a mildly spicy flavor. Harvest baby leaves in about 20 days, and full-size leaves in 40 days.

GREEN WAVE These beautiful bright-green leaves add spice to fresh salads, but its peppery flavor mellows with cooking. Tender baby leaves are ready in 20 days, and mature leaves in 45 days.

GOLDEN FRILLS The lacy, light-green leaves have a sharp, peppery bite when raw. It is heat resistant and slow to bolt. Start harvesting baby leaves in 20 days, and full-size leaves in 40 days.

JAPANES GIANT RED MUSTARD Native to China, but commonly known as Japanese Giant Red Mustard, this is a cool weather variety that has a pungent peppery mustard taste.

IN THE KITCHEN

A staple food in the Southern cuisine of the United States, mustard greens are prepared much like collards. Add them fresh to spice up a salad, or sauté them for a mellower flavor.

SELECTING
Choose plump, crisp bunches of bright-green leaves with no yellowing or browning of the leaf tips. Look for a unblemished core with few or no brown spots. Smaller leaves are the most tender.

PREPARING
Rinse mustard greens under cold water to remove trapped dirt. Pat the greens dry if using them in a salad, but leave them wet if cooking—the excess moisture will help them wilt without browning. Remove the tough, bitter central stem by folding each leaf in half lengthwise and then trimming away the vein.

STORING
Wrap unwashed mustard greens in a paper towel, and place them loosely in a produce bag. Store them in the crisper drawer of the refrigerator for up to a week.

PRESERVING
To freeze the leaves, blanch them for three minutes in boiling water, plunge them into ice water, and dry. Store them in an airtight container for up to six months.

USES
Toss a few fresh mustard greens into any green salad to brighten its flavor. Citrus vinaigrettes pair well with these bitter greens, balancing out their sharpness.

For a simple sauté, heat olive oil over medium heat, and sauté chopped onion, minced garlic, red pepper flakes, and salt. Add mustard greens and chicken stock. Cook for about five minutes, or until the greens are tender.

Try this Asian sauté: Roast sesame seeds in a dry hot skillet or wok; remove from heat and set aside. Heat sesame oil, and cook mustard greens until wilted. Add minced garlic, soy sauce, rice wine vinegar, sake, and sugar. Cover and simmer for 10 to 15 minutes. Sprinkle with sesame seeds. Serve warm.

IN THE GARDEN

Mustard greens are not flowering plants so they tolerate shade a bit better than other vegetables. Provide mustard with a rich, fertile soil and you'll be rewarded with the most tender young greens.

 CLIMATE
Mustard greens can grow in either full sunlight or partial shade in most growing zones.

SOIL
Prepare a fertile bed with well-draining soil. Amend with several inches of compost. The optimal pH range is between 6.5 and 6.8.

PLANTING
Start seeds indoors about four weeks before the last frost date, and every two weeks. Sow at a depth of ½ inch (13 mm).

Space seedlings every 3 inches (8 cm), and rows every 12 inches (30 cm).

GROWING
Keep mustard plants evenly moist. Mulch to protect the delicate roots. Feed with a general purpose fertilizer every two weeks.

HARVESTING
Cut young 6-inch (15 cm) leaves for baby-size leaves, removing the outer leaves first. Harvest full-size plants promptly—mature leaves quickly become tough and woody.

NUTRITIONAL VALUE

Serving size 100 g (3/4 cup)
Calories 26   Protein 2.6 g   Fiber 2 g

Vitamin K 590% DV   Vitamin E 12% DV
Vitamin A 69% DV   Iron 9% DV
Vitamin C 33% DV   Vitamin B-6 8% DV
Calcium 19% DV   Phosphorus 6% DV

HEALTH BENEFITS

Provides antioxidants
Lowers cholesterol
Aids digestion
Benefits cardiovascular system
Boosts immune function
Strengthens bones
Supports healthy vision

OKRA

Abelmoschus esculentus

This hairy, herbaceous flowering plant belongs to the mallow family and is grown for its mucilaginous fruit pods. Known as Lady's Fingers, okra likely originated in Western Africa, and is now cultivated in tropical regions around the world. Okra is rich in dietary fiber, vitamin C, and vitamin K.

VARIETIES

CLEMSON SPINELESS
A longtime favorite, this vigorous variety grows to 4 feet (1.2 m) tall. Clemson yields an abundance of succulent, spineless 3-inch (8 cm) pods that mature in about 56 days.

RED BURGUNDY
A tall and striking plant in the vegetable garden. Its slender, wine-red pods grow to 7 inches (18 cm) long. This award-winning plant grows to 5 feet (1.5 m) tall. The fruits mature in about 55 days.

GO BIG This majestic okra (right) grows up to 7 feet (2.1 m) tall and boasts enormous 7-inch (18 cm) pods in lush emerald green. The large yellow blossoms of this okra make it a welcome sight as an ornamental plant as well.

SILVER QUEEN OKRA
This okra can grow to a height of 6'. Well branched plants carry unique white/green pods. Very productive if picked young. Plant in fertile soil with compost or manure; keep well watered.

IN THE KITCHEN

This slender vegetable is the essential ingredient in gumbo—a hearty Louisiana soup. Okra is also a favorite vegetable in African, Asian, Indian, and Caribbean cuisines.

SELECTING
Try to select individual pods rather than prepackaged okra. Choose firm, bright-green pods. Avoid okra that looks dull or is bruised or blemished. If you're cooking okra whole, choose longer pods; for stir-fries, opt for the shorter pods, which will cook faster.

PREPARING
Rinse the fruit pods to remove dirt and the fuzzy hairs on the surface. To cook whole okra, carefully trim the ends without piercing the seed pod; when cut, the pod oozes a mucilaginous goo. For cooking stews and soups, slice the pod, retaining the goo to use as a thickening agent.

STORING
Place fresh okra in a paper bag, and store in the refrigerator for up to three days. Or wrap it in a paper towel, and store in a mesh bag in the refrigerator.

PRESERVING
Flash-freeze okra pods individually, then store them together in an airtight container.

USES
The most basic method for cooking okra is boiling or steaming. Okra is also delicious sautéed, grilled, or roasted.

Combine with any of the following to complement cooked okra: a garlic, lemon, and butter sauce; herbs such as sweet basil and parsley; a vegetable medley of tomatoes, corn, and eggplant; a tangy vinaigrette; or a creamy hollandaise sauce.

Try this easy okra sauté: In a skillet, sauté chopped red onion in olive oil. Add halved cherry tomatoes, corn kernels, and chopped okra. Cover, and cook for 12 minutes. Season with oregano, salt, and pepper.

Here's a rich gumbo recipe: In a soup pot, whisk olive oil and flour; cook until thick. Add broth, chopped onions, celery, green pepper, and garlic; cook for three minutes. Add chopped tomatoes, okra, bay leaf, basil, salt, and pepper; simmer for one hour. Add cooked chicken pieces and sausage slices; heat through. Garnish with chives and parsley.

NUTRITIONAL VALUE

Serving size 100 (2/3 cup)
Calories 22   Protein 1.9 g   Fiber 2.5 g

Vitamin K 40% DV	Thiamin 11% DV
Vitamin C 22% DV	Magnesium 9% DV
Vitamin B-6 14% DV	Calcium 8% DV
Folate 12% DV	Niacin 6% DV

HEALTH BENEFITS

Provides antioxidant
Benefits cardiovascular system
Protects against cancer
Regulates blood sugar
Aids digestion
Boosts immune function

IN THE GARDEN

This succulent warm-weather vegetable is a towering beauty with dazzling yellow blossoms. Plant okra where it won't shade other vegetables but where you can appreciate its flowers.

CLIMATE
Okra prefers warm tropical climates, but it can grow well from zones 6 to 11. Okra needs full sunlight.

SOIL
Okra is an adaptable plant, but is grows best in well-draining soil rich in organic matter. Amend poor or very alkaline soil before planting. The optimal soil pH is between 5.8 and 7.0

PLANTING
Soak okra seeds overnight before planting. Sow seeds ½ inch (13 mm) deep, and 24 inches (60 cm) apart. Space rows 18 inches (46 cm) apart.

GROWING
Water okra regularly, and mulch around the plants. Feed with a general-purpose fertilizer every few weeks.

HARVESTING
In about two months, begin harvesting okra pods at 3 inches (8 cm) long. Pull off the lower leaves from the plant after the first harvest to encourage new growth.

ONION

Allium cepa

The onion is a herbaceous perennial of the amaryllis family (Amaryllidaceae). Since ancient times, the onion has been cultivated for its sharp-flavored bulb—a tightly formed bundle or concentric leaf layers. Native to Southeast Asia, onions have adapted in temperate regions throughout the world.

VARIETIES

Ancient Egyptians viewed the onion as a symbol of the universe. The name *onion* likely derives from the Latin word *unus*, meaning "one." Onions have been regarded not only as a culinary necessity in so many cuisines but also as a medicinal plant with curative powers. Today, onions are known to be nutritious vegetables loaded with vitamins, minerals, and antioxidants. Grouping onions according to taste is one way to select onions. There are basically two options: the strong-flavored kinds and the milder (and usually bigger) ones.

SOUTHPORT RED GLOBE This heirloom onion has a crisp, mildly pungent interior with pink-tinged rings. Southport is a long-day onion that's easy to grow in containers, and is ready to harvest in 120 days.

PURPLETTE This lovely pearl onion is an early mini with a glossy burgundy skin. A short-day variety, Purplette can be harvested early as a bunching green onion or at 60 days as a mature mini.

TOKYO LONG WHITE
Tokyo Long White is a favorite Japanese bunching variety with a mild, sweet flavor. Long, juicy slim stalks grow 14""-16"" tall. Moderate bolting resistance. Delicious in soups, stir-fries, and stews.

SHALLOT The reddish-brown shallot has a sharp, crisp bite when raw, but its flavor mellows and sweetens with cooking, and has a hint of garlic. From the outside, a shallot looks a bit like a misshapen red onion, but once you peel it, you will see that instead of rings, it divides into cloves as garlic does. Small bulbs will have two to three individual cloves and large shallots can have up to six cloves. Each clove is flat on one side and rounded on the other.

NUTRITIONAL VALUE

Serving size 100 g (1 cup)
Calories 40   Fiber 2.7 g

Vitamin C 10% DV   Phosphorus 4% DV
Vitamin B-6 9% DV   Potassium 3% DV
Folate 8% DV   Calcium 2% DV
Thiamin 4% DV   Iron 2% DV

HEALTH BENEFITS

Provides antioxidants
Benefits heart health
Protects against cancer
Boosts immune function
Regulates blood sugar
Strengthens bones

WHITE CASTLE
This short-day jumbo onion has a medium pungent flavor. White Castle is disease resistant and is good for short- or medium-tern storage. It's white color is enhanced when cured.

RED LONG OF TROPEA
This tall and oblong onion hails from the Mediterranean and is a favorite red onion in Italy and France. It's an excellent onion fresh or for bunching, and is ready in 90 days.

SIERRA BLANCA
This large, snow-white hybrid has an excellent flavor. Highly adaptable and disease resistant, it produces uniform bulbs with thick, juicy rings. It's ready to enjoy in 109 days.

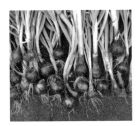

RED BARON
A medium-size red onion with lovely purple scallions, Red Baron can be grown for bunching or for full-size onions. At 12 inches (30 cm) tall, the plants start forming delicious small bulbs.

AILSA CRAIG
This heirloom yellow onion can reach enormous proportions—5-pound (2.3 kg) globes are not unusual for this variety! First introduced in 1887 by DAvid Murray, the gardener of the Scottish Marquis of Ailsa, this globe-shaped onion has been a favorite ever since. Ailsa Craig has a pale yellow skin and a sweet, mild flesh. The key is to growing large onions is to plant it early and never let it slow down—feed them lots of nitrogen.

IN THE KITCHEN

Onions add a savory flavor to any meal: You can add onions to breakfast omelets, lunch sandwiches, and fresh green salads. It's also an essential ingredient in most sauces and dressings. But onion can also be the foundational food in a recipe—such as the famous French onion soup.

SELECTING

When choosing onions, look for firm and dry bulbs with glossy, paper-thin skin. The "neck," or top, should be dry and tightly closed. If it's damp, soft, or discolored, it's not fresh. Avoid onions that have green sprout popping out of their tops.

Select onions that are most appropriate for your recipe. If you're using onions raw, select the mildest varieties such a red onions or sweet yellow onions.

For a more robust flavor, try white onions, which have a strong, pungent flavor that does not sweeten with cooking.

The tiny, mild pearl onions are great for tossing in with roast vegetables.

PREPARING

Slice off about an ½ inch (13 mm) from the top of the onion, then cut it lengthwise, from the top to root. Fold away the skin to reveal the onion. To dice onion, place the onion half on a cutting board, and make several horizontal cuts almost to the root of the onion; then make several vertical cuts from the root to the top. Now slice down to dice the onion.

STORING

Store whole onions out of the sun in a cool, dry location, such as a pantry. Place onions and shallots in mesh bags or in paper bags with holes punched in them. Onions can keep for up to four weeks. Store peeled onions in airtight containers in the refrigerator for up to two weeks.

PRESERVING

To freeze onions, you don't need to blanch them first. Simply diced them, and then place them in airtight containers. Frozen onions will keep for a year.

Alternatively, you can preserve onions by pickling them. In a bowl, whisk together cider vinegar, water, sugar, and salt. Pack thinly sliced red onion into a sterilized Mason jar, and pour the liquid over the onions. Cover, and let sit at room temperature for an hour or more. Refrigerated pickled onions last for a few weeks. Serve with salads, sandwiches, or nachos.

USES

Add onions to any dish you like for a savory or sweet flavor.

If you really onions, try this French onion soup recipe: In a large soup pot, sauté onion in butter until caramelized, about 20 to 30 minutes, adding stock as needed. Add garlic; stir in wine, scraping the pan; add beef stock, thyme sprigs, and bay leaf; simmer for 15 minutes; remove herbs. Add white wine vinegar, salt, and pepper. Broil baguette slices for two minutes. Ladle soup into individual over-proof bowls, place bread slice on top, and sprinkle with Gruyère cheese. Place on baking sheet, and heat for three minutes. Serve warm.

IN THE GARDEN

Growing onions in your garden is rewarding—because onions are a foundational ingredient in so many recipes, it's great to have fresh onions when you need them. Onions are excellent companion plants for cruciferous vegetables, tomatoes, and lettuce.

 CLIMATE With so many varieties of onion to choose from, gardeners can find just the right type for their climate and growing season. Generally, the cool-season onion is planted in the spring for a late fall harvest. In warmer zones, onions can be planted in the fall for a spring harvest. Find an open location in your garden with full sunlight.

 SOIL Like so many bulb-type vegetables, onions prefer a loose, fertile, well-draining soil. Till the soil several inches down, and remove any rocks in the planting bed. Amend the soil the manure or compost and nitrogen-rich fertilizer before planting. The ideal soil pH for onions is between 5.5 and 6.5,

 PLANTING Start seeds indoors about six to eight weeks before the last frost date. Sow seeds ¼ inch (6 mm) deep. Gently separate onion seedlings without damaging their fragile roots. Plant them in shallow furrows, and cover their roots immediately. Space transplants 4 inches (10 cm) apart, in rows 12 to 18 inches (30 to 46 cm) apart.

 GROWING Keep onion plants evenly moist, but not wet— onions tend to rot easily if their roots are standing in water. In the absence of rain, water onions every other day, either in the early morning or early evening. Mulch to preserve moisture and protect the roots. Every two to three weeks after planting, feed plants with a nitrogen-rich fertilizer.

 HARVESTING Once the tops become yellow, bend the tops down to speed up the ripening process. Loosen the soil around the onions to facilitate drying out. When the tops are brown, pull up the onions. If onions send up flower stalks, they have stopped growing, and you should pull them out and use them right away.

 FUN FACT
You can peel or cut an onion without crying if you cut the root end last, if the onion is refrigerated, or you cut the onion while holding the it under cold running water.

PARSNIP

Pastinaca sativa

The long, tuberous parsnip is a biennial root vegetable that of the carrot family (Apiaceae). Its cream-colored flesh has a nutty, earthy flavor that sweetens when kissed by frost. Parsnips require a long growing season, and can be harvested through winter—as long as the ground doesn't freeze over.

VARIETIES

GLADIATOR The flavorful creamy-white taproots of this vigorous plant have a clean, crisp sweetness. The smooth, tapered roots grow to 7 inches (18 cm) long and mature in about 100 days.

COBHAM A later-maturing variety, Cobham is bursting with mouth-watering sugars. The 8-inch (20 cm) roots do well even in heavy soils. Cobham is highly disease resistant, and matures in about 120 days.

GUERNSEY HALF LONG This heirloom originated in France and dates back over 200 hundred years. It has a sweet, nut-like flavour and considered to be one of the very best roasting varieties.

HOLLOW CROWN A common species in temperate and tropical climates, livid amaranth tolerates a wide range of soil pH and soil quality. The green leaves and stems are especially tender.

IN THE KITCHEN

Parsnips taste a bit like carrots and sweet potatoes except earthier and nuttier. Smaller parsnips are good for eating raw, but cook more mature parsnips to bring out the best flavor.

 SELECTING Choose the whitest parsnips you can find—the whiter their color, the sweeter their flavor. Smaller parsnips are also generally sweeter, and larger ones are tougher and woodier. Opt for parsnips with the roots still intact, with no yellowing or browning at the core. Avoid parsnips with cracks or bruises, or those that look shrivelled.

 PREPARING Rinse parsnips under cold water, and use a vegetable scrubber to gently rub away dirt and debris. Slice off the ends, and peel the skin as you would a potato. Then slice, dice, or julienne the parsnips as required.

 STORING Place unwashed parsnips in a produce bag and store them in the refrigerator for up to two few weeks.

 PRESERVING To freeze parsnips, first blanch them in boiling water for three minutes, plunge them into ice water, and dry well. Store them in airtight containers for up to eight months.

 USES Fresh parsnips are delicious tossed in a salad or grated into coleslaw.

To cook parsnips, the best options are steaming, roasting, and boiling. Parsnips pair well with apples, potatoes, and carrots and are an excellent addition to soups.

Try this simple recipe for mashed parsnips: Steam cubed parsnips for about 10 minutes or until tender. Combine with heavy cream, butter, salt, and grated nutmeg; mash until smooth. Sprinkle with chopped chives or parsley.

Roast parsnips with winter vegetables such as butternut squash, carrots, turnips, and potatoes. Cut parsnips into matchsticks, toss with olive oil, garlic powder, salt, and pepper. Roast at 425°F (220°C) for 40 to 50 minutes.

IN THE GARDEN

The cool-weather parsnips are best planted in midsummer for a late fall harvest. Trim off their tops for some delicious salad greens while you wait for your parsnips to sweeten.

 **CLIMATE** Parsnips grow best in full sun in zones 3 to 9. They perform best in northern climates.

 **SOIL** Parsnips prefer well-draining, fertile soil. Amend with compost, and loosen the soil so the roots can grow freely. The soil should be slightly acidic with a pH between 6.0 and 6.8.

 PLANTING Start seeds indoors to avoid sowing outdoors in summer heat. Sow ½ inch (13 mm) deep. Set transplants 6 inches (15 cm) apart. Space rows 18 inches (46 cm) apart.

GROWING Keep plants evenly moist. Feed parsnips with a low-nitrogen fertilizer after thinning and again every few weeks.

HARVESTING In late fall, cut off the tops, and pull out roots with a fork. Or leave parsnips in the ground through the winter to let the cold weather sweeten their flavor.

NUTRITIONAL VALUE

Serving size 100 g (1 small)

Calories 71	Fiber 3.6 g

Vitamin C 17% DV	Thiamin 7% DV
Folate 15% DV	Vitamin B-6 7% DV
Phosphorus 10% DV	Vitamin E 7% DV
Potassium 8% DV	Magnesium 7% DV

HEALTH BENEFITS

Provides antioxidants
Aids digestion
Boosts immune function
Benefits cardiovascular system
Supports nerve function
Supports healthy vision

PEAS

Pisum sativum

Peas are herbaceous annuals of the Fabaceae family and are native to Eurasia. Cultivated for more than 9,000 years, peas are now grown worldwide for their juicy seeds and crunch pea pods. Peas, are botanically fruit, as they contain seeds and develop from the ovary of a flower.

VARIETIES

Flowering pea vines are a pretty addition to any garden. And the sweet peas are fun and delicious to snack on right from the vine. Plant one or all of these three basic varieties: Garden peas (also called English or shelling peas) have plump peas but inedible pods; snow peas have edible pods but tiny peas; and sugar snap peas, which are a cross between garden and snow peas and both pod and peas are edible.

OREGON GIANT This vigorous snow pea variety yields plenty of 5-inch (13 cm) flat pods on white-flowered vines that reach 30 inches (76 cm). The flavorful, crunchy pods are ready to enjoy in 60 days.

SUGAR ANN The earliest of the snap peas, the award-winning Sugar Ann produces mouth-watering peas and tender pods. The vines grow to 24-inch (60 cm) and don't need staking. Start harvesting in 51 days.

SWEET HORIZON An outstanding snow pea, this is a European hybrid with straight, flat pods that grow in sets. The sugar-sweet 4-inch (10 cm) pods are dark-green and easy to harvest at 65 days.

MAXIGOLT A superb late-variety, Maxigolt is known for its huge, super-sweet peas in plump 3½-inch (9 cm) pods. The 4-foot (1.2 m) vines don't need a lot of support. The peas mature in 65 days.

AVALANCHE These tender, dark-green snow peas grow to 5 inches (13 cm) long but can be harvested earlier. Enjoy high yields of snow peas on semi-leafless 30-inch (76 cm) vines in 59 days.

SUGAR DADDY The double pods of this bush vine yield sweet, nutty-tasting peas at each plant node. Sugar Daddy's sweet pods grow at the top of the plant, making harvesting a snap. Enjoy in 60 days.

OREGON SUGAR POD 2 A vigorous and disease-resistance variety, Oregon Sugar Pod yields tender, sweet pods that grow to 4½ inches (11 cm). Enjoy them fresh or in stir-fries. Harvest in 60 days.

ROYAL SNOW Garnet pods contrast nicely with the lush 30-inch (76 cm) vines for easy harvesting. The sweet 3-inch (8 cm) pods have a pleasing, mildly bitter taste and are ready to enjoy in 61 days.

SUGAR SNAP

The immensely popular Sugar Snap produces lush, round peas in thick, juicy pods that reach 3 inches (8 cm) in length. The tall vines grow up to 6 feet (1.8 m). Enjoy a long harvest of delicious peas beginning in about 60 days.

IN THE KITCHEN

"Eat your peas!" Peas should be enjoyed, not maligned—peas are nutritious and delicious, provided they are well prepared. Overcooking peas is a sure way to deplete all the flavor and crunch, not to mention all the nutrients. Eat peas fresh or just lightly cooked so they retain their great crunchy taste.

 SELECTING
When selecting garden peas or snap peas, look for plump, firm, bright-green pods. Avoid soggy or shrivelled pods. Loose shelled peas don't last very long: Their sugar quickly turns to starch. So if you purchase them, be sure to eat them soon.

When selecting snow peas, look for smaller, shiny, flat pods; these are the sweetest and most tender. Avoid cracked, extra-large, or droopy pods.

 PREPARING
Wash peas just before using. For garden and snap peas, pinch off the ends, pull away the string, and the pop out the peas.

 To prepare snow peas, wash them first, trim the ends, and enjoy them raw or toss them in a stir fry.

 STORING
Shelled peas should be eaten right away, or stored in the original packaging or an airtight container and refrigerated for just one or two days.

For snow peas and whole snap peas, wrapped in a paper towel, and store in a produce bag in the refrigerator. Pea pods will keep for three to five days.

 PRESERVING
Freezing is the best way to preserve the sweet crispness of fresh shelled peas. First, blanch loose peas in boiling water for about 30 seconds, plunge into ice water, and dry. Flash-freeze them by arranging them in a single layer on rimmed baking sheet; this ensures the peas don't freeze into a big clump. Store in an airtight container for up to six months.

USES
Garden peas and snap peas are delicious raw as a snack or sprinkled into fresh green salads.

When cooking snow peas, it's best to sauté them very briefly so they keep their crunchy texture. They'll retain more nutrients too. Try this quick recipe for snow peas with almonds and shallots: In a skillet, melt butter; add slivered almonds, and cook until golden, stirring frequently, for about one minute. Add minced shallot and snow peas; sauté briefly until tender. Drizzle with lemon juice, and season with salt and pepper.

Snow peas are a common ingredient in Asian stir-fries. Here's a tangy recipe for snow peas and mushrooms: In a skillet, heat olive oil with some sesame oil, and sauté sliced shiitakes for one to two minutes. Add minced ginger, and cook for one minute. Add snow peas and soy sauce, and cook for two to three minutes. Season with salt, pepper, and sesame seeds.

VEGETABLE · PEAS

IN THE GARDEN

Cool-weather peas are some of the first spring vegetables that you can plant, yet their growing season is quite short. Choose a variety of early- to late-season cultivars to extend your harvest. Great companion plants for peas are beans, carrots, and cucumbers.

 CLIMATE Cool-weather peas grow well in zones 2 to 9. Peas perform best when the temperatures are below 70°F (21°C), and they will stop producing when the weather tops 80°F (27°C).

SOIL Peas prefer a fertile, sandy loam that is well-draining, but they tolerate poorer soils. Work in plenty of compost or bonemeal at planting. Aim for a pH of 6.0 to 7.5.

PLANTING At planting time, set up a trellis or netting to support the vines—their tendrils need a surface to wrap around, plus harvesting will be easier.

Start seeds outdoors four to six weeks before the last spring frost date, when the soil can be worked and the soil temperature is at least 45°F (7°C). Sow seeds 1 inch (2.5 cm) deep, and about 2 inches (5 cm) apart. Sow seeds in wide bands of 3 inches across. (Peas grown close together crowd out weeds.) Space rows 12 to 24 inches (30 to 60 cm) apart. If cold weather kills your seeds, reseed right away. For a fall crop, sow seeds 10 weeks before the first frost date.

 GROWING Water peas lightly until the pods emerge, and then water daily if needed. Mulch around the plants to conserve moisture. Peas are light feeders and don't require fertilizer; avoid nitrogen-rich fertilizer. Gently weed around the plants so as not to disturb the roots. Protect peas from birds with a light netting draped over the plants.

 HARVESTING Pick garden peas when the pods are plump with bulging seeds. Pinch off the pods from the stems while holding the stem with your other hand. Harvest often to encourage continued growth. Pick peas in the morning, when they are crispest. Pick snow peas then the pods are thin and the seeds are still small.

PEPPERS, CHILI

Capsicum annuum, C. chinense, C. frutescens

The chili pepper is the fiery fruit of Capsicum plants in the nightshade family. Chilis are native to Mesomerica, where they were first cultivated 9,000 years ago. Also called chiles, chili peppers have varying intensities of heat—from fairly mild to scorching hot—depending how much capsaicin they contain.

VARIETIES

Of the five species of chili peppers, three are the mostly commonly cultivated today. *Capsicum annum* includes many of the more popular varieties such as jalapeño and cayenne. Some of the hottest peppers belong to the species *C. chinense,* including habanero and Datil. And in the *C. frutescens* are tabasco and piri piri. In many chili cultivars, the peppers ripen from green to red, acquiring heat as they mature.

ANAHEIM This meaty chili pepper is mildly hot and perfect for roasting or frying. Anaheim produces high yields of large chilis that grow to 7 inches (18 cm) long. The peppers are ready to harvest in 80 days.

RED HABANERO One of the hottest habaneros, this chili ripens to red rather than the usual gold. The fruit is sizzling hot with some smoky and citrus notes. This chili grows to less than 2 inches (5 cm) in 80 days.

PIRI PIRI Also known as African bird's eye, and Thai chili, this fiery-hot pepper is a compact sliver of pure heat. Measuring just 1-inch (2.5 cm) long, Piri Piri ripens from green to red and is ready to harvest in 120 days.

POBLANO The mild, heart-shaped Poblano is the traditional pepper in stuffed chili rellenos. When dried, Poblano turns a chestnut color and can be ground into chili powder. It grows to 5 inches (13 cm) in 75 days.

JALAPEÑO This popular chili is named after Xalapa, the capital of Veracruz, Mexico. This 4-inch (10 cm) chili is usually harvested green, when it's still fairly mild, in about 70 days. At 93 days, you get full red heat.

MIRASOL In Spanish, *mirasol* means "looking at the sun"—this 5-inch (13 cm) chili grows upward from its stem. Mirasol is mildly hot with a berry flavor and is essential in mole sauce. It's ready to pick in 90 days.

SERRANO Intensely hot with a uniquely pungent flavor, Serrano is a finger-shaped chili with medium-thin walls and is easy to dry. Green chilis are ready to enjoy in 75 days, and red chilis in 90 days.

ACI SIVRI A Turkish heirloom, Aci Sivri is a cayenne-type of chili that grows to 7 inches (18 cm) long. The pods curl and wrinkle as they ripen from yellow-green to red. It matures in about 90 days.

TABASCO
Scorching-hot Tabasco scores 40,000 on the Scoville heat scale. This fiery Louisiana heirloom grows as a perennial in frost-free regions and can set fruit for several years. The bushy plant reaches 5 feet (1.5 m) in height and sets hundreds of fruits per season. The 1½ inch (15 cm) fruits ripen from green to scarlet red in 85 days. Pick with gloves!

IN THE KITCHEN

Cooking with chili peppers can add a lot of fiery character to your food. But be forewarned: Handle scorching-hot chilis with care! Wear gloves and keep your fingers away from your eyes.

 ### SELECTING
Look for peppers with the deepest color and the smoothest, firmest skin. Avoid damaged, wrinkled, or bruised chilis. Select your heat intensity not just by the variety of the pepper but also by its size: Smaller chili peppers are hotter than their larger counterparts because their heat is more concentrated.

PREPARING
If you want to get the most heat out of your chilis, use the entire pepper: the wall, the seeds, and the spongy white pith. The pith is actually the hottest part of the chili, not the seeds. If you'd rather not play with fire, scoop out the pith and seeds and use only the wall.

 ### STORING
No need to wash chili peppers before storing them. Place them in an airtight container, and store them in the produce drawer of the refrigerator for two to three weeks. Whole chili peppers will stay fresh longer than cut peppers. Keep in mind that the thicker the walls of the chili, the longer it will keep.

PRESERVING
To freeze chilis, first slice them, then arrange them in a single layer on a baking sheet. Flash-freeze chilis for a few minutes, then store them in an airtight container for up to a year.

To brine chilis, cut them in half, and place them in a sterilized jar; cover with water, add salt, and stir. Cover and refrigerate for up to four weeks.

Dried chilis will keep for several months: First blanch them for four minutes, then pat them dry. Cut them in half or in quarters, and place them on a baking sheet lined with parchment paper. Dry peppers at 200°F (100°C) for up to three hours. Remember: dried peppers have more heat.

 ### USES
You can spice up any dish with fresh chopped chili peppers. Add chilis to omelets, sandwiches, burgers, stir-fries, or soups.

Try roasting chilis: Simply place them whole on a baking sheet, and roast at 375°F (190°C). Check on them every 15 minutes, and turn them when the top has charred. Once all the sides are charred, remove the peppers. Place them in a bowl, put a tight-fitting lid on it, and let the steam loosen the skin for 15 minutes. Peel the skin from the peppers, and enjoy.

Try stuffed chiles rellenos: Roast whole peppers (see above), cut off the tops, and place them in a baking pan. Combine shredded Monterey Jack, cheddar cheese, and paprika; stuff into peppers. Whisk together eggs, milk, and flour; add salt and pepper; pour into the baking pan. Bake at 400°F (200°C) for 30 to 40 minutes. Allow to cool, and serve with salsa.

IN THE GARDEN

Some like it hot—and some like it hotter. Plant a few types of chili peppers in your garden and see what kind of heat you can handle in your kitchen. Chili peppers can be tough to grow from seed, however, so you might want to consider starting out with seedlings.

 ### CLIMATE

Chili peppers are hardy, warm-season plants that require full sunlight. Keep in mind that the hottest chili varieties often have the longest growing periods. Provide chilis plenty of warmth to get them started. Chili peppers grow best when air temperatures are between 70° and 95°F (21 to 35°C).

SOIL

Chilis like fertile, well-draining loam that is rich in organic matter. Work in aged compost into beds before planting. Chilis prefer a neutral soil with a pH of about 5.5 to 6.8. The minimum soil temperature for peppers to germinate properly is 65°F (18°C).

PLANTING

Start sowing seeds indoors as early as January, at least eight to 10 weeks before the last frost date. Sow seeds ½ inch (13 mm) deep, 18 to 24 inches (46 to 60 cm) apart. Space rows 24 to 36 inches (60 to 90 cm) apart. Sow two seeds per spot, and thin to the strongest seedling. Transplant chilis peppers into the garden when they are 4 to 6 inches (10 to 15 cm) tall, about two weeks after the last frost.

 ### GROWING

Chilis grow well in containers, raised beds, and in-ground gardens. Keep plants evenly moist but not wet, especially when blossoms and fruit appear. If the soil goes too dry, it can result in flower drop. Add aged compost to beds before planting and again midseason. Water more often after the fruit forms. Tip: Water heavily a few hours before harvest to turn hot peppers milder; withhold watering before harvest to turn up their heat. Mulch the plants, but avoid nitrogen fertilizer.

 ### HARVESTING

Cut chili peppers off the vine when they have reached their mature size and color. Remember that green peppers are milder, and red are red-hot.

 **FUN FACT**

The Scoville Scale measures the heat intensity of chilles. In 2017, a Welsh fruit grower named Mike Smith accidentally grew the world's hottest chilli. His creation, Dragon's Breath, topped the Scoville Scale with 2.48 million units!

PEPPER, SWEET

Capsicum annuum

Sweet peppers are the fruits of capsicum plants in the nightshade family. Their bright, glossy skin is consists of either three or four large lobes. Unlike other pepper varieties, sweet peppers don't produce the heat inducing compound capsaicin, which is why they're sweet instead.

VARIETIES

Sweet peppers come in a variety of shapes, size, and colors. Many of them are bell shaped—thus "bell peppers"— and others are elongated or round. But they all start out green peppers. As they ripen, sweet peppers go from green to yellow to orange and, finally, to a mature deep red. And with that maturity comes extra sweetness. That's why red and orange peppers are sweeter than green.

KING OF THE NORTH This early-season heirloom dates back to 1934 New England. The King thrives in cooler summer climates and yields plenty of crisp 6-inch (15 cm) peppers that ripen from green to red in 68 days.

CUBANELLE Also called Cuban pepper, this variety has a rich, sweet flavor with a touch of heat. Its thin walls are great for quick cooking. Cubanelle grows to 8 inches (20 cm) and ripens to bright orange-red in 80 days.

BULL NOSE Modern forms of this pepper have become increasingly elongated when compared to the original short and stout form. Bull Nose peppers have a smooth, thick-walled skin.

COMO DI TORO GIALLO Very early maturing yellow sweet Italian pepper. Long tapered fruits with easy to remove skin. A nice sweet flavor that is excellent either fresh, grilled or roasted. .

SWEET SUNRISE Medium-large fruits are blocky to slightly elongated. The flavor is fruity and sweet. Sweet Sunrise is a sturdy, medium-sized plant with good leaf cover. Yields well and fruits ripen early.

CARMEN Carmen peppers feature a deep red color and an elongated shape, hence their Italian name Corno di Toro, which translates to "horn of the bull." They have no heat and have rich, robust sweetness.

NUTRITIONAL VALUE

Serving size 100 g (2/3 cup)
Calories 26   Fiber 2.1 g

Vitamin C 170% DV	Vitamin E 11% DV
Vitamin B-6 22% DV	Riboflavin 7% DV
Folate 12% DV	Niacin 7% DV
Vitamin A 17% DV	Thiamin 5% DV

HEALTH BENEFITS

Reduces inflammation
Promotes mucilage
Provides antioxidants
Prevents against cancer
Benefits cardiovascular system
Regulates blood sugar

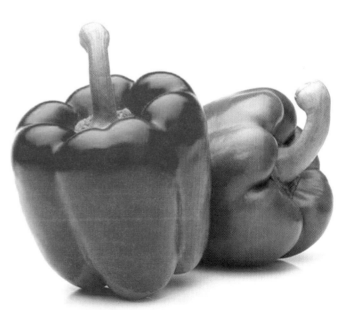

GOURMET These bright tangerine fruits have thick, juicy walls and a luscious flavor. The bountiful Gourmet is easy to grow in a variety of conditions. Pick orange fruits in 85 days, and green ones in 65 days.

ISLANDER The thick walls of this pepper ripen from lavender to orange to scarlet red. The light-yellow flesh is mild and sweet. A medium-tall plant, Islander yields violet fruit in 56 days, and red fruit in 81 days.

SUPER SHEPHERD A large Italian sweet pepper that matures from green to red. They grow to about 7 inches and have a sweet and very palatable flavor with thick flesh, making them perfect for stuffing.

SWEET BANANA The banana pepper is a mild, medium-sized chili pepper with a tangy, slightly sweet taste. It is typically bright yellow, it matures to green, red, or orange. Plants will typically reach 1 to 2 feet tall.

CALIFORNIA WONDER
California Wonder is the gold standard for bell peppers—its sweet flavor, thick-walled flesh, and bright colors are all outstanding. Introduced in 1928, it's now so popular that it can be found in most grocery stores in the United States. The upright, ever-bearing plants grow to 26 inches (66 cm) tall and produce high yields of 4-inch fruits. The glossy peppers ripen from deep green to scarlet red in about 75 days.

IN THE KITCHEN

Sweet peppers are a treat to cook with—they're crunchy, colorful, and sweet. They're delicious all on their own but they also lend a crispy texture and sweet flavor to just about any dish.

SELECTING
Look for peppers with the deepest color and the smoothest, firmest skin. Avoid damaged, wrinkled, or bruised peppers. If you're looking for the sweetest pepper, opt for red, which s the richest or the sweet peppers—and has the most concentrated nutrients. The next sweetest are orange and yellow peppers. The least sweet, and slightly bitter, are green peppers.

PREPARING
Wash peppers just before using, and scrub off any waxy coating. With a paring knife, cut out the stem. Slice the pepper in half, from top to bottom, and scoop out the pith and the seeds. Slice as needed.

STORING
No need to wash peppers before storing them. Place them in an airtight container, and store them in the produce drawer of the refrigerator for two to three weeks. Whole peppers will stay fresh longer than cut peppers.

PRESERVING
To freeze peppers, first slice them, and arrange them in a single layer on a cookie sheet. Flash-freeze the peppers for a few minutes, then store them in an airtight container for up to a year.

To brine peppers, cut them in half, and place them in a sterilized jar; cover with water, add salt, and stir.

Dried chilis will keep for several months: First blanch them for four minutes, then pat them dry. Cut them in half or in quarters, and place them on a baking sheet lined with parchment paper. Dry the peppers at 200°F (100°C) for up three hours.

USES
Sweet peppers are excellent raw: Snack on fresh peppers wedges, slice peppers into matchsticks for crudités with dip, or purée them into a romesco sauce. Peppers are often added to foods to lend a sweet, crunchy texture—such as omelets, salsa, chili, stir-fries, or pizzas.

To bring out a rich flavor, try roasting your sweet peppers: Place whole peppers on their sides on an oiled baking sheet, and roast at 400°F (200°C). Check on them every 15 minutes, turning them as the tops char. Once all the sides are charred and the peppers look collapsed, remove the peppers, and place them in a bowl. Place a tight-fitting lid on the bowl, and let the steam loosen the skin for 15 minutes. Peel the skin from the peppers, and enjoy.

Roast peppers (see above). Remove the stems, and cut the peppers in half. Discard the seeds, and cut the peppers into strips. In a bowl, combine olive oil, minced garlic, chopped Italian parsley, salt, and pepper. Toss peppers with marinade, and refrigerate for at least two hours.

IN THE GARDEN

Sweet peppers are rewarding to grow in the garden. They have a compact form and are easy to grow once you get the seeds going. Peppers do have a fairly long growing season, but the rainbow display of fruit is worth the wait.

CLIMATE
Peppers are hardy, warm-season plants that require full sunlight. Keep in mind that red peppers will take the longest to grow. Provide peppers with plenty of warmth to get them started. Peppers grow best when air temperatures are between 70° and 95°F (21 to 35°C).

SOIL
Peppers like fertile, well-draining loam that is rich in organic matter. Work in aged compost into beds before planting. Peppers prefer a neutral soil with a pH of about 5.5 to 6.8. The minimum soil temperature for peppers to germinate properly is 65°F (18°C).

PLANTING
Start sowing seeds indoors as early as January, at least eight to 10 weeks before the last frost date. Sow seeds ½ inch (13 mm) deep, 18 to 24 inches (46 to 60 cm) apart. Space rows 24 to 36 inches (60 to 90 cm) apart. Sow two seeds per spot, and thin to the strongest seedling. Transplant peppers into the garden when they are 4 to 6 inches (10 to 15 cm) tall, about two weeks after the last frost.

GROWING
Peppers grow well in containers, raised beds, and in-ground gardens. Keep plants evenly moist but not wet, especially when the blossoms and fruit appear. If the soil goes too dry, it can result in flower drop. Add aged compost to beds before planting and again midseason. Water more often after the fruit forms. Mulch the plants, but avoid nitrogen fertilizer.

HARVESTING
Begin to harvest peppers when they are 3 to 4 inches (8 to 10 cm) and the fruit is firm and green. If the pepper feels thin, it is not ripe. If it feels soggy, it's over-ripe. To harvest peppers, cut them off the vine when they have reached their mature size and color. Remember that green peppers are less sweet and nutritious than red.

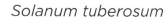

POTATO

Solanum tuberosum

The potato is a herbaceous perennial that belongs to the nightshade family (Solanaceae) and is related to eggplant and tomato. Although it's commonly called a root vegetable, it's actually a starchy tuber that develops along the stem of the potato plant—that's where the plant stores its nutrients.

VARIETIES

Potatoes are the largest tuber crop in the world. More than 200 varieties of potatoes are sold in the United States alone. The following seven varieties are the most common: Russet, Red, White, Yellow, Blue, Fingerling, and Petite. Each has a distinctive flavor, texture, and color.

ALL BLUE A gorgeous potato with deep-blue skin and moist, meaty flesh that turns lighter blue when cooked. All Blue is excellent for salads and mashing. The 4-inch (10 cm) tubers mature in about 100 days.

DÉSIRÉE This longtime European favorite is an early-season potato with satiny pink skin and smooth, creamy-yellow flesh. Désirée is great for roasting and baking, and is ready to harvest in 80 days.

KING EDWARD These are one of the oldest varieties grown, dating back to 1902. They are recognized as one of the most versatile varieties for cooking and growing at home and have a pleasing flavor.

PRINCESS LARATTE A culinary superstar, Princess Laratte is an early-season fingerling with a sweet, complex flavor reminiscent of chestnuts and almonds. It's ready to harvest in 90 days.

RED NORLAND

The attractive and reliably uniform Norland has smooth crimson skin and pearly white flesh. The medium-size potato is high yielding and ready to harvest in 85 days.

SIFRA
The Sifra potato variety has a medium late ripening period, which allows gardeners to harvest its crop 95 - 115 days after planting. As a rule, Cifra varieties are not watered before flowering.

RUSSIAN BANANA

This heirloom fingerling hails from the Baltic region. It has a thin buff skin and a firm flesh with a rich chestnut flavor. Versatile in the kitchen, Russian Banana is ready in 95 days.

YUKON GOLD
A star among yellow-flesh potatoes, Yukon Gold has a thin, buff skin and a dry, creamy-yellow interior. This early-season variety is great any way you cook it. Enjoy it in 100 days.

GERMAN BUTTERBALL

This award-winning heirloom was introduced in 1988 and has been a favorite all-purpose potato ever since. The pale-yellow skin of German Butterball is smooth and netted, and the buttery-tasting, golden flesh has a moist, slightly flaky texture that holds up well when cooked. This luscious late-season variety is ready to enjoy in 95 days.

IN THE KITCHEN

The mellow flavor and smooth texture of potatoes make them perfect to add to any meal: Cook them up in egg frittatas for breakfast, make a creamy potato salad for lunch, or mash them up for dinner. No wonder the humble potato is a staple food in so many cuisines—it's versatile and delicious, too.

 ### SELECTING
Choose a variety that will suit your cooking method. For mashing potatoes, one of the best is Russet. For roasting or baking, select waxy types such as new potatoes and fingerling. You can also choose all-purpose potatoes, which have a medium amount of starch and hold up well under various cooking methods. Yukon Gold is a great all-purpose potato.

Look for potatoes with smooth, firm skin and an even tone. Avoid those with green or brown spots, and pass on the damaged or bruised potatoes. And don't buy potatoes that have already sprouted, unless you eat them right away.

 ### PREPARING
Rinse sweet potatoes under cold water, and gently brush away dirt with a vegetable scrubber. If your potatoes are organic, there's no need for you to peel them. Conventional potatoes, however, will have chemical residues in their skin, so you might want to peel those. Use a paring knife to cut out the eyes.

 ### STORING
Do not store potatoes in a refrigerator— the cold temperature turns the starch into sugar. Instead, store your potatoes in a cool, dark, humid area. The ideal temperature is 45° to 50°F (7°to 10°C). An unheated basement or insulated garage should . work fine through winter.

 ### PRESERVING
To freeze potatoes, cut them into equal-size cubes, and simmer them in salted boiling water for five minutes. Place them in a single layer on a baking sheet, and flash-freeze them for about 30 minutes. Place them together in an airtight container, and freeze for up to a year. When using frozen potatoes, don't thaw them; cook them frozen so they don't become discolored.

 ### USES
Potatoes are truly versatile in the kitchen. They can be steamed, sautéed, baked, roasted, or mashed. The simplest way to enjoy potatoes is to bake them: Poke holes around the potato, wrap it in foil, and bake at 425°F (220°C) for 55 minutes. Sprinkle with chopped parsley, and serve with a pat of butter.

To roast potatoes, slice red or white potatoes at an even thickness. Toss them with olive oil, minced garlic, sprigs of fresh rosemary or thyme, salt, and pepper. Spread the potatoes in one layer on a baking pan, and roast at 400°F (200°C) for 30 to 40 minutes, turning twice during cooking.

Mashed potatoes are a great comfort food: To make them, boil Russet potates in salted water until tender. Drain, and start mashing. Slowly add hot milk, until you've reached the desired consistency. Add softened butter, salt, and pepper. Sprinkle with parsley.

IN THE GARDEN

With so many varieties to choose from, you'll need to do a little planning before planting your potatoes. Select a potato variety that will best suit your culinary tastes. Whether you prefer roasting, baking, or mashing them, there's a perfect potato just for you.

CLIMATE
Potatoes need full sun and cool weather to thrive. Potatoes grow well in zones 1 through 7.

SOIL
Prepare a planting bed with loose, well-draining sandy soil. Potatoes prefer a soil pH between 5.8 and 6.5, although they will tolerate a slightly more acidic pH. Amend the soil with compost or manure and fertilizer at planting time.

PLANTING
Plant bare-root slips after the last frost. Dig a trench about 6 inches (15 cm) wide and 8 inches (20 cm) deep, tapering at the bottom to 3 inches (8 cm) wide. Plant the slips cut-side down, every 12 to 14 inches (30 to 36 cm) and cover with 3 to 4 inches (8 to 10 cm) of soil. Potatoes perform best when grown in rows. Space rows about 36 inches (90 cm) apart.

Two weeks after planting, when sprouts appear, gently fill in the trench with another 3 inches (8 cm) of soil, but leave a few inches of the plants exposed. Repeat in a few weeks, so the soil mounds up about 5 inches (13 cm) above garden level; this process is called "hilling."

GROWING
As you are hilling, be sure to protect the growing tubers from sunlight, which will cause them to turn green. Water regularly during the growing season, especially once the sprouts appear. Potatoes are heavy feeders: Use a mixture of cotton seed meal and bone meal to side dress and add between rows. Mulch to conserve moisture and control weeds.

HARVESTING
Harvest potatoes on a dry day. Dig carefully, so you don't puncture or bruise the potato skin. The soil should be loose, so digging should be easy. Smaller new potatoes will be ready to harvest about two weeks after flowering has stopped. To harvest the largest and best potatoes, wait until the foliage dies back before carefully digging them up.

✋ FUN FACT ✋
It's alive! When you buy a potato, it's not dead—it's just dormant. That's why it can start sprouting if it's exposed to warmth and moisture.

PUMPKIN

Cucurbita pepo

Pumpkins are probably the most well known of all the squashes—the bright, cheerful colors and unusual shapes are a welcome sight on farmstands and in markets all through the fall season. But pumpkins are not just decorative; they are sweet and delicious and loaded with nutrients, too.

VARIETIES

LONG ISLAND CHEESE
This New York heirloom resembles a wheel of cheese. Its sweet orange flesh is a favorite for making pies. This medium-size pumpkin is ready to harvest in about 108 days.

CINDERELLA Also called Rouge vif d'Etampes, this French heirloom looks like a fairytale pumpkin coach. Its deep-orange flesh is delicious in both sweet and savory pies. Cinderella matures in 110 days.

JARRAHDALE BLUE
This slate-blue pumpkin has a flat top and deep ribs, and grows to about 10 pounds (4.5 kg). Its excellent flavor is well suited to all sorts of savory dishes. It stores well, too. Enjoy it in 100 days.

MARINA DI CHIOGGIA
An Italian heirloom, this blue-green squash hails from a fishing village south of Venice. This beautiful squash is also delicious baked or in pies. It's ready to harvest in 95 days.

IN THE KITCHEN

The next time you feel like baking a pumpkin pie, try making it with freshly roasted pumpkins. Once you've tasted the mouth watering flavor of fresh pumpkin, you'll never go back to store-bought.

SELECTING
Pumpkins should feel firm and heavy for their size. Look for smooth, dull skin without any soft spots; shiny skin suggests that the squash may have been picked too early. The stem should be green, not black, and should not be dried out.

PREPARING
Wash the pumpkin, and scrub off any dirt. To make it easier to cut through the hard rind, pierce the skin in a few spots, and microwave for three minutes. Allow the squash to cool, then cut it lengthwise, from stem to end, with a large, sharp knife. Remove the fibers and seeds before cooking.

STORING
Pumpkin can keep for up to two months in a cool, dry location. Once it has been cut or cooked, wrap it and refrigerate it for up to four days.

PRESERVING
Baked, cubed, or puréed pumpkin can be frozen for up to 12 months.

USES
Pumpkin is most often associated with the savory-sweet pumpkin pie. To make pumpkin pie, first roast the pumpkin. Soften the hard rind in the microwave for three minutes, and cut the squash in half, from top to bottom. Scoop out the seeds and strings, but save the seeds for roasting. Brush the insides of the pumpkin with coconut or avocado oil, and place them cut side down on a baking sheet. Pierce several holes in the flesh to allow steam to escape. Roast at 400°F (200°C) for 30 to 45 minutes. Scoop out the flesh and purée until smooth. It's now ready to add to your favorite pumpkin pie recipe.

To make a pumpkin purée, combine roasted pumpkin with melted butter, maple syrup, and brown sugar. Spice it up with cinnamon and nutmeg, or with stronger spices such as paprika and cayenne. Add pumpkin purée to foods like oatmeal, applesauce, and pancakes. You can also use pumpkin as a ravioli filling or as the base for a soup.

IN THE GARDEN

Big, gleaming pumpkins are a joy to grow in the garden. Just remember that they have a long growing season, and they need quite a bit of space to spread out.

CLIMATE
Select a location in full sun, but rotate squash in your garden every couple of years. Squash grows well in zones 4 and higher.

SOIL
Pumpkin needs fertile, well-drained soil with a pH of 6.0 to 6.8. Till the soil down to 8 inches (20 cm).

PLANTING
Sow outdoors after the last frost, or indoors three weeks before the last frost in 3-inch (8 cm) pots. Plant three to five seeds on a mound to protect the roots. Space mounds 36 inches (90 cm) apart. Cover with 1 inch (2.5 cm) of fine soil.

GROWING
Keep the soil evenly moist. Apply a 10-10-10 fertilizer after seedlings emerge and again after blossoms appear.

HARVESTING
Pumpkin is ready to pick when your fingernail can't pierce its skin. Cut it from the vine, leaving part of the stem intact.

RADICCHIO

Cichorium intybus

Native to the Mediterranean region, radicchio is a variety of leaf chicory in the daisy family (Asteraceae). This elegant lettuce has tight, cabbage-like heads with crisp leaves in shades of burgundy, magenta, and bronzy green that contrast against the pure-white veins. Radicchio has a pleasing bitter flavor.

VARIETIES

BEL FIORE In Italian, the name "beautiful flower" refers to the dramatic display of the variegated pink and crimson leaves. Bel Fiore performs well in warm weather, and is ready to harvest in 60 days.

LEONARDO This gorgeous chioggia variety has burgundy leaves with show-white veins. The large, round heads reach 5 inches (13 cm) across and average a pound (0.5 kg) each. It matures in 85 days.

PERSEO An extra-early chioggia variety, Perseo boasts compact, uniform heads that grow to 4 inches (10 cm) wide. It's very popular in Europe for salads and grilling. Perseo is ready to harvest in 55 days.

IN THE KITCHEN

The vibrant burgundy-red leaves of radicchio are a visual and culinary delight. Liven up everyday green salads with some crispy, peppery radicchio leaves.

 SELECTING
Choose crisp, firm heads with brightly colored leaves. Avoid heads with wilting or brown leaves. The base of the head should look fresh and green.

 PREPARING
Remove the outer leaves, and run the head under cold water to remove debris. Cut the head in half lengthwise, and remove the tough core. Slice radicchio to the desired thickness.

 STORING
Wrap the whole radicchio unwashed in a produce bag in the coldest section of the refrigerator. Radicchio will keep for up to two weeks; however, the bitter flavor tends to intensify over time.

 PRESERVING
To freeze the leaves, boil them for three minutes, cool them in ice water, and strain the water before placing them in an airtight containers.

 USES
Add a spicy note to green salads and pasta sauces with sliced raw radicchio leaves.

Combine radicchio with kale to balance out the bitterness. Drizzle with a pungent blue cheese dressing to complement its strong flavor.

Cooking radicchio reduces the bitterness. Sauté or grill radicchio with olive oil and salt. Add some garlic, basil, or chopped bacon. It's a delicious addition to omelets.

IN THE GARDEN

This striking purple lettuce is a cool-season plant that prefers the mild temperatures of early spring and late fall. In cooler climates, radicchio can be grown year-round.

 **CLIMATE**
Radicchio is a hardy lettuce that grows especially well in cooler areas. Plant it in full sunlight in zones 3 to 9.

SOIL
Radicchio is not too particular about soil type, but nutrient-rich soil is best. Its wide pH range is between 5.0 and 7.0.

PLANTING
Sow seeds indoors two to four weeks before the last frost date, or outdoors as soon as the soil can be worked. Sow seeds ⅛ inch (3 mm) deep, and 1 inch (2.5 cm) apart. Space rows 18 inches (46 cm) apart. Thin seedlings to 8 inches (20 cm) apart.

GROWING
Water plants using a drip irrigation system. If watering from above, water early in the morning or in the evening. Feed with a general purpose fertilizer.

HARVESTING
Pick outer leaves as needed. Harvest the heads when they are firm to the touch, in about 60 to 65 days after sowing.

 NUTRITIONAL VALUE

Serving size 50 g (1 1/4 cups)

Calories 12	Fiber 0.5 g

Vitamin K 128% DV	Iron 3% DV
Folate 8% DV	Phosphorus 3% DV
Vitamin E 85% DV	Potassium 3% DV
Vitamin C 5% DV	Zinc 3% DV

 HEALTH BENEFITS

Provides antioxidants
Reduces pain
Aids digestion
Strengthens bones
Regulates blood sugar
Promotes brain function

RADISH

Raphanus sativus

The small, red root vegetable was first cultivated in Asia thousands of years ago. A member of the mustard family (Brassicaceae), radish is grown primarily for its round, succulent taproot. The quick-growing spring varieties have a sharp, warming flavor that is a bit milder than the pungent winter types.

VARIETIES

CHERRY BELLE The award-winning Cherry Belle yields smooth, scarlet radishes with juicy white flesh. This extra-early variety is very adaptable. The radishes grow to 1 inch (2.5 cm) wide in 22 days.

BLACK SPANISH ROUND An heirloom since the 1500s, this dramatic ebony radish has a luscious, warming white flesh. This winter radish grows to 4 inches wide (10 cm) and is ready to enjoy in 55 days.

DAIKON An longtime favorite in Asia, white daikon radishes have been cultivated for use in salads, soups, and stir-fries, and for pickling. The thick white taproots can grow to 14 inches (36 cm) long. Daikon is not only a delicious radish but also an excellent cover crop. Its large taproots loosen the soil and enrich it with nutrients. It's ready to harvest in 40 days.

IN THE KITCHEN

The peppery heat of radish pairs well with creamy cheeses, rich avocados, and cool cucumbers. Toss sliced radishes in salads with leafy greens and tomatoes for a juicy crunch.

SELECTING
Chose radishes in bunches. They should be smooth and unblemished and have a bright color. The tops should be green and fresh, not yellow or slimy. Avoid those with dark spots.

PREPARING
Soak radishes in a bowl of cool water. Trim the tops, leaving an inch (2.5 cm), and cut off the roots. Rinse under cold water, using a brush or knife to scrape away dirt or spots.

STORING
Store radishes in one of two ways. (1) Keep their tops and roots intact, and place them in a bowl of water; refrigerate for up to 10 days, changing the water as needed, or (2) cut off the tops and roots, wrap them in a paper towel, and place them in a produce bag; refrigerate for two weeks.

PRESERVING
Blanch radish slices for three minutes in boiling water, plunge into ice water, and dry before freezing. Radishes will keep for six months in the freezer.

USES
Fresh radishes have such a crisp texture and delicious bite that they are best eaten raw. Whole radishes are a quick and nutritious snack, and sliced radishes go great in any tossed salad. Try these herbs on your radishes: dill, parsley, cilantro, or thyme.

Try adding grated radish to a grain dish, or make this easy radish slaw: In a medium bowl, combine grated radishes, grated carrots, and shredded cabbage. In a small bowl, combine chopped red onion, coriander, olive oil, lemon juice, sugar, salt, and pepper. Toss together.

If your radishes are past their prime, they'll be more bitter but will sweeten up when cooked. Try this roast radish recipe: Toss together halved radishes, halved garlic cloves, avocado oil or melted butter, salt, and pepper. Spread radishes is a single later on a baking sheet, and roast at 425°F (220°C) for 20 minutes, turning once. Sprinkle with chopped fresh parsley and chives, and serve with a dallop of crème fraîche.

IN THE GARDEN

Grow radishes from spring through fall. Plant spring radishes early and enjoy a spring crop in three to four weeks, then plant winter radishes in midsummer for a late-fall harvest.

CLIMATE
Radish grows well in zones 2 to 10 in full sun. Avoid planting radishes in shade, which leads to lush foliage but small taproots.

SOIL
Prepare a bed with loose, fertile, and well-draining soil. Amend with compost, and remove rocks. Aim for a soil pH between 6.6 and 7.0.

PLANTING
Sow seeds directly so as not to disturb the roots after the last frost.

Sow seeds ½ inch (13 mm) deep, 2 inches (5 cm). Space rows 12 inches (30 cm) apart. Sow every two weeks.

GROWING

Water regularly, keeping the soil evenly moist. Thinly mulch after seedlings emerge.

HARVESTING

Pull out radishes once they measure about 1 inch (2.5 cm) across and are popping out of the soil. Harvest radishes promptly, before they turn woody.

ROMAINE

Lactuca sativa var. longifolia

Romaine belongs to the daisy family (Asteraceae) and is one of the oldest varieties of lettuce. It's also known as Cos, the Greek island where the lettuce presumably originated some 5,000 years ago. Unlike many other lettuce varieties, the sturdy Romaine is generally very heat tolerant and slow to bolt.

VARIETIES

ROUGE D'HIVER This French heirloom dates back to 1885. In cool weather, the colors deepen to rich burgundy and emerald green. It tolerates cold well, but not heat. Harvest between 20 and 50 days.

MONTE CARLO The deep-green, savoyed leaves of this compact variety grow in an attractive whorl. Harvest Monte Carlo's dense, uniform heads as minis, or wait for them to mature in 46 days.

DRAGOON The heads of this mini green Romaine are dense, compact, and uniform. Dragoon has an excellent flavor and a crispy texture. This bolt-tolerant variety is ready to harvest in just 43 days.

COASTAL STAR This large, sturdy Romaine has heavy heads of delicious dark-greens leaves and crispy hearts. Coastal Star is heat-tolerant and matures in about 57 days. Plant for a spring or late-summer crop.

IN THE KITCHEN

Romaine lettuce is the delicious foundation of caesar salad. The refreshing flavor and crisp texture of Romaine is a perfect canvas for rich cheesy dressings and crunchy roasted nuts.

SELECTING
Choose fresh, crisp Romaine with moist, firm green stems. Avoid bunches with damaged, dried-out, or yellowing leaves. Whenever possible, purchase lettuce at a farmer's market, especially if you can find bunches with the roots still intact.

PREPARING
Rinse leaves in cold water to remove dirt trapped between curls. Remove the tough stems. Tear the leaves into bite-size pieces—chopping lettuce with a knife bruises the fragile leaves.

STORING
Wrap the bunch in a paper towel, and store it in a produce bag in the refrigerator for up to five days. Avoid the coldest part of the refrigerator, because freezing temperatures cause lettuce to wilt.

PRESERVING
Romaine does not freeze well. The cell walls break down when frozen, causing the leaves to become mushy. To keep lettuce crisp, it should be stored above freezing temperatures.

USES
Romaine lettuce tastes great fresh as a salad green and pairs well with just about any vegetable—tomatoes, cucumbers, and corn are particularly good combinations.

Here's a recipe for the classic caesar salad: In a salad bowl, combine crushed garlic, egg yolk, crushed anchovies, and Dijon mustard. Whisk in olive oil and lemon juice, and season with salt and pepper. Tear Romaine leaves into bite-size pieces and place into the bowl. Add croutons and freshly grated Parmesan cheese. Toss together and enjoy.

Try this Mediterranean salad: Combine Romaine lettuce with tomatoe wedges, artichokes hearts, sliced red onions, and kalamata olives. Toss with a lemon Dijon vinaigrette.

IN THE GARDEN

The quicker Romaine grows, the crisper its leaves. For optimal growing conditions and the best-tasting lettuce, provide Romaine with rich, fertile soil and plenty of moisture in cool weather.

CLIMATE
Romaine prefers cool weather but some varieties tolerate summer heat. Plant Romaine in full sun in zones 3 to 9.

SOIL
Prepare a well-draining fertile bed with loose soil. The optimal pH for Romaine is between 5.8 and 6.5 .

PLANTING
Start seeds indoors four weeks before the last frost date, or outdoors when the soil is workable.

Sow seeds ¼ inch (1 cm) deep. Space rows 12 inches (30 cm) apart.

GROWING
Keep the soil moist; mulch to preserve moisture and discourage weeds. Sprinkle the leaves on hot days to cool the leaves. Apply a nitrogen-rich fertilizer at planting and every few weeks.

HARVESTING
Pick outer leaves as needed, cut the plant to within 1 inch (2.5 cm) of the base, or pull up the full head at maturity.

NUTRITIONAL VALUE

Serving size 1cup (30 g)

Calories 4	Fiber 0.3 g

Vitamin K 39% DV	Thiamin 2% DV
Vitamin A 12% DV	Riboflavin 2% DV
Folate 3% DV	Vitamin C 1% DV
Iron 3% DV	Niacin 1% DV

HEALTH BENEFITS

reduces inflammation
boosts nerve function
lowers cholesterol
promotes restful sleep
provides antioxidants
protects against cancer

RUTABAGA

Brassica napus var. napobrassica

Rutabaga is a sweet root vegetable with smooth, waxy leaves and a bulbous taproot with a rippled neck. Developed in the 1600s, rutabaga is a cross between wild cabbage and turnip and belongs to the mustard family (Brassicaceae). Rutabaga is also known as Swedish turnip and swede.

VARIETIES

GILFEATHER This 1860s New England heirloom features apple-green tops on round roots. Gilfeather's creamy-white flesh has an exceptional flavor that's sweeter than most varieties. It matures in 95 days.

HELENOR The productive globes of this variety have a sweet, golden-orange flesh that is quick to develop its color. Helenor's uniformly sized roots are tinged with red on top and grow to 6 inches (15 cm) in 90 days.

LAURENTIAN A uniformly round hybrid, Laurentian has purple tops and creamy yellow flesh with a sweet, mild flavor that's similar to cabbage. It grows to 6 inches (15 cm) long in about 95 days.

AMERICAN PURPLE TOP This 100-year-old heirloom has a bright-yellow flesh that's sweet and mellow. The leafy tops grow to 20 inches (51 cm) tall and the roots to 6 inches (15 cm). It's ready in 80 days.

IN THE KITCHEN

Not sure what to do with rutabagas? Use them much as you would potatoes—either roasted or mashed. Rutabagas taste a bit milder than turnips and have a crunch similar to carrots and radishes.

 SELECTING
Choose a firm rutabaga that's no bigger than a grapefruit. If it's any larger than that, it won't have much flavor. Avoid rutabagas with cracks or bruises and those that look shrivelled.

 PREPARING
Rinse the rutabagas under cold water. Slice off the ends, and peel the skin as you would a potato, then slice or dice as needed.

 **STORING**
Place unwashed rutabagas in a produce bag and store them in the refrigerator for up to two few weeks.

 PRESERVING
To freeze rutabagas, first blanch them in boiling water for three minutes, plunge them into ice water, and dry well. Store them in airtight containers for up to eight months.

 USES
Raw rutabagas are a delicious tossed into a salad or grated into coleslaw. For a nutritious snack, cut rutabagas into sticks and drizzle with olive oil, lemon juice, and salt.

To cook rutabagas, steaming, roasting, and boiling are the best options. Rutabagas pair well with apples, potatoes, and carrots and are an excellent addition to soups.

Try this simple recipe for mashed rutabagas: Steam cubed rutabagas for about 10 minutes or until tender. Combine with heavy cream, butter, salt, and grated nutmeg; mash until smooth. Sprinkle with chopped chives or parsley.

Roast rutabagas with winter vegetables such as butternut squash, carrots, parsnips, and potatoes. Toss with olive oil, garlic powder, salt, and pepper. Roast at 425°F (220°C) for 55 minutes.

IN THE GARDEN

Rutabagas are a cool-weather vegetable that are best planted in midsummer for a fall harvest. They're a bit slower growing than turnips, however, and can take up to 12 weeks to mature.

 CLIMATE
Rutabagas grow best in full sun in zones 3 to 9. They perform best in northern climates.

 SOIL
Well-draining fertile soil is best. Amend with compost or manure loosen the soil so the roots can grow freely. The soil should be slightly acidic soil with a pH between 5.5 and 6.5.

 PLANTING
Start seeds indoors to avoid sowing outdoors in summer heat. Sow ½ inch (13 mm) deep. Set transplants 6 inches (15 cm) apart. Space rows 18 inches (46 cm) apart.

 GROWING
Keep plants evenly moist. Feed rutabagas with a low-nitrogen fertilizer after thinning and every few weeks.

 HARVESTING
Rutabagas are ready to harvest when they reach about 3 inches (8 cm) in diameter. They will be at their most tender at this size.

SORREL

Rumex acetosa

Sorrel grows wild throughout the grasslands of Europe. Its slender, arrow-shaped leaves are forest-green and have a tart, lemony flavor. The perennial sorrel plant belongs to the buckwheat family (Polygonaceae) and is also referred to as common sorrel and spinach dock.

VARIETIES

FRENCH SORREL
This tangy, earthy heirloom is excellent in soups and salads. French Sorrel grows to about 12 inches (30 cm) tall, and its baby-size leaves are ready for harvesting in 30 days.

GARDEN SORREL Also known as common sorrel, this early variety has narrow, arrow-shaped leaves that grow in clumps. Garden Sorrel has a zesty, lemony flavor and is ready to enjoy in 35 days.

RED-VEINED SORREL
Emerald green leaves contrast beautifully with burgundy stems and veins.

This variety is best for its baby-size leaves. Older leaves can be tough but are pretty as an ornamental.

IN THE KITCHEN

Sorrel is a zesty green that tastes like a cross between lemons and kiwis. It gets its tart bite from oxalic acid—which is mildly toxic. Use is sparingly to liven up blander dishes.

 SELECTING
Choose crisp, small bright-green leaves, which will be the most tender. Avoid leaves that are yellow or wilting, and stems that look woody.

 PREPARING
Soak the leaves in cold water and a spoonful of vinegar. Rinse, and pat dry. Remove the stems by folding the leaf in half and pulling off the stem.

 STORING
Wrap unwashed sorrel leaves in a paper towel and store in a produce bag in the refrigerator for up to three days.

 PRESERVING
To freeze the leaves, blanch them for two minutes in boiling water, plunge them into ice water, and dry before placing them in an airtight containers.

 USES
Add sorrel leaves to fresh green salads mixes for a zesty flavor.
Sorrel pairs very well with cool, creamy sauces and dressings. For a French sorrel sauce, cook sorrel leaves in butter until wilted, add cream and chicken stock, and stir.
Add sorrel to potato and leek soup or to any cream-based vegetable soup.

IN THE GARDEN

Sorrel is a cool-season perennial that is often grown as an annual. Be sure to harvest this leafy green before hot weather sets in—this sensitive plant is quick to go to seed.

 CLIMATE
The cold-hardy sorrel plant grows as a perennial in zones 4 through 9. It performs well in full sun or part shade. Established plants can tolerate cold temperatures as low as –20°F (–29°C).

SOIL
Prepare a fertile, well-draining planting bed. Loosen the soil and amend it with compost and a general-purpose fertilizer at planting. Aim for a pH between 5.5 and 6.8.

PLANTING
Sow seeds directly in the garden two weeks before the last frost date or as soon as the soil can be worked. Sow seeds at a depth of ½ inch (13 mm), and 2 to 3 inches (5 to 8 cm) apart. Space rows 12 to 18 inches (30 to 46 cm) apart. Sorrel grows well in containers.

GROWING
Keep sorrel plants evenly moist to insure the best flavor. Side-dress with compost midseason. Mulch to control weeds and protect roots. Remove flowers to encourage leaf growth. Divide established sorrel in the springtime.

HARVESTING
Harvest leaves in about 60 days. Pick tender young leaves when they reach a height of 4 to 5 inches (10 to 13 cm). Sorrel is a great cut-and-come-again plant.

 NUTRITIONAL VALUE

Serving size 100 g (1/2 cup) cooked
Calories 23   Fiber 2.2 g

Vitamin K 480% DV	Iron 27% DV
Vitamin A 52% DV	Riboflavin 15% DV
Folate 49% DV	Vitamin B-6 15% DV
Vitamin C 37% DV	Vitamin E 13% DV

 HEALTH BENEFITS

Lowers blood pressure
Aids digestion
Provides antioxidants
Supports healthy vision
Improves circulation
Boosts immune function

SPAGHETTI SQUASH

Cucurbita pepo

Native to Mexico and Central America, spaghetti squash is a type of winter squash. When spaghetti squash is cooked, the fibers in the flesh peel apart in long, pasta-like strands—which is, of course, how it got its name.

VARIETIES

PRIMAVERA This high-yielding variety produces fruits with vibrant canary-yellow skin. The fruits are very uniform in size and in shape, and reach up to 3 pounds (1.4 kg). Primavera matures in 93 days.

SMALL WONDER A compact, golden-orange squash that's perfect for a dinner for two. Bountiful fruits reach about 6 inches (15 cm) in length on vigorous vines. It's ready to harvest in about 75 days.

ORANGETI This pumpkin-colored squash has delicate spaghetti-like flesh that's loaded with beta-carotene. Fruits reach up to 10 inches (25 cm) in length and are ready to enjoy in about 90 days.

TIVOLI The pale-yellow fruits of this bush-type hybrid are medium to large and weigh up to 5 pounds (2.3 kg) each. The fruits reach maturity in 98 days, but you can harvest them much earlier if desired.

IN THE KITCHEN

Arguably the most fun vegetable to cook and eat, spaghetti squash looks and feels like real noodles. Roast the squash, scrape out the "noodles," and toss it with your favorite marinara sauce.

SELECTING
Look for smooth, dull skin without any soft spots. The squash should feel heavy for its size. The stem should be green, not be dried out.

PREPARING
Wash the squash, and scrub off any dirt. To make it easier to cut through the hard rind, pierce the skin in a few spots, and microwave for three minutes. Allow it to cool, then cut it in half lengthwise with a large, sharp knife. Remove the seeds before cooking.

STORING
Freshly picked winter squash must be cure for 10 days in a warm area before storing. Cured squash can stored for up to two months in a cool, dark, and dry location. Precut squash should be wrapped, and refrigerate for up to four days. Cooked squash will also keep for four days.

PRESERVING
Baked, cubed, or puréed squash can be frozen for up to 12 months.

USES
To cook the squash quickly, microwave it for five minutes, then cut it in half lengthwise, and remove the seeds. Place it cut side down in a baking dish with water, and microwave for about five more minutes.

To roast the squash, cut it in half lengthwise, and place it on a baking sheet, cut side up. Brush the inside with olive oil, sprinkle with salt, and roast at 400°F (200°C) for 45 minutes, or until tender.

Try this easy recipe for spaghetti squash primavera: Heat olive oil in a skillet, and sauté chopped onion; add minced garlic. Stir in diced zucchini and green bell pepper. Season with Italian herbs, salt, and pepper. Add chopped tomatoes and cooked squash. Top with feta cheese.

NUTRITIONAL VALUE

Serving size 100 g (2/3 cup)
Calories 27   Fiber 1.4 g

Vitamin B-6 8% DV   Iron 3% DV
Vitamin C 5% DV   Magnesium 3% DV
Niacin 5% DV   Potassium 3% DV
Thiamin 3% DV   Zinc 2% DV

HEALTH BENEFITS

Provides antioxidants
Aids digestion
Lowers blood pressure
Regulates blood sugar
Boosts immune function
Supports healthy vision

IN THE GARDEN

Spaghetti squash is quite a substantial fruit—it can weigh as much as 5 pounds (2.3 kg). Be sure to provide enough space for each of your plants so they can reach their full potential.

CLIMATE

Select a location in full sun. Squash grows best in zones 3 and higher.

SOIL

Squash prefers fertile, well-draining soil with a pH between 6.0 and 6.8. Amend the soil and till down to 8 inches (20 cm).

PLANTING

Sow seeds in late spring after the last frost date and when the soil is warm—seeds rot in cool soil, wet soil. Sow seeds 1 inch (2.5 cm) deep, and every 12 to 36 inches (30 to 90 cm), depending on size. Space rows 6 to 12 feet (1.8 to 3.7 m) apart.

GROWING

Keep the soil evenly moist. Fertilize after seedlings emerge and after blossoms appear.

HARVESTING

Fruits are ready to harvest from late summer to early fall. Cut fruits from the vine once the stems begin to crack and the skin hardens. The color will also intensify at maturity.

SPINACH

Spinacia oleracea

Spinach is a dark-green leafy vegetable that originated in Ancient Persia and belongs to the amaranth family. Its glossy, leathery leaves can be either smooth and flat or wavy savoy. A true superfood, spinach is loaded with nutrients—most famously iron and vitamin A.

VARIETIES

BLOOMSDALE
An old-time favorite since 1925, Bloomsdale has glossy, deep-green leaves that are heavily savoyed. This luscious variety grows upright and is ready to harvest in about 30 days.

NOBLE GIANT This award-wining heirloom dates back to 1926 and lives up to its name—Giant soars to 25 inches (64 cm) tall in 46 days. The large, smooth leaves are good for fresh salads, cooking, or canning.

MALABAR This variety is not a true spinach but rather a vining Asian plant that is just as delicious and nutritious as the real thing. Malabar is very heat tolerant and is ready to harvest in about 70 days.

NEW ZEALAND
A heat-tolerant variety of spinach, New Zealand has a sharp flavor that improves with cooking. It produces all summer long, and matures in about 50 days.

IN THE KITCHEN

Spinach is a versatile, nutritious green—you can eat it raw in fresh salads, sauté it with some garlic, cream it with a bit of nutmeg, or add it to your favorite egg dishes.

 SELECTING
Choose crisp, small leaves that are deep green. Avoid yellow, wilted, or soggy leaves.

 PREPARING
Soak leaves in cold water, and rinse several times—spinach is notorious for trapped dirt.

 STORING
Wrap spinach in paper towels and store it in a produce bag. Refrigerate for up to five days.

 PRESERVING
Blanch spinach for two minutes, and dry. Freeze for up to six months.

 USES
Make a fresh salad with tender baby spinach leaves. Spinach pairs well with citrus vinaigrettes and pungent cheese dressings.

For a quick sauté, heat olive oil in a skillet, add minced garlic, and cook briefly. Add spinach, cover, and cook until tender. Squeeze out excess liquid.

Spinach tastes great when creamed. Try this recipe: In a skillet, cook chopped sweet onion; add garlic and cook briefly. Add chopped spinach, cover, and cook for two minutes. Stir in heavy cream, salt, pepper, and nutmeg. Cook until reduced by half.

IN THE GARDEN

Cold-hardy spinach is one of the first leafy greens you can plant in your garden. You'll see seedlings emerge in about five days. Sow every few weeks for a continuous harvest.

 CLIMATE
Spinach is very cold-hardy and grows well in zones 2 to 9 in full sun or light shade. Plant in early spring and again for a late-fall harvest.

 SOIL
Plant spinach in fertile, well-draining soil. Spinach prefers a neutral to alkaline soil with a pH of 7.0 or higher. Work in a general-purpose fertilizer at planting.

 PLANTING
Sow seeds directly as soon as the soil can be worked. Sow seeds ½ inch (13 mm) deep, and 1 inch (2.5 cm) apart. Space rows every 14 to 18 inches (36 to 46 cm). Thin seedlings to 4 inches (10 cm) apart.

 GROWING
Water plants regularly. Side dress with a general-purpose fertilizer every few weeks.

 HARVESTING
Pick young leaves as needed. Don't allow the leaves to get too large—spinach turns bitter soon after it matures.

NUTRITIONAL VALUE

Serving size 100 g (1/2 cup) cooked
Calories 23   Fiber 2.2 g

Vitamin K 480% DV	Iron 27% DV
Vitamin A 52% DV	Riboflavin 15% DV
Folate 49% DV	Vitamin B-6 15% DV
Vitamin C 37% DV	Vitamin E 13% DV

HEALTH BENEFITS

Lowers blood pressure
Aids digestion
Provides antioxidants
Supports healthy vision
Improves circulation
Boosts immune function

SQUASH: WINTER

Cucurbita pepo

These hard-skinned squashes are called "winter squashes" because after a fall harvest they can be stored through the winter. These slow-growing, vining plants generally produce heavy fruits with a sweet, firm flesh that must be cooked before eating. Their deep-orange flesh is rich in beta-carotene.

VARIETIES

BLUE HUBBARD
A favorite in farmer's markets, this blue-skinned heirloom is moderately sweet and dry. The fruits of Blue Hubbard weigh up to 15 pounds (7 kg) in about 110 days.

BUTTERCUP This small variety has creamy, dark-orange flesh with a rich, sweet flavor that tastes like chestnuts. The fruits average about 4 pounds (1.8 kg). Harvest Buttercup squashes in 95 days.

CABOCHA Sweeter than butternut, Cabocha is a Japanese squash with a bright golden-orange flesh and a sweet potato texture. The mottled 3-pound (1.3 kg) fruits are ready to enjoy in about 85 days.

DELICATA An heirloom squash from 1891, the oblong Delicata is known as the "sweet potato squash" because of its similarly sweet flavor. This squash reaches just 2 pounds (0.9 kg) in 80 days.

IN THE KITCHEN

Cooking with winter squash may seem overwhelming—just cutting through their tough skin is a challenge. But with a few quick tips, you'll be ready to enjoy these sweet fruits.

 SELECTING
Squash should feel firm and heavy for its size. Look for smooth, dull skin without any soft spots; shiny skin suggests that the squash may have been picked too early. The stem should be green, not black, and should not be dried out.

 PREPARING
Wash the squash, and scrub off any dirt. To make it easier to cut through the hard rind, pierce the skin in a few spots, and microwave for three minutes. Allow the squash to cool, then cut it lengthwise, from stem to end, with a large, sharp knife. Remove the fibers and seeds before cooking.

 **STORING**
Winter squash can keep for up to two months in a cool, dry location. Once the squash is cut, wrap it and refrigerate it for up to four days. Cooked squash can also be refrigerated for up to four days.

 PRESERVING
Baked, cubed, or puréed squash can be frozen for up to 12 months.

 USES
Winter squash is most often baked or roasted, and its bowl shape makes it easy to stuff with various fillings.

For a sweet side dish, cut the squash halves on a baking sheet. Combine melted butter, maple syrup, and brown sugar, and brush it on the flesh. To spice it up, sprinkle with cinnamon and nutmeg, or some paprika and cayenne. Roast at 400°F (200°C) for 50 to 60 minutes until a fork easily pierces through the flesh.

If you prefer savory squash, drizzle it with olive oil, salt, and pepper, and add some cumin, coriander, or smoked paprika.

IN THE GARDEN

To maximize your squash yield, encourage pollination of squash blossoms by planting bee-attracting flowers such as beebalm, mint, or coneflowers nearby.

CLIMATE
Select a location in full sun, but rotate squash in your garden every couple of years. Squash grows well in zones 4 and higher.

SOIL
Squash needs fertile, well-drained soil with a pH of 6.0 to 6.8. Till the soil down to 8 inches (20 cm).

PLANTING
Sow outdoors after the last frost, or indoors three weeks before the last frost in 3-inch (8 cm) pots. Plant three to five seeds on a mound to protect the roots. Space mounds 36 inches (90 cm) apart. Cover with 1 inch (2.5 cm) of fine soil.

GROWING
Keep the soil evenly moist. Apply a 10-10-10 fertilizer after seedlings emerge and again after blossoms appear.

 HARVESTING
Harvest when your fingernail can't pierce the squash's skin. Cut the squash from the vine, leaving about two inches (5 cm) of the stem intact.

NUTRITIONAL VALUE

Serving size 100 g (2/3 cup)

Calories 27	Fiber 1.4 g

Vitamin B-6 8% DV	Iron 3% DV
Vitamin C 5% DV	Magnesium 3% DV
Niacin 5% DV	Potassium 3% DV
Thiamin 3% DV	Zinc 2% DV

HEALTH BENEFITS

Provides antioxidants
Boosts immune system
Supports healthy vision
Nourishes skin
Strengthens bones

SWEET POTATO

Ipomoea batatas

Sweet potato is a root vegetable with a dense, sugary flesh that ranges in color from creamy white to scarlet red. Sweet potatoes grow on traveling vines and belong to the morning glory family (Convolvulaceae). They are often confused with yams, which are not as sweet and have a courser skin.

VARIETIES

BEAUREGARD Probably the most popular variety of sweet potato, Beauregard is a standout for its high yield of reddish-purple potatoes and rich orange flesh. They mature in 90 days and stores well.

SATSUMA This Japanese variety has reddish-purple skin and white, creamy flesh with a nutty flavor. Satsuma sweet potatoes are robust and disease resistant. They are ready to harvest in about 90 days.

YELLOW JERSEY The creamy-white flesh of this longtime favorite stays firm even after cooking. Dating back to 1780, this "old-fashioned" variety whose skin color fades while in storage.

VARDAMAN This compact variety has a deep red-orange flesh and exceptionally sweet flavor. Its golden skin darkens after digging. Vardaman is ready to harvest in 100 days.

IN THE KITCHEN

The options are endless when cooking with sweet potato. You can sauté them with savory spices, bake them into sweet pies, or roast them with other root vegetables.

 **SELECTING** Choose small or medium sweet potatoes, which are sweeter and creamier than larger, starchy ones. Look for smooth, firm skin and an even tone. The deeper the color, the more beta carotene.

PREPARING Rinse sweet potatoes under cold water, and gently brush away dirt with a vegetable scrubber.

STORING You can store sweet potatoes right on your kitchen counter as long as they are out of the sun. They should remain fresh for up to three weeks.

 PRESERVING Store sweet potato in a cool, dark place for up to two months.

 USES Sweet potatoes are really versatile in the kitchen. They can be steamed, sautéed, roasted, or grilled. The simplest way to enjoy them is to bake them: Poke holes around the potato, wrap it in foil, and bake at 425°F (220°C) for 55 minutes. Serve with a pat of butter.

To sauté sweet potatoes, heat olive oil in a skillet, and add cubed sweet potato. Sprinkle with salt, pepper, garlic powder, and curry powder. Cook until tender.

IN THE GARDEN

Sweet potatoes are tropical plants that thrive in hot and humid climates. They require at least four frost-free months to thrive. To grow them in cooler climates, protect plants with row covers.

 CLIMATE Sweet potatoes prefer full sun in hot, humid climates. They perform best in zones 7 and warmer.

 SOIL Well-draining loam is best. The ideal soil pH is between 5.8 and 6.2, although sweet potatoes will tolerate a more acidic pH.

 PLANTING Plant the bare-root slips after danger of frost has passed. Plant slips 3 to 4 inches (8 to 10 cm) deep, in raised ridges 12 inches (30 cm) high, and in rows 36 inches (90 cm) apart.

 GROWING Water moderately during the growing season, but stop watering two weeks before harvest. Feed sparingly with a low-nitrogen fertilizer.

 HARVESTING Harvest "baby baers," or small roots, anytime. Dig up the mature roots in the fall before a hard frost and before the soil temperature drops below 50°F (10°C).

SWISS CHARD

Beta vulgaris subsp. vulgaris

The tall, fast-growing Swiss chard is admired for its rainbow of colorful stems and rich flavor. Chard belongs to the amaranth family (Amaranthaceae) and tastes a lot like its relative beet greens—but it doesn't have the same fleshy roots. Chard performs well not only in cool weather but also hot temperatures.

VARIETIES

FORDHOOK GIANT
This heirloom is the standard Swiss chard. Its thick, savoyed leaves are medium green with white veins and stems. It yields through summer and is ready to enjoy in 60 days.

PEPPERMINT
A dazzling sight in the garden, this pink-and-white-stemmed Swiss chard has deep-green leaves that contrast beautifully against white ribs. Harvest baby leaves in 33 days.

BRIGHT LIGHTS
An outstanding Swiss chard, this variety has savoyed green or bronze leaves. Its colorful stems can be gold, orange, pink, red, or purple. The bolt-resistant Bright Lights is can be harvested for baby leaves in 28 days, or full size in 55 days.

IN THE KITCHEN

The sweet-tasting Swiss chard has a similar flavor to spinach and beet greens but with a bit more bitterness. Use Swiss chard in recipes that call for spinach.

 SELECTING
Choose crisp, small leaves that are deep green. Avoid yellow, wilted, or soggy leaves.

 PREPARING
Soak leaves in cold water, and rinse several times to remove trapped dirt and debris.

 STORING
Wrap the leaves in paper towels and store them in a produce bag. Refrigerate chard for up to five days.

 PRESERVING
Blanch Swiss chard for two minutes, and dry. Freeze for up to six months.

 USES
Make a fresh salad with the tender young leaves. Swiss chard pairs well with citrus vinaigrettes and pungent cheese dressings.
For a simple sauté, heat olive oil in a skillet, add minced garlic, and cook briefly. Add Swiss chard, cover, and cook until tender. Serve warm.

IN THE GARDEN

The fast-growing Swiss chard is one of the first leafy greens you can plant in your garden. Enjoy the bright colors popping up in no time. Sow seeds every few weeks for a continuous harvest.

 CLIMATE
Swiss chard is quite cold-hardy and grows well in zones 3 to 10 in full sun or light shade. Plant in early spring and again for a late-fall harvest. Swiss chard is fairly heat tolerant but will slow down in hot summers.

SOIL
Plant chard in fertile, well-draining soil. Swiss chard prefers a neutral pH of around 6.5. Work in a general-purpose fertilizer at planting.

PLANTING
Sow seeds directly as soon as the soil can be worked. Sow seeds ½ inch (13 mm) deep, and 1 inch (2.5 cm) apart. Space rows every 14 to 18 inches (36 to 46 cm). Thin seedlings to 4 inches (10 cm) apart.

GROWING
Water plants regularly. Side dress with a general-purpose fertilizer about halfway through the growing season. Mulch around the plants to conserve moisture. Cut plants back once they reach 12 inches (30 cm) tall.

HARVESTING
Pick young leaves as needed. Don't allow the leaves to get too large—Swiss chard turns bitter soon after it matures.

NUTRITIONAL VALUE

Serving size 100 (3/4 cup)
Calories 20   Fiber g

Vitamin K 329% DV	Iron 23% DV
Vitamin A 34% DV	Magnesium 20% DV
Phosphorus 33% DV	Vitamin E 13% DV
Vitamin C 24% DV	Potassium 12% DV

HEALTH BENEFITS

Provides antioxidants
Aids digestion
Lowers blood pressure
Regulates blood sugar
Boosts immune function
Supports healthy vision

TOMATILLO

Physalis philadelphica

Native to Mexico and Central America, the tomatillo belongs to the nightshade family (Solanaceae) and is only a distant cousin of the tomato. Also known as Mexican husk tomato because of its papery covering, the tomatillo resembles a delicate Chinese lantern dangling from the plant.

VARIETIES

GRANDE RIO VERDE This vigorous heirloom produces high yields of large, apple-green fruits on determinate vines. Grande Rio Verde fruits have a rich flavor and grow to 4 ounces (113 g), maturing in 85 days.

PINEAPPLE The tiny fruits of this heirloom weighs only 1 ounce (28 g), but they're bursting with juicy pineapple flavor. The golden fruits have good texture and mature from green to yellow in 75 days.

PURPLE TOMATILLO The attractive amethyst skin of these unique tomatillos have deep-purple veins and are covered in pale husks. Their sweet-tart flavor is excellent in salsas. Harvest fruits in 70 days.

DE MILPA A popular Mexican heirloom, De Milpa produces abundant medium-size apple-green fruits that are tinged with purple. It's excellent for long-term storage. Fruits mature in 70 days.

IN THE KITCHEN

The essential ingredient in salsa verde, tomatillos are popular in Asian and Mexican cuisines. Its sweet-tart flavor is more akin to green apple than tomato. Enjoy tomatillos raw or cooked.

SELECTING
Open the husk slightly to examine the surface of the flesh. Tomatillos should be firm and bright green. Avoid fruits that look blemished, dried out, or shriveled up.

PREPARING
Peel off the husk just before using. Rinse the tomatillos to remove the sticky coating and debris.

STORING
Store tomatillos in their husks in a paper bag in the refrigerator for up to two weeks. You could also store unripe tomatillos at room temperature so they could continue ripening.

PRESERVING
To freeze tomatillos, peel their husks, wash them, then dry well. Store them in airtight containers in the freezer for up to six months.

USES
Make this classic salsa verde recipe: Remove the tomatillo husks, rinse well, and cut in half. Roast cut side down with garlic close at 400°F (200°C) for about five minutes to blacken the skin. In a blender, combine tomatillos, chopped white onion, lime juice, garlic, cilantro, chili peppers, and pulse until finely chopped and mixed Season with salt, and store in the refrigerator.

IN THE GARDEN

To grow the zesty, tangy tomatillos, you'll need at least two plants for proper pollination. Each plant will produce about a pound (0.5 kg) of luscious little fruits. Tomatillos grow well in containers.

 CLIMATE
Tomatillo grows best in zones 3 to 9 in full sunlight. If you are using transplants, be sure to harden off, or acclimate, your seedlings before planting.

SOIL
Prepare a fertile, well-draining bed. Aerate and amend your soil with compost before planting. Aim for a soil pH of 7.0.

PLANTING
Start seeds indoors six to eight weeks before the last frost. Sow seeds at a depth of ¼ inch (1 cm). Space plants 36 inches (90 cm) apart. Stake around the plants with trellises to keep the fruits off the ground. Be sure to position trellises at planting so as not to disturb the roots later.

GROWING
Water plants regularly, and mulch to conserve moisture. Fertilize only very poor soil.

 HARVESTING
Harvest tomatillos when the fruit is green, but has filled out the husk.

NUTRITIONAL VALUE

Serving size 100 g (3 fruits)

Calories 32	Fiber 1.9 g

Vitamin C 16% DV	Phosphorus 6% DV
Niacin 12% DV	Potassium 6% DV
Vitamin K 10% DV	Magnesium 5% DV
Iron 6% DV	Thiamin 4% DV

HEALTH BENEFITS

Regulates blood sugar
Provides antioxidants
Boosts immune function
Increase energy levels
Prevents against cancer
Supports healthy vision

TOMATO

Solanum lycopersicum

The tomato is one of the most popular vegetables to cultivate in home gardens. A flowering plant of the nightshade family (Solanaceae), the tomato is native to Central and South America. Although it's really a fruit, the luscious tomato is commonly treated as a vegetable in cuisines worldwide.

VARIETIES

Thousands of heirloom and hybrid tomatoes are cultivated worldwide in a vast array of sizes (from the tiny grape to the giant beefsteak) and a rainbow of colors (yellow, pink, purple, and, of course, red). But they all fall into two main categories: determinate bush types and indeterminate vining types. When choosing your varieties, remember that bush tomatoes mature all at once, whereas the vining varieties grow continuously for a longer harvest.

BIG RAINBOW A huge, beefy heirloom, Big Rainbow has a magnificent marbled flesh. The flavor is mild and sweet, and it makes a lovely presentation. The large fruits mature to 22 ounces (0.6 kg) in about 85 days.

PERSIMMON This Russian heirloom has a radiant persimmon color and an outstanding low-acidity flavor. Persimmon is a hefty beefsteak variety whose fruits mature to 1 pound (0.5 kg) in 80 days.

PRINCIPE BORGHESE This Tuscan heirloom grape tomato is perfect for making sauces and for drying. A determinate variety, it boasts relatively few seeds and nice dry meat. It's ready to harvest in 75 days.

BLOODY BUTCHER Harvest these heirloom cherry tomatoes in just eight weeks. The superb fruits have a rich flavor and a scarlet-red color. Enjoy up to nine 3-ounce (85 g) fruits per cluster.

YELLOW PEAR This prolific pear-shaped cherry tomato is an old heirloom that's still popular.

The golden-yellow fruit is refreshingly tangy and sweet. The indeterminate vines mature in 78 days.

ROMA The perfect variety for making tomato paste, the egg-shaped Roma has a thick, dry flesh and very few seeds. The fruit of this determinate variety is a compact 3 inches (8 cm). Enjoy it in 73 days.

CHEROKEE PURPLE

This heirloom dates back to the Cherokee tribe. Its vigorous vines yield about 20 fruits per plant. This variety boasts rich-tasting, deep-purple fruits that mature in about 80 days.

DRUZBA A 4-inch (10 cm) mini beefsteak, Druzba is an outstanding heirloom with perfect form, rich flavor, and smooth skin. The indeterminate vines produce for a long harvest, maturing in 80 days.

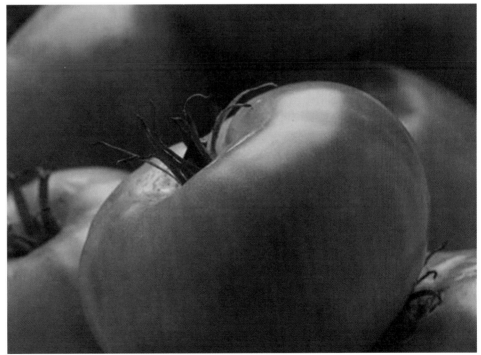

BRANDYWINE RED

A longtime favorite, Brandywine Red is a great-tasting heirloom. This large beefsteak variety can reach up to 2 pounds (0.9 kg), and is a great slicing tomato. Brandywine Red has a thin, pink-red skin and a juicy flesh that's not too acidic. The vigorous indeterminate vines benefit from cages or trellises, and mature in 85 days.

IN THE KITCHEN

Why wait until you get to the kitchen to start enjoying your tomatoes? Start nibbling on those cherry tomatoes straight from the vine. Tomatoes are arguably at their most delicious when they're sunkissed warm, but they are also divine in fresh salads, soups, pasta sauces, and countless recipes.

 SELECTING
Look for plump, fairly firm, heavy fruits with a bright color. The skin of tomatoes should be smooth and free of blemishes, bruises, and cracks.

 PREPARING
Rinse tomatoes under cold water, and gently rub to remove debris. Don't soak tomatoes because the tomato will absorb surrounding contaminants. Pat tomatoes dry until they are ready to use.

 STORING
Unripe tomatoes should be stored with their stem side down in a paper bag or a cardboard box at room temperature. Perfectly ripe tomatoes can be stored on a kitchen counter, provided they are out of direct sunlight. Very ripe tomatoes that are soft to the touch should be stored in the refrigerator inside a produce bag.

 PRESERVING
Blanch firm, ripe tomatoes in boiling water for 30 seconds; remove the skins; core and peel. Freeze tomatoes whole or in quarters in airtight containers.

Try making sun-dried tomatoes—in your oven: Halve tomatoes, and squeeze out the seeds. Place them on a nonstick baking sheet, and sprinkle with salt. Bake at 200°F (95°C) until leathery, which could take several hours.

 USES
Tomatoes can be eaten with any meal: Add them to a breakfast omelet, enjoy them in a lunchtime quiche, or toss them in a dinner salad.

The classic Italian tomato salad is the Caprese salad (from the island of Capri): On a platter, arrange alternating slices of buffalo mozzarella and slices of fresh tomato, overlapping loosely; tuck fresh basil leaves between the layers. Drizzle with olive oil, salt, and white pepper.

Roast tomatoes in the oven for a savory side dish: Place tomatoes on a nonstick baking sheet. Drizzle with olive oil, and sprinkle with salt and pepper. Toss with fresh herbs such a basil, rosemary, or thyme, and if desired, garlic cloves for added flavor. Roast at 400°F (200°C) for 20 to 40 minutes, depending on the size of the tomatoes.

Fresh marinara sauce is easy to prepare and tastes so much richer and fresher than store-bought sauce. Make an extra-large pot of sauce, and store it in the freezer so it's ready for your next pasta meal. To make marina sauce, heat olive oil in a large pot, sauté chopped onions, then add minced garlic; add freshly chopped tomatoes, red wine, honey, chopped fresh basil, oregano, and thyme; season with salt and pepper. Simmer for 30 to 45 minutes. Serve over pasta.

IN THE GARDEN

Tomatoes are vigorous plants that are fairly maintenance-free. And your efforts will be mightily rewarded with bountiful harvests of mouth-watering fruits. Be sure to plant several different varieties for a continuous harvest all summer long.

CLIMATE

Tomatoes grow well in zones 4 to 11. Tomatoes are a heat-loving, long-season plant that need warmth and at least six hours of sunlight to thrive. Time your harvest before the first frost—tomatoes do not tolerate freezing temperatures.

SOIL

Tomatoes prefer fertile, acidic soil. Till the soil at least 12 inches (30 cm), and amend with compost or manure. Add a 5-10-5 fertilizer at planting. The soil pH should be between 6.0 and 6.8.

PLANTING

Start seeds indoors six to eight weeks before the last spring frost date. Sow two to three seeds per growing container. Cover the seeds with about ¼ inch (6 mm) of soil, and gently press down over the seeds. Use a heating mat, and keep the soil evenly moist. Thin the seedlings. Before transplanting outdoors, harden off the plants, gradually acclimating them to sunny weather. Space plants 3 feet (90 cm) apart, and bury two-thirds of the plant—roots will grow from the buried leaves.

GROWING

To produce those luscious fruits, tomato plants need a lot of water and plenty of food. Water tomato plants deeply every morning. In extreme heat, water tomato plants twice a day. Mulch around plants to help retain moisture and to discourage weeds. Apply a 5-10-5 fertilizer every week.

HARVESTING

Look at the base of a tomato for ripeness: A red tomato will have a fully, or almost fully, red base. Feel the tomato to see if it's still hard or if it's beginning to soften. You're better off picking tomatoes a day too early rather than a day too late: overly mature tomatoes will start to crack and develop rot.

 FUN FACT

The tomato is originally from Peru, where its Aztec name translates to "plump thing with a navel."

TURNIP

Brassica rapa subsp. rapa

The turnip is a hardy biennial plant that belongs to the mustard family (Brassicaceae). It's cultivated for its sweet fleshy roots and tender green tops. Originally from Asia, the turnip is now grown in temperate regions worldwide. Its flavor is reminiscent of carrots and potatoes.

VARIETIES

BOULE D'OR This lovely European favorite, Golden Ball has been grown for more than 150 years. Its deep-yellow flesh has a fine, sweet flavor and a nice texture. Boule D'Or is ready to enjoy in 60 days.

HAKUREI The perfect turnip for a gourmet: Hakurei turnips has a smooth surface, a neat top, and uniformly round roots. Its pure-white skin has a pleasant crunch. This hybrid is ready to eat in 35 days.

PURPLE TOP
A traditional American turnip, the 4-inch (10 cm) roots are smooth and round. The tops are purple, and the bottoms are white below the soil line. Purple Top is ready in about 50 days.

SCARLET QUEEN
The crisp, delicious Scarlet Queen has spicy red skin with flattened ends. The flesh of this salad turnip features pretty splashes of color. Scarlet Queen matures in 43 days.

IN THE KITCHEN

Turnips have a reputation for being bitter. In reality, young turnips are quite sweet, and they mature to a potato-like flavor. Only stale turnips taste bitter—so choose your turnips wisely.

 SELECTING
Choose a firm turnip that's no bigger than 3 inches (8 cm) across. If it's any larger than that, it won't have much flavor. Avoid turnips with cracks or bruises and those that look shrivelled.

PREPARING
Rinse turnips under cold water. Slice off the ends, and if desired, peel the skin as you would a potato, then slice or dice as needed.

 STORING
Place unwashed turnips in a produce bag and store them in the refrigerator for up to two few weeks.

PRESERVING
To freeze turnips, first blanch them in boiling water for three minutes, plunge them into ice water, and dry well. Store them in airtight containers for up to eight months.

 USES
Raw turnips are a delicious tossed into a salad or grated into coleslaw. For a nutritious snack, cut turnips into sticks and drizzle with olive oil, lemon juice, and salt.

To cook turnips, steaming, roasting, and boiling are the best options. Turnips pair well with apples, potatoes, and carrots and are an excellent addition to soups.

Try this simple recipe for mashed turnips: Steam cubed turnips for about 10 minutes or until tender. Combine with heavy cream, butter, salt, and grated nutmeg; mash until smooth. Sprinkle with chopped chives or parsley.

Roast turnips with winter vegetables such as butternut squash, carrots, parsnips, and potatoes. Toss with olive oil, garlic powder, salt, and pepper. Roast at 425°F (220°C) for 55 minutes.

IN THE GARDEN

Turnips are a cool-weather vegetable that can be planted in early spring for a late spring harvest, or in midsummer for a fall harvest. Enjoy your turnip crops in 30 to 60 days.

 CLIMATE
Turnips grow best in full sun in zones 2 to 9. They perform best in northern climates.

 SOIL
Well-draining fertile soil is best. Amend with compost or manure loosen the soil so the roots can grow freely. The soil should be slightly acidic soil with a pH between 5.5 and 6.5.

 PLANTING
Sow seeds directly as soon as the soil can be worked. (Seedlings do not transplant well.) Sow ½ inch (13 mm) deep. Thin seedlings to 6 inches (15 cm) apart. Space rows 18 inches (46 cm) apart.

 GROWING
Keep plants evenly moist. Feed turnips with a low-nitrogen fertilizer after thinning and every few weeks. Mulch well.

 HARVESTING
Harvest when turnips are about 3 inches (8 cm) in diameter. Early varieties are ready five weeks after planting.

WATERCRESS

Nasturtium officinale

The dark, cruciferous watercress grows wild along springs and rivers and is cultivated for the tender, young leaves; mature leaves have an undesirable bitterness. Often watercress is merely used as a plate garnish, but it actually is a powerhouse of nutrients related to superfoods such as kale and spinach.

VARIETIES

TRUE WATERCRESS

A cool-season perennial, True Watercress is the standard, traditional watercress that is commercially available. Its crispy, peppery leaves are best when harvested early as baby-size greens. It's excellent in salads and gourmet sandwiches. Plant True Watercress in late spring or early fall. The plants mature in 60 days. Watercress or yellowcress is an aquatic plant species with the botanical name Nasturtium officinale. Watercress is a rapidly growing, aquatic or semi-aquatic, perennial plant native to Europe and Asia, and one of the oldest known leaf vegetables consumed by humans.

IN THE KITCHEN

Watercress is most often eaten raw, although, like kale or spinach, it can be cooked. All parts of the cress are edible: the leaves, the stems, and even the flowers.

 SELECTING
Choose crisp bunches with small leaves and thin, tender stems for the freshest flavor. Avoid those with obvious insect damage. Thick, more mature stems may have a slightly bitter taste.

 PREPARING
Just before using watercress, rinse the leaves in cold water to remove any trapped debris; spin or shake dry.

 STORING
Place watercress upside-down in a bowl of cold water, with the stems submerged and the leafy tops covered with a plastic bag. Store it in the refrigerator for up to five days. Or wrap leaves in a paper towel and store them in a plastic bag in the refrigerator.

 PRESERVING
To freeze the watercress, blanch the leaves in boiling water for one minute, plunge into ice water, and dry. Store in airtight containers for up eight months.

 USES
Try adding raw, young watercress leaves to fresh salads or light summer pasta sauces that call for spinach or kale.

Mature watercress leaves are astringent, so these are best cooked. The leaves do hold up well under heat. The simplest method of cooking watercress is to sauté it: In a skillet, sauté minced garlic and minced ginger in some olive oil. Add a chopped tomato, and cook. Then add watercress, and cook until wilted. Season with salt, and pepper.

Liven up sandwiches, salads, and soups with this tangy leafy green.

IN THE GARDEN

Watercress is a unique, cool-season vegetable that requires constant moisture. A little extra work spent on these leafy greens will pay off handsomely with the first tender crop.

 CLIMATE
Watercress grows best in hardiness zones 5 to 9 in full sunlight. If you have a water feature such as a fountain in your garden, cultivate watercress there.

SOIL
Watercress needs fertile, humus-rich, limy soil with a pH between 6.5 and 7.5. Amend with compost.

PLANTING
Sow directly after the last frost about ¼ inch (6 mm) deep, and ½ inch (13 mm) apart, or simply broadcast the fine seeds. Thin seedlings to 4 inches (10 cm) apart. Or sow seeds indoors, and transplant to containers, a cold frame, or a field.

GROWING
Keep the soil moist or place the planting pots in pans of water and refresh the water daily.

 **HARVESTING**
Begin picking young leaves three weeks after the seedlings first emerge. Cut the plants to 4 inches (10 cm) to encourage new growth.

NUTRITIONAL VALUE

Serving size 1 cup (35 g), raw
Calories   4   Fiber 0.2 g

Vitamin K 85% DV	Riboflavin 3% DV
Vitamin C 20% DV	Phosphorus 3% DV
Thiamin 8% DV	Magnesium 2% DV
Vitamin A 6% DV	Potassium 2% DV

HEALTH BENEFITS

Improves hormonal function
Benefits cardiovascular system
Protects against cancer
Helps alleviate depression
Provides antioxidants
Strengthens bones

YAM

Dioscorea polystachya

Yams are edible tubers of perennial herbaceous vines in the lily family (Dioscoreae). These vines are cultivated for their elongated, starchy tubers in temperate and tropical regions, especially in Africa, Asia, and Oceania. Many yams are believed to have phytonutrients with medicinal value.

VARIETIES

CHINESE YAM
This starchy root has been used in Ancient Chinese medicine as a curative for various ailments such as menopausal symptoms. It can baked, steamed, or broiled.

GUINEA YAM Also known as Yellow Yam, this tuber grows from a spiny vine that trails 6 feet (12 m). The roots have a rough outer skin and a pale yellow flesh. It matures in seven to 12 months.

INDIAN YAM Also known as air-potato yam or winged yam, this root is most widely used in tropical and subtropical countries. The tubers can weigh up to 100 pounds (45 kg).

LESSER YAM This perennial, climbing plant can reach 8 feet (2.4 m). It has heart-shaped leaves and a tuber with attractive yellow or white flesh and a sweet chestnut flavor.

IN THE KITCHEN

Yams and sweet potatoes are entirely different vegetables, but they are often prepared in a similar manner. Yams, however, are starchier and drier than sweet potatoes.

SELECTING
Choose small or medium yam roots, which are sweeter and creamier than larger, starchy ones. Look for smooth, firm skin and an even tone. The deeper the color, the more beta-carotene.

PREPARING
Rinse yams under cold water, and gently brush away dirt with a vegetable scrubber.

STORING
You can store yams right on your kitchen counter as long as they are out of direct sunlight. They should remain fresh for up to three weeks.

PRESERVING
Store yams in a cool, dark place for up to two months.

USES
Yam are quite versatile in the kitchen. They can be steamed, sautéed, roasted, or grilled. The simplest way to enjoy yams is to bake them: Poke holes all around the yams, wrap it in foil, and bake at 425°F (220°C) for 55 minutes. Serve with a pat of butter.

To sauté yams, heat olive oil in a skillet, and add cubed yams. Sprinkle with salt, pepper, garlic powder, and curry powder. Cook until tender.

IN THE GARDEN

Yams are tropical plants that thrive in hot and humid climates. They require at least four frost-free months to thrive. To grow them in cooler climates, protect plants with row covers.

CLIMATE
Yams prefer full sun in hot, humid climates. They perform best in zones 7 and warmer.

SOIL
Well-draining loam is best. The ideal soil pH is between 5.8 and 6.2, although yams will tolerate a more acidic pH.

PLANTING
Plant the bare-root slips after danger of frost has passed. Plant slips 3 to 4 inches (8 to 10 cm) deep, in raised ridges 12 inches high, and in rows 36 inches (90 cm) apart.

GROWING
Water moderately during the growing season, but stop watering two weeks before harvest. Feed sparingly with a low-nitrogen fertilizer.

HARVESTING
Harvest "baby baers," or small roots, anytime. Dig up the mature roots in the fall before a hard frost and before the soil temperature drops below 50°F (10°C).

ZUCCHINI

Cucurbita pepo

Also called courgette, zucchini is a type of summer squash that belongs to the gourd family (Cucurbitaceae). Zucchini is widely grown for its earthy-tasting fruits, which are prepared as a vegetable in most cuisines. Squash blossoms are also edible—and delicious when fried.

VARIETIES

COCOZELLE This gorgeous variegated squash is excellent when harvested for baby-size fruit at just 2 inches (5 cm). An Italian heirloom, it's also known as Cocozella di Napoli. It matures in 45 days.

GOURMET GOLD A bright-yellow zucchini, Gourmet Gold boasts a high yield over a long harvest. The bushy plant produces gleaming fruits that grow to 8 inches (20 cm) long in 55 days.

BLACK BEAUTY
An heirloom zucchini, Black Beauty is admired for its crisp, white flesh and glossy, black-green skin. Its fruits are slender, and reach up 8 inches (20 cm) long. Prolific and early-maturing, this zucchini is ready to harvest in 48 days.

MAGDA This Cousa-type zucchini has a wonderfully sweet and nutty flavor. The chunky, pale-green fruits are tapered, and are best picked when small, up to 4 inches (10 cm) long. Magda is ready to harvest in 45 days.

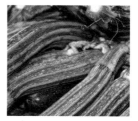

ITALIAN RIBBED The nutty-flavored heirloom is revered by Italians. Known as Costata Romanesco, this variety boasts slices that are shaped like stars. The fruits reach 8 inches (20 cm) and mature in 58 days.

ROUND DE NICE
This vigorous old heirloom yields over a long season. The bountiful pastel-green round zucchini have a distinctively rich flavor. Harvest baby-size fruit at 2 inches (5 cm).

IN THE KITCHEN

Zucchini is a remarkably versatile vegetable. Its flesh is juicy with a mild, earthy flavor, and it tastes just as delicious in savory dishes as it does in sweet muffins and quick breads.

SELECTING
Choose zucchini with firm, shiny, bright-yellow skin that is blemish-free; avoid those with bruising. Look for zucchini with a fresh, green stem that's not dried out. Hold the squash: It should feel heavy for its size.

PREPARING
Handle the zucchini gently—its thin skin is fragile and easily damaged. Some squash have small prickles on the skin—gently rinse these off under cold water. No need to peel the rind unless it's rather thick. Trim off the ends.

STORING
Wrap the squash in a produce bag in the refrigerator, where it will keep for up to two weeks. If you have squash blossoms, use those right away.

PRESERVING
To freeze zucchini, wash and slice it first. Then steam it or blanch it in boiling water for three minutes. Plunge the zucchini slices into ice water, then dry thoroughly. Place them into an airtight container and freeze for up to 12 months.

USES
For an easy summer sauté, heat olive oil in a skillet, and add chopped onion and garlic. Add thinly sliced zucchini, salt, pepper; and fresh marjoram, dill, or cumin seed. Sauté for five minutes, or until tender.

Use julienned zucchini as a crudités or add to salads, slaws, and soups. Zucchini is equally tasty in sweet baked goods such as muffins and quick breads. Try sweet spices like cinnamon, nutmeg, cloves, or ginger.

To roast, place diced zucchini on a baking sheet; toss with olive oil, lemon juice, salt, garlic powder, paprika, and cayenne. Bake at 400°F (200°C) for 45 minutes, or until tender.

IN THE GARDEN

Harvest zucchini when it's still young for its delightfully tender flesh and mild, nutty flavor. This compact, bush-type squash is ideal for smaller beds and container gardening.

CLIMATE
Zucchini squash prefers a location in full sunlight. It grows well in almost any climate, from zone 3 through 11.

SOIL
Zucchini prefers rich, well-draining soil. Amend the top 3 inches (8 cm) with compost. The ideal pH is from 6.0 to 6.8.

PLANTING
Sow seeds directly after the last frost date. Plant four seeds per hill at a depth of 2 inches (5 cm).

Space rows 36 inches (1 m) apart. Thin to one or two seedlings per hill.

GROWING
Water zucchini at least once a week, and more often during dry spells and hot weather. Use low-nitrogen 5-10-10 fertilizer at planting time and every four weeks. Plant bee-friendly flowers nearby for better pollination.

HARVESTING
Cut the stem just above the young squash about eight days after the plant flowers.

NUTRITIONAL VALUE
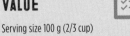

Serving size 100 g (2/3 cup)

Calories 5	Fiber 1 g

Vitamin C 17% DV	Potassium 6% DV
Folate 7% DV	Magnesium 5% DV
Vitamin B-6 6% DV	Phosphorus 5% DV
Vitamin A 6% DV	Iron 4% DV

HEALTH BENEFITS

Provides antioxidants
Benefits cardiovascular system
Lowers blood pressure
Lowers cholesterol
Helps control weight
Boosts immune function

APPENDICES

FRUIT INDEX

E

VEGETABLE INDEX

FRUIT INDEX

The publishers wish to thank Jo Walton for her efforts with picture research, Tina Vaughan for working on yet another impossible schedule, and the three authors, Sophie and Karen (Fruit) and Audra (Vegetables). Thanks also to Finn for the index, and to Philippa for creating the template and the original cover design.

The book is dedicated to Dill.

PHOTO CREDITS

Credits for all of the images in this book can be found at www.moseleyroad.com/Fruit_and_Vegetable_Bible/credits

Every effort has been made to identify the owners of the images included in this book—any errors will be rectified in future editions.